INDIAN PIPUNCULIDS (DIPTERA : PIPUNCULIDAE)

A COMPREHENSIVE MONOGRAPH

V. C. Kapoor

J. S. Grewal

S. K. Sharma

Department of Zoology,
Punjab Agricultural University,
Ludhiana-141 004, INDIA.

Atlantic Publishers & Distributors (Regd.)
New Delhi-110 027, INDIA.

Rs. 150
$ 25

Published by : Atlantic Publishers, B-2, Vishal Enclave, Najafgarh Road,
New Delhi-110 027, INDIA.
& Printed at : Kanav Printers, Ludhiana, INDIA.

Foreword

I am pleased to write the foreword for the present monograph on the Indian pipunculid flies (Diptera : Pipunculidae) by Prof. V. C. Kapoor, Drs. J. S. Grewal and S. K. Sharma. This is the first comprehensive monographic work on these flies in India (after Brunetti, 1923) dealing with 91 species. It is heartening to note the discovery of two new subgenera, 54 new species and 9 new records in this work Since these flies are of great economic importance in being parasitoids of various homopteran pests (especially rice leafhoppers), this study will go a long way in knowing the pipunculid fauna of India. With the present complete taxonomic knowledge, it will become easier for the applied workers to utilise the desired species as biocontrol agents of many leafhopper pests.

This unique work will be of great use to entomologists not only in India but all over the world.

1987

Sukhdev Singh
Vice-Chancellor
Punjab Agricultural Uuiversity
Ludhiana.

Preface

Pipunculids or big-headed flies are of great economic importance. Majority of them are exclusive parasitoids of various homopteran pests and thus play an important role in nature in checking the populations of these pests, especially rice leafhoppers and mango hoppers. In some countries efforts are being made for their mass rearing for release purpose for the control of rice leafhoppers. In India, the use of these flies is not yet thought of. This is particularly due to the inadequately known fauna of these flies in our country. Only 28 species were known from India before the present work was undertaken. This monograph not only deals with the taxonomy of 91 species under 6 genera but also establishes their importance as potential biocontrol agents of leafhopper pests especially those of rice. Majority of the species are new to science besides some new records and two (one described earlier by the authors) new subgenera. The taxonomy of these taxa is mainly based on their genitalic characters. Keys to all these taxa have also been drawn. From now onwards this monograph will not only be useful in knowing the present pipunculid species of India but also stimulate others to discover more and more species in the near future. It will also be possible to use the competent species as biocontrol agents of homopteran pests.

V. C. K.
1987 J. S. G.
S. K. S.

CONTENTS

1. INTRODUCTION

The Pipunculidae is a small but very distinct family of the order Diptera and superfamily Syrphoidea with a world wide distribution. The members of this family can be distinguished by their large, spherical or hemispherical head which is extremely mobile and composed almost entirely of compound eyes. These flies are therefore also called big headed flies.

The family name is based on the genus *Pipunculus* Latreille (1802). According to Cammerson (1974), the name *Pipunculus* means "little pumpkin" due to the characteristic and peculiar head resembling pumpkin. The name of this family was a subject of much controversy for quite a long period. Some workers used the family name Dorilaidae based upon Meigen's genus *Dorilas* and some workers preferred the family name Pipunculidae based upon Latreille's genus *Pipunculus*. The name *Dorilas,* on which the name Dorilaidae was based, is a reference to "Mithradates IV of Pontas", a friend of Doryloas. There were also Proposed many other names like Megacephali, and Cephalopsida etc. as indicated by Verrall (1900) in his catalogue of European Pipunculidae. The name Pipunculidae is well accepted today.

Economically this family is a very important group of dipterous insects in being exclusive endoparasites of various families of Homoptera including Cicadellidae, Delphacidae, and Fulgoridae. Some pipunculids have been found quite effective in suppressing rice leafhopper population. Esaki and Hoshimato (1936) reported 65 per cent parasitism of a *Pipunculus* species in rice green leafhopper, *Nephotettix cincticeps* Uhler in Japan. Koizumi (1959) described *T. itoi* reared from zigzag striped leafhopper, *Inazuma dorsalis* (Motsch.) in Japan. Hardy (1971) reported 10 pipunculid species associated with rice leafhoppers from the Oriental region. Wan (1972) reported parasitization of common rice leafhoppers and planthoppers due to pipunculid flies in Sarawak. Liu (1974) found 8 species of these flies as natural enemies of *N. cincticeps* and *Nilaparvata lugens* (Stal) in Taiwan. Hsich (1975), while studying the seasonal fluctuation of the green rice leafhoppers, found that two pipunculid species, *E. javaensis* de Meijere and *T. oryzaetora* (Koizumi) are greatly responsible for reducing the population of *N. cincticeps.* Chandra (1978, 1979) reported 5 pipunculid species, i. e. *E. roralis* (Kertesz), *E. mutillatus* loew. *E. javaensis* de Meijere, *T. oryzaetora* Koizumi and *T. subvirescens* (Loew) as effective parasitoids of rice leafhoppers in Philippines. He reported 36% parasitization. Yano (1979) found 8 species of pipunculids in the rice fields of Thailand. Even Brunetti in 1922 reported *Pipunculus (Cephalops) annulifemur* (Brunetti) parasitizing the leafhoppers from Bangalore and Subramaniam in the same year reported it as a parasitoid of mango hoppes.

2. HISTORICAL RESUME

WORK DONE IN INDIA

The taxonomy of these flies is largely neglected in India. Only 32 species out of 600 from the world are known from India. Brunetti (1912) was the first to work on the Indian pipunculids when he described 21 new species from Oriental region including 12 from India. Brunetti (1915) added one more new species, *Pipunculus uniformis* from Shimla (H. P.) and another, *P. annulifemur* parasitizing leafhoppers, from Bangalore in 1922. Subramaniam (1922) also reported *P. annulifemur* as a parasitoid of mango hoppers. It was only in 1923 when Brunetti published his comprehensive work on these flies in "Fauna of British India" series in which he included 24 species under 3 genera, of which only 19 were truly Indian.

Since 1923 no work was done on the Indian pipunculids till 1971 when Hardy published a review of the oriental pipunculids. His work included 4 species from India, i. e. *T. oryzaetora*, *T. subvirescens*, *P. (Eudorylas)** *javaensis* and *P. (E.) orientalis* along with their synonyms and hosts. He in 1972 b puplished a monograph on the oriental pipunculids in which he described 6 species from India, i. e. *P. (Cephalops) subaeneus* Brunetti, *P. (E.) filicornis* Brunetti, *P. (E.) macropygus* de Meijere, *P. (E.) uniformis* Brunetti, *T. limpidipennis* (Brunetti) and *T. nitens* (Brunetti). He with Delfinado in 1975 brought out a catalogue of the Oriental Pipunculidae which included 131 species; of these only 23 were from India, 2 were widespread oriental & 2 cosmopolitan.

Kapoor *et al.* (1977) added two new species, namely *P. (E.) ranikhetiensis* and *P. (E.) kumaonensis* from Kumaon hills of Uttar Pradesh (both synonymised here with *E. mutillatus* Loew). Kapoor *et al.* (1985) again described one new subgenus *Clareosphaera* and one new species of the

---

* *Eudorylas* treated as a genus in this work.

genus *Dorylomorpha* Aczel from India.

WORK DONE ABROAD

A good amount of work has been done on these flies in other countries. As mentioned earlier Meigen (1800) described the genus *Dorilas* and Latreille (1802) erected the genus *Pipunculus*. Later, few more genera were added by different workers uptil 1864, viz. *Micronesia* Meigen (1803), *Cephalops* Fallen (1810), *Chalarus* Walker (1834), *Atlenevra* Macquart (1834), *Nephrocerus* Zettersted (1838), *Alloneura* Rondani (1856) and *Prothechus* Rondani (1856) along with 56 species under all these genera.

Later, Loew (1865, 1872) described 8 new species from America and Europe including the well known one, *P. subvirescens*. Becker (1884) worked on the Egyptian pipunculids, while Johanneson in the same year described two new species of *Nephrocerus* from New York.

Kowarz (1887) described 14 species (including 4 new) from Bohemia, along with a checklist of Bohemian species. Giard (1889) worked on the parasitic castration of hymenopterous larvae by *Atlenevra spuria* Meigen (now *Chalarus spurius*). William (1893) described 6 new species of *Pipunculus* from North America. Mik (1899) proposed the name *Verrallia* for *Prothechus* which was preoccupied. Hough (1899), while dealing with the pipunculids of North America, described 3 new species of *Pipunculus*.

Becker again in 1900 published another comprehensive work on these flies giving tables and lists of species of different genera and included 69 species along with 16 new ones from the Palaearctic region. Kertesz in the same year proposed some new names along with synonymies. It was the first major work on these flies when Verrall (1900) brought out a catalogue of the flies of the Europe. He again in 1901 worked on the British Pipunculidae and described 37 species including 5 new ones belonging to 4 genera *(Chalarus*, *Verrallia*, *Nephrocerus*, and *Pipunculus)* along with key and synonymies. He mentioned *Cephalops* Fallen, *Micronesia* Meigen, and *Allonevra* Rondani as synonyms of *Pipunculus* Latreille, and *Atlenevra* Macquart as the synonym of *Chalarus* Walker.

Kertesz (1903) described 7 (including 6 new) species of the genus *Pipunculus* along with their key from SriLanka. Perkins (1905) described 26 new species from Australia and 5 new species from Hawaii. He also presented a key along with information on their biology and in 1906, he reported them as natural enemies of leafhoppers along with one new species, *P. eutrichodus* from Queensland. In 1910, he again added 4 new species from Hawaii. de Meijere (1907) described one new species from Holland and 2 new species of *Pipunculus* from Java and again in 1914, 6 new species from Java.

Becker (1907) reported one species of *Pipunculus* from Tunis; in 1908, while working on the Diptera of Hungary, described 2 new species of *Pipunculus*; and in 1910, one new species from Corsica. He, again in 1914, added one new species from Africa. Kertesz (1907) described one new species from Formosa and two from Africa and in 1910 published a catalogue of the Diptera of Africa including Pipunculidae, Syrphidae, Platypezidae, Oestridae and Conopidae.

Strobl (1909) added *P. argyrostictus* from Monistrol while Wahlgren (1910) worked on the Swedish Pipunculidae and described one new species. Cresson (1911, 1912) described 31 species of *Pipunculus* from North America, out of which 9 were new. Malloch (1912, 1913) described 4 new species from North America. Becker, again in 1915, described the synonymy of *Dorilas (D.) ater* and Kertesz (1912, 1915) described 21 more species from Formosa, of which 15 were new. Banks (1915) described 4 new species of *Pipunculus* and *Verrallia* from United State. In the same year, Hurting and Severin worked on the natural enemies of the sugarbeet leafhoppers in California.

Johnson (1915) described one new species of *Nephrocerus* from the United States while Knab, in the same year, descrided 2 new species from the same country. Muir (1918, 1921) worked on the pipunculids and stylopids parasitizing Homoptera, while William (1918) worked on the pipunculids parasitizing cane leafhoppers at Pahala, Hawaii. Johnson (1919) published a revised list of the Diptera of Jamaica which included 2 new species of *Pipunculus.* Collin (1920) worked on the British species of sylvaticus group which included one new species as well. Stahl (1920), while studying the life history and habits of beet leafhoppers, made biological observations on *P. industrius* and *P. vagabundus* parasitizing *Eutettix tenella.*

Becker (1921) described 6 new species from Palaearctic region and again in 1924 described 5 new species from Formosa. Lamb (1922) described 4 new species from Seychelles, and Tonnoir (1925) added

3 from New Zealand. Curran (1927), while working on North American Diptera, described 2 new species of *Pipunculus* from Canada along with a key to the North American species and in 1928a, b, worked on the African Pipunculidae. Brunetti (1927) and Shanon (1927) added 4 species each from Pahang and Argentina, respectively.

Collin (1929, 1931a, b, c, 1937, 1938) described many new species, proposed new synonymies, and erected new genera from various parts of Nearctic and Palaearctic regions. Frey (1932) worked on the pipunculids of England. Curran (1934, 1936) added few new species from Africa. Sack (1935) revised the Palaearctic Dorylaidae and described few new species. Enderlein (1936) erected two new genera i. e. *Cephalosphaera* for *Pipunculus campestris* Latreille and *Jassidophaga* for *Verrallia pilosa* Zettersted. Knab (1937) worked on the biological control of beet hoppers, using mainly the pipunculid parasitoids.

Aczel (1939a, b, c.) erected 3 new tribes, Chalarini, Dorylaini and Nephrocerini, and a new genus *Tomosvaryella* or *Dorilas sylvatica* Meigen besides describing new species, new names and synonymies from Hungary. Hardy (1939), in his work on Nearctic Pipunculidae, described 4 new species a d 2 new subspecies of the genus *Pipunculus* and one new species of the genus *Verrallia* from USA. He again with Knowlton (1939 a, b) added 8 more new species from USA.

Duda (1940) described 4 new species of *Pipunculus* from Germany and also erected a new genus *Strandimyza*. Hardy (1940) described 7 new species of *Tomosvaryella* and 1 new species of *Dorylas* from USA besides synonymising some others. Aczel in the same year erected 4 new genera viz. *Anacephalops, Claraeola, Collinas* and *Eudorylas* besides describing a new species of *Cephalosphaera* from Europe. Brooks and Jagnes (1941) worked on the Pipunculidae of Iowa, U.S.A. while Collin (1941) worked on the Pipunculidae and Empidae of Ussuri region of USSR describing 4 new species of *Pipunculus* and one of *Verrallia*.

Rapp (1943) described two new species from Quebec and one from New Jersey. He again worked on the Pipunculidae of New Jersey in 1944; and in 1945 studied the types of genera and subgenera of pipunculids. Rapp and Cooper (1943) published a catalogue of African pipunculids. Aczel (1943) worked on the ecology, bionomics and early stages of Dorylaidae; in 1944, he revised the Palaearctic species of *Tomosvaryella* giving keys, synonymies, new combinations and new species; in 1948, he published a monograph of Dorilaidae of Europe; and in 1952, brought out a catalogue of pipunculids of Neotropical region. Collin (1945) synonymised *Alloneura* Rondani with *Tomosvaryella* Aczel, *Strandimyza* Duda with *Pipunculus* Latreille and *Jassidophaga* Enderlein with *Verrallia* Mik.

From early forties, Hardy has been a very active worker on the taxonomy of these flies on the world basis. He (1943) did commendable work on Nearctic Dorilaidae which included keys to the subfamilies, genera and subgenera of the world and keys to the species and subspecies of the Nearctic genera, including 14 world genera, 1 subgenus and 117 species; of these *Allomethus* was a new genus and 27 were new species under different genera. He in 1946, 1947, 1948 $_{a, b, c}$, 1949 $_{a, b, c}$, 1950 $_{a, b}$, 1952 $_{a, b, c, d}$, 1953, 1954$_{a, b}$, 1955, 1956$_{a, b}$ 1958, 1959 $_{a, b}$, 1960, 1961, 1962 $_{a, b, c}$, 1964$_{a, b}$, 1965$_{a, b}$, 1966$_{a, b}$, 1967, 1968, 1971, 1972$_{a, b}$, with Delfinado in 1975 & 1980 described several new species, genera, synonymies, new names, new combinations, keys, checklists and biological notes etc. from various parts of the world Collin (1956) again worked on these flies describing many news pecies of *Alloneura*, *Cephalops* and *Pipunculus* from Palaearctic region which also included synonymies, new combinations and new names. He, again in 1958, described 2 new species from Yugoslavia (1 of *Alloneura* and 1 of *Cephalops*). Koizumi (1959) described 2 new species of *Eudorylas* and one of *Tomosvaryella* from Japan. He, again in 1960, made useful observations on paddy inhabiting Dorilaidae from Japan and described 3 species (including 2 new ones).

Coe (1966$_a$) published a handbook for the identification of British insects which also included Pipunculidae comprising descriptions and keys to subfamilies, 6 genera, and 17 species (including 13 new ones). He, again in 1966$_b$, worked on the British species of *Chalarus* and *Verrallia* giving key to the species, along with 6 new species and 4 new records; and again amended this work in 1967. In 1969, he described some pipunculids from southern Spain as well. Cole (1969) presented a key to the Nearctic genera of Pipunculidae while Whittaker, in the same year, described life cycle of *Verrallia aucta* and *V. setosa* along with their relationship to cercopid hosts in England. Bankowska (1972) reviewed the the Polish species of Pipunculidae and listed 47 species under 8 genera, out of which 13 were new; and again in 1973a, b gave their systematic list, keys and distribution. In this he included 48 species belonging to 8 genera from Poland proper. Lyenborg (1975) worked on the Danish Pipunculidae and described 6 species (incl. 2 new ones) under 2 genera. Rald (1977, 1979) worked on the Pipunculidae of Denmark and described some rare species along with a checklist. Thompson (1977) considered *Verrallia virginica* Banks as a valid species differing distinctly from V. *aucta* (Fallen) with which it was synonymised by Hardy (1943) in the Nearetic rcgion.

Albrecht (1979a, b) described 8 new species of *Dorylomorpha* from Finland while Chandra in the same year worked on the taxonomy and bionomics of the Pipunculidae of Philippines. Yano (1979) did faunal and biological studies of the insects of paddy fields in Asia which also included keys and notes of 10 pipunculid flies belonging to 3 genera from Thailand. May (1979) studied the biology of *Cephalops curtifrons*. McLean (1979) described a new pipunculid, *Nephrocerus flavicornis* from Norfolk, Britain. Jervis (1980a, b) studied the life history of *Chalarus* species in relation to leafhopper hosts and also studied their oviposition behaviour and larval development. Stubbs (1980) recorded *Nephrocerus scutellata* (Macq., 1834) for the first time from Britain.

Kozanek (1981a, d & c), while working on the Pipunculidae of Czechoslovakia, described 10 species (including 5 new) of *Pipunculus* and *Nephrocerus*. Lauterer (1981) gave a list of 17 species under 2 genera from Czechoslovakia while Shatalkin in the same year described one new species of *P.* (*Claraeola*) from USSR. Czechowski *et al* (1981) gave a good account of the fauna, zoogeography and ecology of pipunculid flies of Warsaw, Poland. Jervis (1986) added 2 new species of the genus *Chalarus* Walker (*C. trilineatus* and *C. orientalis*) from Burma. Speight (1986) found *Dorylomorpno maculata* as new to Ireland.

3. BIONOMICS

Habits and Habitat

Acording to Verrall (1900), these flies do not have any fixed habitat. They usually fly alone in low herbage or among the foliage or in shrubs and trees. In areas where the host bugs are concentrated, these are found in large numbers. William (1918) observed both sexes of these flies feeding on dew or honey dew, on sugarcane leaves in Hawaii. Hardy (1943) reported that all the grassy areas usuall have one to many species depending upon the time and the season. The specimens of *Pipunculus* (*Pipunculus*) *ater* (Meigen) and *Chalarus latifrons* Hardy were occassionally found at light, but this was not a certain behaviour, while Coe (1966) mentioned that they are not at all attracted to light. According to Lundbeck (1922) these flies are most active when the day is calm and sunny. Some species are more active during morning hours, some from 11 a m. to 3 p.m. and some in the evening. Our own observations are that they are never attracted to light, but are more common on low herbage under shady places during calm and sunny days.

Mating and Oviposition

Bristowe (1950) noted that mating in *Eudorylas zonatus* lasts for about 6.5 minutes in air. Coe (1966) also mentioned that mating in most of the species usually occurs in air, although couples of *Eudorylas semifumosus* (Kowarz) were sometimes observed hovering and at other times resting on the leaves of shrubs during the mating. During copulation the piercer of the female ovipositor getsinto the genital cavity of the male, so that the aedeagus might reach the vagina.

For the oviposition, the female pipunculid fly suddenly pounces upon the host nymph and then flies up holding the host in its legs and then oviposits. After oviposition the host is dropped and the fly repeats the similar process with other hosts. According to Hardy (1943), the flies prefer nymphal stages which are their actual targets for attack and oviposition as compared to adult stages. Jervis (1980_{b}) reported such observations in the genus *Chalarus* which attacks *Eupteryx* species of leafhoppers. According to him, the flies may attack any of the nymphal stages from 2nd to 5th instar but 4th and 5th are preferred. The eggs are laid in the abdomen directly through the skin of the host. The process involves a unique maternal care as the host is not injured and the larva is securely left with abundance of food (i.e. in the host). We, too, have confirmed these findings with regard to *T. troangulatus* and *T. subvirescens* which prefer and oviposit in the abdomen of 4th or 5th instars of rice leafhoppers. Williams (1918) and Jenkinson (1903) made interesting observations on these aspects in the pipunculid parasites of sugarcane leafhopper, *Perkinsiella saccharicida* in Hawaii and *Verrallia aucta* (Fallen) on froghoppers, respectively. They suggested that the female pipunculid might be able to discriminate between a parasitized and unparasitized host. However, multiple attack has been reported in a single typhlocybid nymph, *Alebra albostriella* (Fall.) by the pipunculid, *Chalarus paramenteri* Coe by Jervis (1980 $_a$). We, too, have confirmed multiple attack of *T. troangulatus* in early instar leafhoppers.

The shape of the egg, larvae etc. are quite controversial. According to Loew (1841) eggs of pipunculids are flask-shaped. While Coe (1966 $_b$) stated that the eggs of *Verrallia villosa* are yolk filled and oval in shape, broadly rounded at one end and narrow at the other end, dull whitish and semi opaque. The eggs of *T. troangulatus* and *subvirescens* are oval.

Larva is oblong subcylindrical and rounded at both extremities, and it is more slender and elongate with smoother and soft skin during the early develpomental stages (Loew, 1841). However, Perkins (1905) stated that, in general one third developed larvae were more contracted than the fully grown ones. He also reported the larva as amphipneustic, small but with very distinct anterior stigmata and the posterior spiracular area dark coloured and very distinct. The mouth is a simple opening at the anterior extremity without definite chitinized parts, but by dissection a pair of triangular chitinized pieces were obtained. Different workers described the larvae of different species, e.g. *Chalarus spurius* Fallen by Keilin and Thompson, 1915; *P. annulifemur* Brunetti by Subramaniam (1922), *T. vagabunda* (Knab) by Hardy (1943); *E. chlorionae* Frey by Lindberg, 1946; *E. mauritianus* Hardy by William, 1957; *E. semifumosus* (Kowarz) by Rothschild, 1964; *Verrallia* species by Coe, 1966 $_b$; *T. frontata* Becker by Parker, 1967 and *V. aucta* Fallen by Whittaker, 1969. In *T. troangulatus* and *T. subvirescens*, the larvae were found to be oblong with clear skin during the early stages (skin became opaque in later stages), a head like structure was formed in the late instars and it became more elongated.

DEVLOPMENT

The eggs may hatch in the nymphal or adult host but the further development does not occur until the host reaches maturity. With the growth of the host, the larva also grows and a fully grown larva occupies the whole abdomen and even some part of thorax (Jervis 1980) Although it is still difficult to recognise a parasitized leafhopper externally, in most cases the males containing fully grown larvae have their abdomens distended. The females look like gravid ones. Sometimes the fully grown larvae can be seen through the skin in cleared specimens (Fig. 1). Rothschild (1964) also observed the decolouration from green to pale yellow among parasitized hosts.

The orientation of the larva is again a matter of controversy. Loew (1841) stated that initially the young moved in the abdominal cavity of the host without showing signs of particular orientation. As the larva approaches maturity, it fills the greater part of the abdomen and often extends into the thorax of its host with its head in the direction of the host's head. Perkins (1905) found that the late first instar larva of *Chalarus* always had its head pointing towards the host's thorax while it was in opposite direction in the 2nd instar larva. Similar observations have been made by Wan (1972) in *Verrallia* and by Waloff (1975) in *E. mauritianus*. Thus, the orientation differs with different genera and species. We have observed that the early instars can be found with their heads pointing towards host's thorax.

According to Perkins (1905), when the larva of *Pipunculus* quits its host, it usually escapes at the junction of the metathorax and abdomen either below or above, as these segments have been found ruptured in leafhoppers. However, in *P. xanthocnemis* the larva escapes from *Liburnia (*Metcalf*)* through a round hole in the mid-dorsal line of abdomen. The hole was irregular as it had been gnawed. Knowlton (1937) observed the emergence of the larva through the middle of the hopper's abdomen apparently by contracting and expanding and thus by exerting pressure on the body wall of the host. Rothschild (1964) stated that the emergence in *E. semifumosus* (Kowarz) occurred between 1st and 2nd abdominal sternites. The larva of *T. troangulatus* and *T. subvirescens* at this stage is a acephalous maggot, with a head like structure (fig. 2) in the front and elongate when extended, but capable of great contraction. Due to this contraction and extension or by rolling movements, it makes sufficient progression and find a suitable spot for pupation. These observations were also recorded by Perkins (1905) for *Pipunculus* but in that case it was pointed at the front and without any head like structure.

The mature larva consumes the contents of host's body, then breaks out the abdomen killing the host. In some cases the larva crawls to the ground and pupates in the soil while in the other cases pupation takes place on or at the bases of leaves of plants or in the debris, fallen leaves etc. Our observations are that the fully mature larva can come out only through the region of metathorax because it fills the abdomen completely and even extends in to the metathorax; when its head is in metathorax, it will natuarally cut the skin there or at the most at the junction of thorax and abdomen.

The puparium is formed by hardening of the larval cuticle, which becomes black, brown or red in colour. In some species its surface has a dense and regular coriaceous sculpture. The dark posterior stigmatic area in many species in deeply depressed, in others not at all and bears one or more small tubercles on elther side. When the fly comes out of the puparium, the letter always appears to be ruptured along the same lines i e. along the front and hind margin of the dorsal segment (Perkins, 1905).

Effect of parasitization on host

Although genital abnormalities have been reported in unparasitized leafhoppers (Kathiritham by, 1974), the developing larvae of pipunculids also cause structural (external as well as internal) abnormalities in their hosts. Parasitic castration in the leafhoppers, *Typhlocyba* species was first reported by Giard (1889) due to the larvae of the pipunculid, *Atlenevra spuria* (now *Chalarus spurius* Fallen). Lindberg (1946) reported extensive aberration of the genitalia in a delphacid, *Chloriona* sp. attacked by a *Pipunculus* sp. There occurred changes in its wing venation and also the normal macroptermales became brachypterous in the delphacids, *Cosmomelus anpeps*, *Delphacodes pellucica* (F.) and *Megamelodes zenosa* (Germar) (Rothschild, 1964). The abdomens of these delphacids become distended, the intersegmental membrance changes from white to yellow owing to colouration of underlying pipunculid larva; sclerites often become poorly pigmented and the length of legs reduced. Besides, the ovipositor is also reduced in size while the male parameres and aedeagus remain unaffected. There is also reduction in the reproductive organs. The larva consumes the entire testes, ducts and part of the accessory glands. The nerve cord and alimentary canal are not affected but pushed on one side allowing the host to perform its normal activity even in advanced stage of parasitoidism. In females there is complete destruction of the ovarioles and in most cases the ovarian follicles never devleop. The spermathecae and accessory glands are occasionally spared by the parasiteoid. The wing venation of these delphacids was not affected. Remane and Schulz (1973) reported that the parasitization of pipunculids causes changes in the ontogenetic development of the genital armature of several females of *Jassargus* Zacher (Cicadellidae). Mityaev (1973) discovered some pathological variability in *Cicadas* due to pipunculid parasites in USSR. Ulmi (1976) reported genital abnormality in the penis other than secondary branch length in forage leafhopper pest, *Diplocolenus (Vedanus) abdominalis* F due to pipunculid parasitization in Italy. Kathirithamby (1978) reported genital abnormality in *Nephotettix* species due to the pipunculid larvae in Malaysia. Although primary internal organs are almost totally destroyed, the host dies only at the emergence of the parasite larva. May (1979) noticed gross distortion of the abdomen of a delphacid, *Stenocranus* parasitized by *Cephalops curtifrons*. Internally there occurs loss of the thoracic musculature and nervous tissue severely restricting host movement. The sex organs are invariably affected although specimens with reduced testes are capable of fertilization. Jervis (1980_b) also reported parasitic castration resulting in genital abnormalities in various leafhoppers due to the parasitization of *Chalarus* in Britain. Baldridge and Blocker (1980) also found damage to genital organs in grassland leafhoppers due to pipunculids in Kansas.

Host Specificity

The host relationship of these flies is still not satisfactorily known. Only a few species of pipunculids have been reared from various homopteran bugs. Some species of leafhoppers are attacked by more than one species of pipunculids. A single species of pipunculid sometimes attacks 2 or more different leafhoppers. Perkins (1905) and Williams and Sweezy (1905) discovered 3 pipunculid species parasitizing the sugarcane leafhopper, *Perkinsiella saccharicida* (Kirk.) in Hawaii. These flies have been found responsible in suppressing the population of leafhoppers to a great extent. Perkins (1905, 1908) was able to establish the association of 15 of 26 pipunculid species with their leafhopper hosts in Australia. He could find only a few species apparently host specific. Waloff (1975) and May (1979) reported *P. (C) curtifrons* Coe as the only host specific parasitoid of the leafhopper, *Stenocranus minutus* (F.)

in Britain. Freytag (1985) gave a list of about 150 species of cicadellids parasitized by various pipunculid species. Huq (1985) reported that *Eudorylas subterminalis* could attack any member of the family Cicadellidae and the number of pipunculid species so far reared from various hosts in West Berlin stood as 3 of *Eudorylas*, 3 of *Pipunculus* and 1 of *Tomosvaryella*. He further added that *E. subterminalis* and *T. sylvatica* had widest host range. Thus the work on the host specificity is still very incomplete and needs immediate attention. The paucity of such works may be attributed to the difficulty in the identification of the larval forms of the fly and the nymphal hosts of the homopterans.

Pipunculid parasitoids of rice leafhoppers

Some pipunculids have been found quite effective in suppressing rice leafhopper's population. Esaki and Hashimato (1936) discovered 65% parasitization of a *Pipunculus* species in rice green leafhopper, *Nephotettix cincticeps* Uhler in Japan. Koizumi (1959) reported 4 pipunculid species parasitizing this leafhopper in Japan. He (1960) again described *Tomosvaryella itoi* reared on zig-zag-striped leafhopper in Japan. Hardy (1972) reported 10 pipunculid species associated with rice leafhoppers from the Oriental region. Shimada (1972) reared 4 pipunculid species on *N. cincticeps* in Japan. Wan (1972) reported the parasitization of common rice leafhoppers and plant hoppers due to pipunculid flies in Sarawak. Liu (1974) found 8 species of these flies as natural enemies of *N. cincticeps* and *Nilaparvata lugens* in Taiwan. Hsich (1975), while studying the seasonal fluctuations of the green rice leafhopper, concluded that the pipunculids, *Tomosvarvella javaensis* and *T. oryzaetora* were greatly responsible in reducing the population of *N. cincticeps*. But Chiu (1977) and Otake (1976) believed pipunculids as specific parasitoids of rice leafhoppers.

Kathirithamby (1978, 1980), while surveying the paddy fields in the Krian District of West Malaysia, found 3 pipunculids, *T. oryzaetora*, *T. subvirescens* and *E. mutillatus* parasitising the nymphs of *N. virescens*, *N. nigropictus*, *N. malayanus* Ishihara and Kawase, *N. parvus* I & K , *Sogotella furcifera* and *N. lugens*. In Sarawak (Anonymous, 1979), the pipunculids *T. oryzaetora* and *P. anomalus* Hardy (1968) together with other insect parasites were found responsible in checking the menace of rice pests, especially *N. virescens*, *N. nigropictus*, *N. lugens*, *Beclia (Inazuma) dorsalis* (Motsch.) and *Cofana spectra* (Dist.). Chandra (1978, 1979) reported 5 common pipunculid species, namely *E. roralis*, *E. mutillatus*, *E. javaensis*, *T. oryzaetora* and *T. subvirescens* as effective parasitoids of rice leafhoppers in the Philippines. He found 36% parasitoidism in green leafhopper in dry land field and 33% in wet land irrigated fields. Hirashima *et al.* (1979) reported ? species of pipunculids as effective parasitoids of *N. virescens*, *N. nigropictus*, *N. lugens* and *S. furcifera* in rice fields of Thailand. Yano (1979) found 8 species of pipunculids in the rice fields of Thailand. Greathead (1983) also rightly felt that the various pipunculid species could be effectively utilized as biocontrol agents of rice leafhoppers. Yano *et al.* (1984) could collect as well as rear some species of pipunculids from the rice fields of Japan. The break up of pipunculids was given as 1 species of *Verrallia*, 6 of *Pipunculus*, 6 of *Tomosvaryella* and 1 of *Dorylomorpha* in association with rice leafhoppers. They, again in 1985, worked out the various changes in the behaviour of *N cincticeps* Uhler due to pipunculid parasitization. In Sarawak, 10% parasitization or lower was reported in *Nephotettix* spp due to various pipunculid species (Anonymous, 1985; Pina and Shepard, 1986 in Philippines). The pipunculids, *T. troangulatus* and *T. subvirescens* have been found to be effective parasitoids of rice leafhoppers in rice fields in Punjab.

Pipunculid parasitoids of homopterans other than rice pests

Few species of pipunculids have been reported as parasitoids of various homopterans which are important pests of many other crops. Subramaniam (1922) noticed 5-15% parasitization by *P. (Cephalops) annulifemur* (Brunetti) on mango hoppers in India. Thompson (1951) listed 8 pipunculid species alongwith their hosts from various parts of the world. Lindberg (1946) described *E. chloriana* Frey as a parasitoid of the delphacid, *Chloriana* sp. from Germany. Williams (1957) reported the attack of *E. mauritiana* Hardy on the sugarcane delphacids like *P. saccharicida* (Kirk.) and *Dicranotropis muiri* Kirk. in Mauritius. Marcos (1953) bred *E. semifumosus* (Kowarz) from the delphacid, *Megamelodes venosus* (Germar). Rothschild (1964) discovered a good percentage of parasitization of *E semifumosus* (Kowarz) on the delphacids, *Conomelus anceps*, *Delphacodes pellucids* (F.) and *M. venosus* (Germar). Whittaker (1969) described some pipunculid parasitoids of Cercopidae. Cantoreanu (1971) reported the pipunculid parasitoidism in *Diplocolenus abdominalis* in Romania. Ulmi (1976), too, reported the pipunculid parasitoidism of this cicadellid in Italy. Kaloostian and Pierce (1972) and Pierce (1971) reported up to 75% parasitoidism of *Tomosvaryella appendipes* (Cresson) on the homopteran, *Scaphytoplus nitridus*, a serious pest of citrus in California. Bull (1973) found that the sugarcane leafhopper is attacked by a different species of *Pipunculus* other thah those described earlier. Kathirithamby (1974, 1978) reared 7 species of *Eudorylas* from the leafhopper, *Errastunus ocellaris* in England. Lyneborg (1975) reported *Verrallia* and *Chalarus* species as effective natural enemies of cercopids and typhlocybids, respectively in Denmark. Waloff (1975) mentioned 19 species of pipunculids as parasitoids of leafhoppers of acidic grasslands in England. Yang and Pan (1979) found frequent parasitoidism of a pipunculid species on the leafhopper, *Matsumuratettix hirogyphicus* (Matsumura), a vector of sugarcane white leaf disease in Taiwan Jervis (1980 a) was able to associate some *Chalarus* species to various leafhoppers in England. Baldridge and Blocker (1980) reared some pipunculid parasitoids from the grassland leafhoppers in Kansas, U.S.A. Waloff and Thompson (1980) also reported the utility of these pipunculids in regulating the leafhopper population on acidic grassland in England. Wilson and Mcphenson (1981) reported the parasitioidism of *E. verius* Cresson in the adults of a delphacid, *Megamelus davisi* van D Meyer and Brun (1984) reported some pipunculids attacking the bugs of economic importance in Belgium. Huq (1984) reared some pipunculid species from a cicadellid, *Euscelis incisus*.

4. MATERIAL AND METHODS

These flies are rarely seen in nature and are often ignored due to their small size. The only best method for their collection is blind sweeping of various spots and then sorting them out. These flies are mostly found in the open grasses as well as those in the orchards under fruit trees, fodder crops and paddy fields in association with homopteran insects. These flies were not collected on stones near rivers or on the coffee cups or empty milk bottles as suggested by Hardy (1943).

The time of their collection is also important. In the morning hours they are generally found after 10 o'clock i.e. when there is enough sunshine and the dew is dry. They remain active upto noon and can be collected in large number. The number again starts declining by the evening.

The netted flies are killed using a cyanide killing bottle or in a bottle containing cotton soaked in chloroform. After sorting, the flies are stored in glass vials or in paper envelopes alongwith crystals of para-dichloro-benzene with complete collection data. These flies are brought to laboratory for further studies. For the present work, different agroclimatic regions of India were surveyed for the collection of the pipunculid flies. The collection was made from different parts of Punjab, Haryana, Jammu and Kashmir, Uttar Pradesh, Rajasthan, Andhra Pradesh, Maharashtra, Tamil Nadu, Karnataka, Kerala, Bihar, West Bengal, Assam, Meghalaya etc. from April, 1982 to Feb. 1987. Besides, the collections of Zoological Survey of India Calcutta, Forest Research Institute, Dehra Dun were also seen.

Preservation and preparation for study

The specimens collected form the field needed to be relaxed first before proceeding further. For relaxing, the flies are placed in an air tight box having a layer of sponge at the bottom. This sponge is soaked with the relaxing fluid (Alcohol (95%) 1060cc+Distilled water 980cc+Benzol 40cc+ Ethyle acetate 380cc).

The relaxed flies are then pinned by inserting a minute needle through the thorax and then mounting this needle on a paper triangle, or mounted directly on the paper triangle. The paper triangle is slightly bent at the tip and this portion is fixed to the pleural region of the fly with the help of insect mounting glue. In this way all the important characters like legs, wings, abdomen, genitalia etc. remain visible for examination of specimen. This method is especially important for the genus *Tomosvaryella* in which hind trochanter and other leg characters are taxonomically very important. The celluloid glue is quite good for fixing the specimens on the triangle due to the fact that the remounting of the specimen, whenever required, is done without damaging it. The method suggested by Curran for pinning of small dipterans to the side of the pin is not good for these flies as the legs gets entrapped in the glue.

For the study of genitalia, the specimen is first relaxed for 24 hrs and then the last abdominal segment is removed very gently with the help of a very fine needle or with microscissors. The best method for removing the genital segments is to place the specimen on a glass slide under a binocular microscope and then using two microneedles at the joints of 5th and 8th segments. One needle pushes the 8th segment backward while the other needle helps to keep rest of body in its position. Care should be taken not to insert the needles very deep, otherwise it will damage the claspers and other parts lying underneath. If we cannot remove this last segment carefully, we need to break last 2-3 segments depending upon how far the claspers have extended on the venter. Dissections can be made easy by putting line of hot caustic potash to make the cuticle soft (Hardy, 1943).

After the last abdominal segment is taken out, it is put into 10% aqueous solution of KOH and is boiled for 5-10 minutes till all the parts become clear; or it is kept for 12 to 24 hrs in KOH depending upon the sclerotization. After that it is again put on the slide and dissected further with the help of microneedles to remove the unwanted parts of the 8th segment. To have the complete view of aedeagus, the claspers and aedeagal basal plates are pushed apart and separated. All these parts are kept in glycerine for further studies. Small glass vials were later used to preserve the parts of genitalia in glycerine. This mathod is useful as the genital structures remain in good condition and can be studied whenever the need be. Mounting of the genitalia on the slides was also tried, but, in this case, the coverslip distroted the various structures of genitalia. To study the chaetotaxy and other minute details of the genitalia, it can be stained in mercurochrome for 5-10 minutes depending upon the need.

The illustrations are made with the help of graph eye piece under a binocular compound microscope or with the help of camera lucida under a monocular compound microscope. Measurements were taken using a stage micrometer.

Host-parasite relationship

To study the host parasite relationship, different species of leafhoppers were dissected to search the pipunculid larvae. It is not difficult to segregate the parasitized leafhoppers from the normal ones. The parasitized leafhoppers become pale and their abdomens distended. Sometimes the larva can also be seen from the clear skin of the abdomen (fig. 1). In majority of the cases, only the young nymphs, preferably 4th and 5th instars, were found parasitized.

The leafhoppers are dissected under binocular compound microscope or under dissecting microscope on a glass slide in a drop of water. One needle is placed on the tip of the abdomen to hold the specimen in its position, while with the help of the other needle, thoracic segments are carefully removed one by one, as sometimes the larva is found even a little inside the thorax; and when the thorax is separated from the abdomen, the head of larva becomes visible protruding out of the abdomen and can be separated by cerefully removing abdominal sclerites one by one. If the larva is not fully developed, it remains in the abdomen only and can be taken out by gently teasing the abdominal tissue.

The leafhoppers can also be dissected in the field simply by breaking the abdomen from the body and then pressing the same from back to forward. If the larva is there, it automatically comes out. The larvae thus taken out are preserved in 70% alcohol.

5. Morphology and Terminology

1) Head (fig. 3 B & E). It is quite large and is formed almost completely of compound eyes. The shape of the head is variable; it is hemispherical in the genus *Chalarus* and almost spherical in other higher genera. The hind margin of compound eyes is almost straight in the genus *Pipunculus* and *Tomosvaryella* i.e. subfamily Pipunculinae, while it is strongly indented in subfamily Nephrocerinae. The width of occiput is also variable. It is very narrow, almost hidden under the compound eyes in the genus *Chalarus* and very much broad and puffed in females of *Cephalosphaera*. In other genera, it may be intermediate of these two cases. The eyes of the male are contiguous on the front except in *Chalarus* and *Dorylomorpha* and in some species of *Pipunculus*. The eyes of females are dichoptic; frons in most of the cases is slightly broad in the middle as compared to its upper end near the ocellar triangle and lower end near antenna. It is variable in colour from dull to polished black, brown etc. and is thinly or densely pollinose. The colour of the eyes is variable from red, brown, dark brown to black. Ocellar bristles are present in the subfamily Chalarinae. Antenna (fig. 4B) is composed of three segments. The first segment is small and seldom visible. The second segment is many times larger than the first segment and is usually with short to strong bristles on upper as well as lower sides (1 to 3 in numbers). The apex of the lower side is such that it fits into the angle of the third segment. The third segment is variable is shape and length. The length varies from 1 to 3x in comparison to 2nd segment and the angle of the tip varies from obtuse to short acute and in some cases the tip is even bristle-like. The shape varies from oval, reniform (kidney-shaped) to long acuminate. The reniform type of antenna is usually found in case of primitive genera in Chalarinae and Nephrocerinae and in few species of *Dorilas* (Hardy, 1943), The third segment is also covered with microscopic pubescence, which may be thin or dense and imparts silvery appearance, especially on the margin. The three segmented arista is fitted into the socket on the upper margin of the 3rd segment; first segment is also called basal segment, and the 3rd segment extends into the flagellum which is wider near the base and tapers apically. The length of arista is also variable. It ranges from 1 to 3x in different species as compared to the length of 3rd segment. Mouthparts are of muscoid type and form a proboscis which is yellow to brown and is also variable in size.

2) Thorax. Chaetotaxy is variable in different species. Thorax with dorsum is usually bare in *Pipunculus* or with microscopic pubescence as in *Tomosvaryella* or with strong bristles as in subfamily Chalarinae and Nephrocerinae. The anterior portion of mesonotum may be densely setose as in *Pipunculus* (*Pipunculus*) or it may be having one or two rows of setae extending down the dorsocentral line as in *Pipunculus* (*Cephalops*). The propleura is usually hidden by broad occiput and possesses a fan-like structure of bristles in *P.* (*Pipunculus*) while it is bare in genera like *Dorylomorpha*, *Tomosvaryella*, *P.* (*Claraeola*), *Beckerias* and in *Eudorylas*. The colour of humeri varies from light yellow to black in different species. The colour of the thorax and scutellum varies from greyish-yellow to polished black. Legs (fig. 4D) are usually simple varying in colour from pure yellow to pure black or in some cases intermediate between the two. The coxae, trochanters and bases of femora have minute to strong bristles mostly in the genus *Tomosvaryella*. The trochanter is quite variable in shape and constitutes an important taxonomic character, although in some cases its shape has been found to vary within the same species. Its bristles are perhaps used by female for holding the leafhopper while ovipositing the eggs into its body or the holding of female at the time of copulation in the air by the male. Femora are gently thickened apically and with rows of short spines on the ventral side of the apical half in most species. The tibiae are gently curved with many rows of short bristles while in T. *curvipatis* sp.n. and T. *contorta* Hardy it is strongly curved. Basitarsus is almost 3x longer than the next tarsal segment. All the tarsal segments possess many rows of long fine hairs. Tarsal claws are well developed The unguitractor or median basal plate of the tarsus widens basally and fits under terminal segment. The spine-like empodium arises from this plate ventrally and extends for 0.75-1.0x the length of claws. Pulvilli are large, lightly to densely pollinose having rounded lobes arising from auxillary plates. Wings (fig 4A) are almost long and narrow, may be equal, small or longer than the body. They vary from brown to hyaline, however, most species have only slight tinge. The wing venation given here is after McAlpine *et al.* (1981) with slight modification. The subcosta (auxillary) and first longitudinal vein (R_1) are of moderate length. The radial sector is two branched, the anterior branch (R_{2+3}) designated as second longitudinal vein and the posterior branch (R_{4+5}), the third vein. The true position of R_4 is not clearly understood whether it is fused with R_3 or with the basal portion of R_5; but its fusion with R_5 seems to be more logical as is seen in the phylogeny of lower groups. The crossveins are r-m (between R_{4+5} and M_{1+2}), m-cu (between M_{3+4} and Cu) and crossvein m (between M_{1+2} and M_{3+4}). The fourth vein (M_{1+2}) is divided into four sections-first section from base to branch of media; second from branch of media upto r-m crossvein; third section from r-m to m crossvein; and fourth section from m crossvein to wing margin. This vein is of great taxonomic importance as the comparative length of 2nd and 3rd sections, which depends upon the position of r-m crossvein in relation to the discal cell, is a good diagnostic character. The presence or absence of an appendage on the last section of vein is an important generic character. This appendage is rudimentary of M_2 and is present in *Prothechus*, *P.* (*Cephalosphaera*), *P.* (*Claraeola*) and subfamily Nephrocerinae. The curvature in the last segment of vein M_{1+2} is a character of specific importance.

The fifth vein (M_{3+4}) can be divided into various sections similar to fourth vein, but these segments do not seem to be of any taxonomic importance. In the light of new interpretation (i e. of Comstock modified by Alexander, Lameere, Martynov and Tillyard), the posterior vein considered Cu_2 by Comstock-Needham is now Cu_1 and their second anal vein is now first anal vein and their anal cell is actually cubital cell.

The costal margin of the wing is divided into 6 sections; first section is from wing base to the humeral crossvein; second from humeral cross-vein to the apex of subcosta; third from end of subcosta to the end of first longitudinal vein (R_1); fourth from R_1 to R_{2+3}; fifth from R_{2+3} to R_{4+5} and sixth from R_{4+5} to M_{1+2}. A stigma may be present or absent and is a generic character; when present it is in a small portion or fills the whole of 3rd costal section.

3) *Abdomen* (fig. 3B and F). It varies very much in shape, but the normal form is subcylindrical, rounded on the sides and widest on segments 2 to 3. Some species have straight sides, some are narrow anteriorly, some are widest at the base. It varies from densely pollinose, opaque, subshining, shining to brightly metallic. It consists of 1-5 and 8th visible segments, 6 and 7 being folded under the 5th. The last segment also called male terminalia

and carries most of the genital portion of abdomen and shows torsion towards left side. The degree of torsion and asymmetry varies, being least in Chalarinae and increasing in higher groups. The 6th tergum is twisted towards the left and gives support to the genital structures. The 7th tergum is lateral in position extending from dorsum to the venter of the left side. The 7th and 8th segments are combined and form a large genital chamber into which folds the ninth segment and copulatory structures. The posterior tip of abdomen is occupied by 8th segment except in Chalarinae in which it is reduced to a relatively small segment occupying left side of the apex. The 8th segment also possesses a small to large membranous area or depression, often referred to as the genital cleft. The particular shape of the 8th segment, its ratio with 5th segment, and shape and position of membranous area are important taxonomic characters. The genital appendages are quite variable in shape and are excellent characters for the separation of species. The herpagones are the appendages of the 9th abdominal segment, their musculature has been studied by Hardy (1943). The herpagones (or claspers, surstyli) (fig. 4F) are usually alike but may be of different shapes as in most of the species of *Tomosvaryella*. The cerci and anal region are located in a convexity between the anterior region of herpagones. The size and chaetotaxy of cerci are also of taxonomic importance. The aedeagus (fig. 4F) varies from simple tube to bifid, trifid (*Tomosvaryella*) or it may be long coiled tube (in *Pipunculus*). The shapes of aedeagal plates and ejaculatory apodemes are also different in different species.

The ovipositing structure of the female is composed of modified 7th, 8th and 9th abdominal segments. The seveth segment forms the basal portion and the 8th and 9th are combined to from the actual piercing structure. The anal opening is on the dorsum of the piercer, near the junction of piercer and base and there is present pilose cercus, a lobe on either side of the anus.

According to Hardy (1943), the vaginal opening is on the ventral side of the ovipositor usually situated in a thickened portion on the piercer. The piercer is having a groove on the above side from the anal opening to the apex which serves as egg tube. The ovipositor consists of two parts resembling a beak as shown in fig. 4C. The upper part of the beak is comparatively smaller in length as compared to the lower half. It may be possible that this beak-like structure opens at the time of copulation because the aedeagus in being very soft and trifid cannot enter small opening as mentioned by Hardy (1943).

During copulation, the ovipositor fits into the genital cavity of the male and claspers hold the terminal portion of female. Ovipositor then opens and aedeagus enters this opening.

6. TAXONOMIC TREATMENT

This is the major part of this work and deals with all the known Indian genera like *Tomosvaryella* Aczel, *Dorylomorpha* Aczel, *Pipunculus* Latreille, *Eudorylas* Latreille, *Chalarus* Walker and *Verrallia* Mik. The systematic position of *Eudorylas* is still not certain. Some treat it as a subgenus of *Pipunculus* Latreille while others give it a generic status But due to its clear-cut taxonomic differences, it is treated here as a fullfledged genus. The genus *Pipunculus* is thus known by only four Indian subgenera like *Pipunculus* Latreille, *Cephalops* Fallen, *Cephalosphaera* Enderlein and *Claraeosphaera* Kapoor and Grewal. *Verrallia* is known by only one subgenus (*Jassidophaga* Aczel) from India The genus *Dorylomorpha* has been split into two subgenera like *Dorylomorpha* Aczel and *Claraeomorpha*, a new one described here. A key is given below for their separation.

KEY TO GENERA & SUBGENERA FROM INDIA (Based on Hardy, 1972)

1. Ocellar bristles present; head hemispherical. occiput narrow, scarcely project beyond eye margin; densely hairy species. Subfamily Chalarinae...2
   Ocellars absent; head nearly spherical, occiput prominent; usually rather sparsely haired species. Subfamily Pipunculinae 3
2. Major portion of vein M_{1+2} and m crossvein lacking .....Genus *Chalarus*
   Wing venation complete.......... ....Genus *Verrallia*
3. Third section of Costa, between apices of veins Sc and R_1, very short compared to fourth section and lacking a distinct stigma; not more than a faint tinge (rarely) in extreme apex of cell Sc. Tribe Tomosvaryellini... 4
   Third section of Costa with stigma and usually equal or longer than fourth section. Tribe Pipunculini..6
4. Crossvein r m situated near middle of cell 1st M_2; eyes of male joined on front................ ....Genus *Tomosvaryella*
   Crossvein r-m situated near basal sixth of cell 1st M_2; eyes of male at least narrowly separated. Genus *Dorylomorpha*...........................5

5. Vein M_1+_2 without an appendix....................Subgenus *Dorylomorpha*
Vein M_1+_2 with an appendix beyond m crossvein........*Claraeomorpha*, new subgenus.

6. Vein M_1+_2 with one or two appendices..7
M_1+_2 without any appendix..8

7. M_1+_2 with appendices, one on crossvein m and the other beyond it...... ....Subgenus *Claraeosphaera* Kapoor & Grewal
M_1+_2 with only one appendix, only beyond crossvein m...................... ....Subgenus *Cephalosphaera*.

8. Propleural fan present. Genus *Pipunculus*..9
Propleural fan absent..Genus *Eudorylas*

9. Anterior portion of mesonotum to at least a level of the suture or notopleural calli densely setose; hairs of dorsocentral row not differentiable... ....Subgenus *Pipunculus*.
Mesonotum sparsely setose by comparison, a single (rarely two rows) row of setae extends down each dorsocentral line and area between is bare... ....Subgenus *Cephalops*

TAXONOMIC DESCRIPTIONS

1. GENUS *TOMOSVARYELLA* ACZEL

Tomosvaryella Aczel, 1939. *Zool. Anz.* 125:22.

Type species: *Pipunculus sylvaticus* Meigen, by original designation.

This genus consists of species without stigma and in which radiomedial crossvein is situated almost in the middle of the cell $1M_2$ The eyes of the male are contiguous on the front for at least short distance forming upper and lower frontal triangles. 2nd antennal segment with 1 or 2 bristles which are comparatively shorter than those in other genera; 3rd segment with acute or acuminate tip and is usually dark coloured with fine pubescence. Occiput is more broader in the upper half because of the indented hind margin of eyes at this point, The dorsum of thorax has sparsely distributed hairs. Scutellum also with few scattered hairs. Colour of the humeri varies from yellow, yellowish-grey to black. Halteres are mostly yellow in colour. Wings are smaller as compared to other genera and mostly hyaline or with slight brownish tinge; 3rd costal section is always shorter than 4th; and the two combined are always shorter than 5th; crossvein r-m slightly before, at or slightly beyond the middle of the discal cell; last section of vein M_1+_2 straight or slightly curved; length of the wing is generally shorter than the body. Legs with front femora of most species having 1-3 small to strong flexor bristles near bases; hind trochanter is variable in shape from rhomboidal, triangular to cylindrical etc. and possesses small setae to strong bristles on ventral side, also with mounds and ridges etc. Abdomen with parallel sides or cylindrical in shape, widest at the segments 2nd or 3rd. First 5 segments are normal in shape and position, while 6th and 7th segments are reduced. Last visible segment is 8th having membranous area at the tip usually on the right side. Male genitalia with symmetrical claspers; aedeagus trifid or tetrafid and not so long as compared to other genera; ejaculatory apodeme simple as compared to other genera. Female ovipositor straight or slightly curved, small to very long.

Before initiating the present work, the genus was known by only six species from India. Of these, *T. coquilletti*, recorded as widespread from the orient, has not been seen in the Indian literature. Here, 28 species have been described including 20 new ones and 2 new records. *T. limpidipennis* Brunetti and *T. nitens* Brunetti could not be collected but their specimens were examined in the museum collection of Zoological Survey of India, Calcutta. Since the specimens were badly damaged, the taxonomic descriptions have been taken from their original works (Brunetti, 1912, 1923). The diagrams of male genitalia of *limpidipennis* (although a doubtful identification) have been taken from Hardy (1972) and that of *nitens* and *coquilletti* from Hardy (1943, 1966 & 1972).

Three species, *T. sylvatica* (Meigen), *T. subvirescens* (Loew) and *T. oryzaetora* Koizumi have been described in detail as their previous descriptions were incomplete. All these 28 species have been divided into 2 groups (Symmetrica and Asymmetrica) on the basis of similarities and dissimilarities of right and left male claspers. These are easily separated by the following key.

KEY TO SPECIES*

1. Both the claspers similar in shape and size. Group Symmetrica............2
   Both the claspers different in shape and size. Group Asymmetrica..... 6
2. Hind trochanter triangular or with strong bristles; claspers straignt or bent inward.................................. 3
   Hi ıd trochanter without such modifications; claspers bent outward......4

**T. longistylus* sp. n. (fig. 32) could not be included as known only by its female but having peculiarly long ovipositor reaching upto the 1st abdominal segment.

3. Hind trochanter with strong bristles; 1st abdominal tergum with 9-10 bristles on each side; claspers short and broader basally; aedeagus tatrafid (fig. 8). India..*T. multisetae* sp. n.
Hind trochanter triangular with many small hairs on the tip; 1st abdominal segment with 5 bristles on each side, claspers beak-like at tip (fig. 9). India ....*T. troangulatus* sp. n.
4. 4th costal section 1.5-2x as long as 3rd costal section 5
4th costal section 3x as long as 3rd costal section; claspers foot-like (fig. 6). India ....*T. equistylis* sp. n.
5. 4th costal section 2.0x as long as 3rd; claspers boot-shaped with inner portion appearing as heal (fig. 5). India..................*T. baderiensis* sp.n.
4th costal seetion 1.5x as long as 3rd, claspers without heal-like portion as in above case (fig.7). India...................... *T. guwahatiensis* sp.n.
6. Humeri grey or black (fig. 23). Oriental, Palaearctic. *T. oryzaetora* Koizumi
Humeri yellow or greyish yellow...7
7. Hind trochanter modified i. e. with small to strong bristles or with rhomboidal shape...8
Hind trochanter without such modifications 16
8. Hind trochanter rhomboidal; claspers very much asymmetrical, left one twisted; hind trochanter of female not rhomboidal but with minute hairs (fig. 28). Cosmopolitan.......................*T subvirescens* (Loew).
Hind trochanter not rhomboidal but with small to strong bristles; claspers not twisted...9
9. 4th costal section 3x as long as 3rd costal section and 5th costal section 1.2x as long as 3rd and 4th combined......................................10
4th costal section 1.5 to 2x as long as 3rd costal section and 5th costal section 1.5 to 2.3x as long as 3rd and 4th combined....................11
10. Cossvein r-m in middle of discal cell; comparatively large sized species; claspers long and spoon-shaped apically. (fig. 17). India...*T. indica* sp.n.
Crossvein r-m at basal 1/3rd; medium-sized species; claspers simple not spoon-shaped. (fig. 10) Oriental, Palaearctic, Nearctic...... ....
....*T. coquilletti* (Kertesz)
11. Claspers with some additional lobe or bent inward; hind trochanter with row of hairs or hairs scattered on mound-like gibbosity.................12
Claspers curved inward or bent inward at the tip; hind trochanter with bristles more concentrated at a particular point...............................14

12. Claspers bent downward and with an additional lobe; hind trochanter without any gibbosity (fig. 31). India...........*T. tattapaniensis* sp. n.
Claspers without any additional lobe but bent outward; hind trochanter with a mound-like gibbosity...13

13. Claspers bent outward at the tip and without any hook-like structure (fig. 22). Oriental..*T nitens* (Brunetti)
Claspers bent inward and with a hook-like structure at the tip (fig. 24). India..T. *ramnagariensis* sp. n.

14. 8th abdominal segment equal in length to 5th abdominal segment; left clasper blunt at tip; right one pointed and bent inward; hind trochanter with 4-5 bristles; crossvein r-m in middle of discal cell (fig. 30). Oriental, Palaearctic, Ethiopian, Nearctic ....T. *sylvatica* (Meigen).
8th abdominal segment about 0.5x as long as 5th abdominal segment; claspers slightly curved inside; hind trochanter with a bunch of hairs; crossvein r-m before middle of discal cell...... 15

15. 8th abdominal segment as broad as 5th segment and with a large membranous area and with small hairs; hind trochanter with one or two tubercles having a bunch of hairs (fig. 13). India......T. *denticulatus* sp n.
8th abdominal segmet 0.5x as broad as 5th segment and with long hairs; hind trochanter without any tubercle; claspers more slender (fig. 15). India...T. *eusylvatica* sp. n.

16. 4th costal section 3 or more than 3x as long as 3rd costal section......17
4th costal section 1.0 to 2.5x as long as 3rd costal section..............20

17. Claspers long and slender; 5th costal section 1.3 to 1.4x as long as 3rd and 4th combined; abdominal segment without any bristle (fig. 25). Oriental...T. *robusta* Hardy.
Claspers small and not slender; 5th costal section 1.1 to 1.2x as long as 3rd and 4th combined; 1st abdominal segment with 3-4 inconspicuous bristles...... 18

18. Both claspers of almost equal length and blunt at tip (fig. 27). India... ....T. *subrobusa* sp.n.
Claspers unequal in length and, out of two one is pointed at the tip...19

19. Left clasper smaller than right one and pointed; right one not pointed apically (fig. 26). India....................................T. *subhectena* sp.n.
Left clasper longer than right one and broader at tip, right one pointed (fig. 14). Oriental, Palaearctic, Australian............T. *epichalca* (Perkins).

20. 4th costal section equal to 3rd costal section; claspers bent outward (fig. 19). Oriental.......................................T. *limpidipennis* (Brunetti).
4th costal section 1.5 to 2.5x as long as 3rd costal section; claspers not bent outward...21
21. 1st abdominal segment with inconspicuous bristles; claspers short and broad (fig. 18). India... ....T. *kashipuriensis* sp. n.
1st abdominal segment with well developed bristles; claspers comparatively long..22
22. Claspers long and slender; last segments of abdomen modified.........23
Claspers not so long and slender, but of such a shape that they appear to fit into each other; last segments of abdomen not modified 24
23. 5th costal section more than 3x as long as 3rd & 4th combined; claspers straight; last abdominal segment with many hairs; hind tibia curved (fig. 11). India...T. *curvipatis* sp. n.
5th costal section about 2x as long as 3rd and 4th combined; clasper long, left one more longer and bent inward at tip; hypopygium long, almost as long as 5th abdominal segment; without long hairs; hind tibia not curved (fig. 20). India...........................T. *longipygiamis* **sp. n.**
24. 4th costal section 2 or more than 2x as long as 3rd costal section; **5th** costal section 1.5x as long as 3rd and 4th combined..................25
4th costal section 1.25 to 1.5x as long as 3rd costal section; 5th costal section 1 75 to 2x as long as 3rd and 4th combined.......................27
25. Claspers very much bent downward, this appears as a separate loop in the dorsal view; ovipositor very much curved upward (fig. 12). India ....T. *dehradunicnsis* sp. n.
Claspers not as above, right one with a cup-shaped structure, where the left one fits; ovipositor of female slightly curved upward (fig 29). India...T. *surstylae* sp. n.
26. Small sized species (less than 2 mm); claspers fit into each other; ovipositor slightly curved downward (fig. 21). India...........T. *minutus* sp. n.
Medium sized species (about 2.5mm); claspers not fitting into each other; ovipositor straight (fig. 16). India.........................T. *genitalis* sp. n.

A. GROUP SYMMETRICA

Tomosvaryella baderiensis sp. nov.

(Fig. 5)

♂. Medium sized, black species. Head 1.15x as broad as thorax, 0.7x as long as broad; compound eyes brown with few black patches, joined on the front for a distance equal to 5 rows of eye facets leaving a small black upper frontal triangle with little pubescence in the lower half; ocellar triangle black; lower frontal triangle black, without any pubescence, more than 2x as long as the joining area of compound eyes; face black with little pubescence in the middle, equal to the lower end of frons near the antenna, getting narrower towards proboscis; proboscis small, brown in colour; occiput dark black, without any pubescence, but with few scattered black small hairs. Antenna : Ist segment small, black; 2nd segment also black; 3rd segment blackish brown, more than 2x as long as 2nd segment, with pubescence on margin and tip, tip acuminate (fig. 5B). Thorax dull black with yellowish pubescence on the lateral margins; scutellum also black, bare; humeri yellow with few small brownish hairs. Halteres yellow. Wings hyaline, 4th costal section 2x as long as 3rd costal section; 5th costal section 1.5x as long as 3rd and 4th combind; crossvein r-m slightly beyond the middle of the discal cell; last section of vein M_{1+2} gently curved (fig. 5A). Legs : coxae, trochanters, femora and tibiae black except for the distal tip of femora and both tips of tibiae which are yellow; tarsii yellow with rows of brownish hairs; pulvilli and claws well developed; hind femora with a row of delicate hairs. Abdomen dull black with scattered small hairs on the hind segments; first abdominal tergum with about 6 strong brownish black bristles on each side; 7th abdominal segment about half as long as 5th segment and also about 2/3rd in width, with a membranous area at the tip. Male genitalia with symmetrical claspers having boot-like tips turned outward and downward as is clear from its dorsal, ventral and lateral views (fig. 5D, E & F); cerci large having rows of bristles on inner as well as outer sides; aedeagus quite long and trifid; the shape of aedeagus and aedeagal basal plates as shown in fig. 5G.

Length. Body 2.6mm; wings 2.7mm.

♀. Ovipositor with black rounded base, piercer brown, curved upward reaching upto the 4th abdominal segment (fig. 5H). Frons black with little pubescence, slightly broader in the mibdle becoming parallel near the antenna. Thorax and first two segments of abdomen more shining than those of male. Bristles on the first abdominal tergum smaller than those in male. Rest description similar to male.

Remarks. This species is quite close to *T. equistylis* sp. n. from Ajnala, Punjab. The wing venation and to some extent shape of claspers also appear to be same but if we see in detail, the claspers of *equistylis* are rounded at tips (fig. 6C) while in this species they are pointed and appear to be boot-shaped with a heel on the back side. The ratio of 3rd and 4th costal sections is also different. The 4th section is 3x as long as 3rd in *equistylis* while it is 2x in this species.

Etymology. Name based on locality.

Specimens examined. Holotype ♂ from Badera near Nahan (H.P.), 25.x 1986, coll. S. K. Sharma. Allotype ♀, same date. Paratypes 1 ♂, same data, coll. S.K. Sharma; 1 ♂, same data, coll. Ashwani Kumar; 1 ♂, Sahastradhara near Dehra Dun, (U.P.), 27.x.1986, coll. S. K. Sharma.

Tomosvaryella equistylis sp. nov.

(Fig. 6)

♂. Medium sized, black. Head almost equal to thorax in width, about 1.2x as long as broad and compressed from the sides; compound eyes brownish black, pollinose, joined on the front for a distance which is equal to the length of lower frontal triangle; upper frontal triangle very small, black, without any pubescence; ocellar triangle also black; lower frontal triangle black with white pubescence; face black with white pubescence, slightly narrow near the antenna, rest slightly broader and parallel-sided; occiput greyish black with pubescence on the lateral sides, more in the lower half. Antenna: 1st segment small, black; 2nd segment brownish black, with little pubescence and with 2 small brown bristles on the upper side; 3rd segment brown, with white pubescence near the margin, acute at apex and about 1.75x as long as the 2nd antennal segment; arista brownish black, more than 2x as long as 3rd antennal segment (fig. 6B). Proboscis not visible externally. Thorax dull black with few scattered brown hairs; pleurae black, densely pollinose; scutellum shining black with little pubescence. Humeri brownish yellow. Halteres yellow. Wings with light brown tinge; 4th costal section about 3.0x as long as 3rd costal section; 5th costal section 1.5x as long as 3rd and 4th combined; crossvein r-m almost in the middle; last section of vein M_{1+2} gently curved (fig. 6A). Legs black; femora with white pubescence; distal tips of femora yellow; proximal 1/3rd and distal tips of tibiae also yellow; all tibiae with rows of yellowish hairs, although hind one with comparatively longer ones; tarsi yellow with brown bristles; claws brown. Abdomen black with brownish tinge, first abdominal tergum with a row of 5-6 yellowish brown comparatively long bristles on each side of the lateral margin; other segments with small black bristles scattered all over the abdomen; 8th abdominal segment less than 0.5x as long as 5th abdominal segment and with a membranous area on the right side of the tip. Male genitalia with long, symmetrical claspers, their tips turned outward, resembling human feet, and with small bristles all over; cerci long, not so broad and with bristles on inner as well as outer sides; aedeagus trifid, and of moderate length; the shape of claspers, aedeagus and aedeagal basal plates as shown in fig. 6C, D & E.

Length. Body 2.7mm; wing : 2.65mm.

♀. Not known.

Remarks. This species comes close to *T. epichalca* (Perkins) as the 4th costal section is 3x as long as 3rd costal section, but differs in having strong bristles on the first abdominal tergum and in the shape of claspers. The shape of claspers does not resemble any species of this genus.

Etymology. Name based on peculiarly shaped symmetrical surstyli.

Specimen examined. Holotype ♂, by sweeping over grasses from Ajnala (Punjab), 18.xi.1985, coll. V. K. Kohli.

Tomosvaryella guwahatiensis sp. nov.

(Fig 7)

♂. Medium sized, black species. Head about 1.2x as broad as thorax, as long as broad, compound eyes dark brown with few black patches joined on the front for a distance equal to 6 eye facets leaving a small upper frontal triangle which is black and without any pubescence; ocellar triangle black; lower frontal triangle black with white pubescence, about 2x as long as the joining area of compound eyes; face black with white pubescence, equal in width at the ends; proboscis not visible externally; occiput black without any pubescence. Antenna: 1st segment small, dark brown, 2nd segment brown; 3rd segment brown with white pubescence near margin and tip, acute, about 2x as long as 2nd segment; arista brown, about 2x as long as 3rd segment (fig. 7B). Thorax dull black with little pubescence on the lateral sides; pleurae black with white pubescence more near the wing base; scutellum black, without any pubescence; humeri brown. Halteres yellow. Wings hyaline; 4th costal section 1.5x as long as 3rd costal section; 5th costal section 1.75x as long as 3rd and 4th combind; crossvein r-m very slightly beyond the middle of the discal cell; last section of vein M_{1+2} almost straight (fig. 7A). Legs: coxae, trochanters, femora and tibiae black with white pubesence except for the distal tip of femora and both tips of tibiae yellow; tarsi yellow with rows of brown bristles; claws brown, pulvilli yellow, well developed. Abdomen black with white pubesence, also with few scattered black bristles; 1st abdominal segment without any bristle; 8th abdominal segment about 2/3rd as long as 5th. Male genitalia with symmetrical claspers turned outward and downward; aedeagus long, trifid; cerci large with long bristles. The shape of claspers, aedeagus, aedeagal basal plates, ejaculatory abdome etc. as shown in fig. 7C, D, E & F.

Length. Body : 2.25mm; wings : 2.15mm.

Remarks. This species is close to *T. equistylis* sp. n. because of symmetrical and outwardly curved claspers but differs in having their tips sharply curved and pointed which in the *equistylis* are not so rounded at the tips. The wing venation is also different; 4th costal section is about 3x as long as 3rd costal section in *equistylis* while in this species only about 1.5x. The shape of antenna is also different (compare figures 6B with 7B).

Specimen examined. Holotype ♂, Guwahati (Assam), 9.iv.1985, coll. S. K. Sharma.

Tomosyaryella multisetae sp. nov.

(Fig. 8)

♂. Medium sized, black species. Head almost equal to thorax in width, as long as broad; compound eyes dark brown, joined on the front for a distance equal to 4 rows of eye facets, leaving a small triangular area below median ocellus, known as upper frontal triangle, which is black and equal in length to joining area of compound eyes; ocellar triangle black; lower frontal triangle black with white pubescence and 2x as long as joining area of compound eyes; face black with little pubesence in lower half, equal in width at both ends and is equal to lower end of frons; occiput black with pubescence on dorsal and lateral sides and with few black bristles on dorsal side near ocellar triangle; hind margin with small greyish hairs. Antenna : 1st segment small, brown; 2nd segment brown with one bristle on upper side; 3rd segment light brown with pubescence in lower half near tip, 2x as long as 2nd segment, acute at apex; arista brown, 2x as long as 3rd antennal segment (fig. 8B). Proboscis small, yellow. Thorax black with little pubescence and with small, light brown hairs on dorsum; pleurae black, bare; scutellum shining black with few scattered brown hairs. Humeri greyish yellow. Halteres yellow. Wings with slight brown tinge; 4th costal section 2x as long as 3rd costal section; 5th costal section 1.5x as long as 3rd and 4th combined; cross-vein r-m distinctly beyond middle of discal cell; last section of vein M_{1+2} slightly curved (fig. 8A). Legs with coxae, trochanters and femora black except for yellow distal tips; tibiae with proximal 1/3rd and distal tips yellow; tarsi light yellow, with rows of yellow hairs; claws brown, pulvilli yellow;

hind trochanter with many strong brown bristles (fig 8C), hind femur and tibia with many small yellowish hairs. Abdomen black, 1st abdominal tergum with about 9 comparatively long black bristles on each side on lateral margin (fig. 8D); other segments with scattered, black bristles; 8th segment less than 1/3rd as long as 5th and with a membranous area an the right side of the tip (fig 8E). Male genitalia with claspers quite broad, symmetrical and with a tooth-like structure in the middle of inner side; both claspers with small hairs on inner side; cerci narrow and with small bristles directed outwardly (fig. 8G); aedeagus tetrafid, not so long; ejaculatory apodeme of small size. The shape of aedeagus, aedeagal basal plates, ejaculatory apodeme etc. as shown in fig. 8F.

Length. Body : 2.6mm; wing : 2.45mm.

♀. Wing venation, bristles on 1st tergum and hind trochanters similar to male. Ovipositor with round base, piercer long, brown, straight reaching upto base of 3rd abdominal segment (fig. 8H). Abdomen not so much shining as in male. Thorax with less hairs. Post scutellar region with little pubescence. Humeri yellow and not grcyish as in male. Other characters similar to male.

Length. Body : 2.6mm; wings : 2.45mm.

Remarks. This species is close to *T. sylvatica* Meigen due to wing venation, and presence of bristles on hind trochanter. It differs from it in the presence of about 9 bristles on each side of the 1st abdominal tergum (only 4-5 in *sylvatica*). The bristles on hind trochanter are more in number and more stronger than those in *T. sylvatica*. The shape of genitalia is also quite different. The claspers are quite long and slender in *T. sylvatica* while broader and not so long in the new species

Specimens examined. Holotype ♂, on weeds, P.A.U., Ludhiana, 18. xi.1983, coll G.B. Singh. Allotype ♀, on weeds, P.A.U., Ludhiana, 18.x.1983, coll. G B. Singh. Patatype 1 ♂, Ludhiana. 18.iv.1981, coll. M. L. Agarwal, 1 ♀, P A.U , Ludhiana, 3.x.1985, coll Balbir Singh and about 30 specimens collected from different localities of Ludhiana district from 1982 to 1986.

Tomosvaryella troangulatus sp. nov.

(Fig. 9)

♂ Medium sized, black. Head about 1.3x as broad as thorax; compound eyes brownish black, joined on front for about 7 rows of facets, leaving a small triangular area below the median ocellus, the upper frontal triangle, which is black and about 0.5x as long as the joining area of compound eyes; lower frontal triangle black with white pubescence and about 2x as long as the joining area of compound eyes; face black with white pubescence, equal in width to lower end of frons; occiput black with white pubescence on lateral side and little on dorsal side. Antenna : 1st segment small, brownish black; 2nd segment brownish black with two bristles on upper side; 3rd segment light brown with white pubescence, more on margins. tapering towards tip, and about 2.5x as long as 2nd segment; arista brown, about 1.5x as long as 3rd segment (fig. 9B). Proboscis not visible externally. Thorax subshining black with little pubescence and with few scattered yellowish hairs on dorsum; scutellum shining black with scattered yellowish hairs; pleurae black with white pubescence; humeri yellow with few yellow setae. Halteres also yellow. Wing with little brownish tringe; 4th costal section about 1.5x as long as 3rd costal section; 5th costal section about 1.75x as long as 3rd and 4th combined; crossvein r-m slightly beyond middle of discal cell; last section of vein M_{1+2} gently curved (fig. 9A) Legs black in ground colour with distal tips of femora and both tips of tibiae yellow; tarsi yellow and with many rows of yellow hairs; claws brown and well developed; pulvilli yellow; hind trochanters almost triangular and with a protuberance on ventral side and with many hairs (fig. 9C). Abdomen shining black with slight pubescence, 1st abdominal tergum with 5 black, well developed bristles on lateral margins; other segments with many small black bristles; 8th abdominal segment less than half as long as 5th segment and with a membranous area on right side of tip (fig. 9D). Male genitalia with symmetrical claspers having broad tips and beak-like projections; cerci narrow and with bristles on inner side (fig. 9E &F), aedeagus trifid, ejaculatory apodeme broad at tip. The shape of ejaculatory apodome, aedeagus, aedeagal basal plates etc. as shown in fig. 9G.

Length. Body : 2.5mm; wing 2.4mm.

♀. Ovipositor with black base and brown piercer which is straight and reaches upto the 3rd abdominal segment (fig. 9I); frons black without any pubescence, less broder in the upper half and slightly more broader in the lower half near the antenna; hind trochanter not with mound or protuberance but with many delicate brown hairs (fig. 9H). Rest of description similar to male.

Length. Body 2.7mm; wings : 2.65mm.

Remarks. This species is close to *T. nitens* (Brunetti) and *T. turgida*

Hardy because of the shape of hind trochanter, but the shape of the genitalia is different from both. It is beak-like at the tip in the new species while it is not so in *nitens* and in *turgida*. The cerci are also not so broad in the new species as in the other two. The shape of trochanters is also not exactly same. The wing venation is also different from that of *nitens*. The 4th costal section is 2x as long as 3rd costal section and 5th is 1.5x as long as 3rd and 4th combined in *nitens* while in the new species 4th costal section is 1.5x as long as 3rd and 5th is 1.75x as long as 3rd and 4th combined.

This species is present in almost all parts of India, but the shape of the protuberance on the hind trochanter is quite variable. It varies from small to large, broad to pointed, little hairy to densely hairy, etc. The wing venation also varies. The ratio of 4th to 3rd costal section varies from 1.5 to 2.75x. The position of r-m crossvein varies from before middle, middle to beyond middle but the genitalia is same in all the cases showing that they all belong to one species.

Etymology. Name based on peculiar shape of hind trochanter. Inspite of showing variation, the peculiar triangular shape persists in all.

Specimens examined. Holotype ♂ on rice, Ludhiana, 17.xi.1985, coll. S.K. Sharma. Allotype ♀, Paddy, P.A.U.. Ludhiana, 15.xi.1985, coll. S. K. Sharma. Paratypes : about 1000 specimens from different localities of Ludhiana Distt. (i.e. Habowal, Jassian, Choorpur, Bhattian, Ladowal, Sunet); Amritsar; Beas; Ajnala; Chandigarh; Phagwara (Distt. Kapurthala); Phillaur (Distt. Jalandhar); Ropar; Raya (Distt. Amritsar); Hoshiarpur, Gagret (HP); Bir Dhandoli (H.P.); Kharak Camp (H.P.); Jahankhealen (Distt. Hoshiarpur, Punjab); Shimla (H.P.); Jhansi, Bilaspur, Kashipur, Afzalgarh (U.P.); Srinagar (J & K); Ramgarh and Ranchi (Bihar); Thekkady and Silent Valley (Kerala) and Delhi from July, 1977 to Nov., 1986.

B. GROUP ASYMMETRICA

Tomosvaryella coquilletti (Kertesz)

(Fig. 10)

Pipunculus coquilletti Kertesz, 1907, Ann. Musei Nationalis Hungarici, 5 : 582

Tomosvaryella coquilletti : Hardy, 1943, Univ. Kansas Sci. Bull., 29 (1):159.

Pipunculus proximus Cresson, 1911, Trans. Amer. Ent. Soc., 36 : 318-319

♂. Face and frontal triangle silvery, front above junction of eyes shining black, as is the vertex; eyes joined for less than half the length of the frontal triangle; 3rd segment of antennae brownish to black, rather slender and long, white, acuminate below (fig. 10B), bristles of 2nd segment very weak. Thorax and abdomen shining black in ground color, very faintly brownish to grey dusted; metanotum, parts of pleurae and 1st abdominal tergum lightly cinereous, sternopleurae entirely shining; humeri and halteres yellow; dorsocentral and marginal hairs distinct on mesonotum, but otherwise sparsely haired Legs chiefly black, apices of femora and tibiae, bases of tibiae and first four tarsal subsegments yellow, last subsegment brown, front femora with a pair of rather strong flexor bristles near bases; mid-coxae with patches of strong, downward projecting bristles on their apices; hind trochanters each with two to several strong bristles on under sides (fig. 10C); femora moderately thickened, bristles rather well developed beneath on apical one third; hind tibiae slightly curved; basitarsi about equal in length to next three tarsal subsegments. Wings faintly iridescent, the 3rd section of costa about 1/3 the lenght of the 4th; 5th section about twice as long as 3rd and 4th combined; crossvein r-m located about half way between the ends of veins R_{1+2} and just before the middle of the discal cell; ultimate section of fourth vein slightly curved (fig. 10A) Abdomen with a faint metallic lustre, sides slightly rounded, widest at segment three; 5th segment scarcely one third longer than 4th. Hypopygium about 3/4 the length of the 5th segment, compressed to the right, asymmetrical with an apical depressed area and a longitudinal groove on the right side as viewed from above (fig. 10D & E). Hypopygium very often extended so that the 9th segment is plainly visible on the right side and the 7th tergum on the left side from dorsal view. From ventral view the hypopygium is very characteristic, the 9th segment is elongate, longer than the eight in length, its anterior margin almost reaching to the membranous area at the apex of the 8th; 9th segment with a deep 'V' shaped cleft on posterior margin and a distinct longitudinal groove down the middle. Harpagones simple, gently curved on inner margins and bluntly pointed (fig. 10F).

Length. body : 3 3mm; wing : 5mm.

♀. Front chiefly silvery, shining on the upper one third, subshining in the middle; hind trochanter with 4 to 5 strong bristles beneath. Ovipositor rather slender, reaching beyond apex of the 2nd abdominal segment; base subglobose, piercer longer than base (fig. 10G); otherwise similar to male. Type locality : Adirondack Mountains, New York. Type in Hungarian National Museum.

Remarks. The above description is from Hardy (1943). It is widely distributed in Oriental, Nearctic and Palaearctic regions.

This species resembles *T. sylvatica* (Meigen) & *T. indica* sp. nov. from India in having bristles on the hind trochanter. The wing venation is close to *T. indica* because of the ratio of the 4th costal section to 3rd costal section but it differs from it in the shape of claspers and the position of r-m crossvein which is in the middle of the discal cell in *T. indica* while at the basal 1/3 in *T. coquilletti.* The general shape of claspers, although not exactly same, brings it somewhat close to *T. sylvatica.*

Tomosvaryella curvipatis sp. nov.

(Fig. 11)

♂. Medium sized, black species. Head slightly broader than thorax, as long as broad; compound eyes dark brown with black patches, fused on the front for a distance equal to 3-4 rows of facets leaving a small triangular area below the median ocellus, known as the upper frontal triangule, which is black and is equal in length to the joining area of compound eyes; ocellar triangle black; lower frontal triangle black, with white pubescence and about 1.5 x as long as the joining area of compound eyes; face black with white pubescence, equal in width at both ends, which is equal to the width of lower end of frons; occiput black with white pubescence on the lateral side, with maximum width along the upper half of compound eyes and with minute greyish setae on the hind margin. Antenna broken. Proboscis not visible externally. Thorax black with few small, scattered, brownish hairs; pleurae black with white pubescence; scutellum shining black with few brown hairs. Humeri yellow. Halteres also yellow. Wings with slight brownish tinge; 4th costal section about 1.5x as long as 3rd costal section; 5th costal section about 2.8 x as long as 3rd and 4th combined; crossvein r-m distinctly before middle of discal cell; last segment of vein M_{1+2} distinctly curved (fig. 11 A). Legs : coxae, trochanters and femora black with distal tips of femora yellow: tibiae with proximal 1/3 and distal tips yellow, rest black, with rows of brownish hairs; hind femora with comparatively long hairs and hind tibia distinctly curved (fiig 11B); tarsi yellow with yellow hairs; claws brown. Metanotum black with white pubescence. Abdomen black, slightly pollinose; 1st abdominal tergum with 4 brown comparatively long bristles on each side on the lateral margin; other segments with small scattered black bristles, segments 3rd to 5th with few brown patches; 5th and 8th abdominal segments with comparatively long brown bristles almost equal in length to those on 1st abdominal tergum; 8th abdominal segment about 0.5x as long as 5th segment and with a membranous area on the right side not visible from dorsal view (fig. 11C). Male genitalia with long, straight asymmetrical claspers (fig. 11D); cerci small with bristles pointed outwardly; aedeagus long, ejaculatory apodeme of small size; shape of ejaculatory apodeme, aedeagus, aedeagal basal plates as shown in fig. 11E.

Length. Body : 2.7mm; wing : 2.5mm.

♀. Not known.

Remarks. This species seems close to *T. contorta* Hardy from Douglas county, Kansas, U S A. (Hardy, 1943) because of resemblance of bent tibia and to some extent shape of claspers but these are not exactly same. They are slightly bent inward in *T. contorta* while they are straight in the new species. Shape of hypopygium and wing venation are also different in both the species. In *contorta*, 4th costal section is 3 to 4x as long as 3rd costal section and r-m is in the middle, while in the new species 3rd costal section is 1.5x as long as 4th costal section and r m is distinctly before the middle of discal cell.

Etymology. Name based on curved hind tibia.

Specimen examined. Holotype ♂ from grasses, Srinagar (J. & K.), 5 xi. 1982, coll. S. K. Sharma.

T. dehraduniensis sp. n.

(Fig. 12)

♂. Medium sized, black. Head 1.1x as broad as thorax; 1.2x as broad as long; compound eyes brown with black patches, joined on the front for a distance equal to 11 rows of eye facets, leaving a small, black upper frontal triangle; ocellar triangle black; lower frontal triangle black with white pubescence, as long as the joining area of compound eyes; face black with white pubescence, almost equal in width at both the ends; occiput black with white pubescence on the lateral side and with minute setae on the hind margin. Antenna : 1st segment small, brownish black; 2nd segment also brownish black, with one bristle on the upper side; 3rd segment brownish black with pubescence in the lower half, acuminate at the tip, 1.5x as long as the 2nd segment; arista dark brown, more than 2x as long as 3rd antennal segment (fig. 12B). Proboscis small, light brown. Thorax dull black with little pubescence near the lateral margins; pleurae black with white pubescence; scutellum black; humeri greyish yellow. Halteres yellow. Wings hyaline; 4th costal section about 2x as long as 3rd costal section; 5th costal section about 1.5x as long as 3rd and 4th combined; crossvein r-m almost in the middle of the discal cell; last section of vein M_{1+2} gently curved (fig. 12A). Legs: coxae, trochanters, femora and tibiae black with white pubescence except the distal tip of femora and both tips of tibia which are yellow; tarsi yellow with brown bristles, ditsal tarsus brown with brown claws; pulvilli yellow. Abdomen dull black with white pubescence and with few scattered small brownish hairs on the last segment; 1st abdominal segment with 3-4 black bristles on each side, other segments with small scatteted bristles Male genitalia: claspers asymmetrical and downwardly curved; dorsally they appear to be having separate lobes and fitting into each other; ventral side with strong bristles; cerci with brown bristles on the inner side (fig. 12C, D & E); aedeagus long, trifid; shapes of aedeagus, aedeagal basal plates and ejaculatory apodeme as shown in fig. 12F.

Length. Body : 2.6mm; wings : 2.8mm.

♀. With strong ovipositor having black base and brown, thick, upcurved piercer reaching upto the 2nd abdominal segment (fig. 12G); frons black with white pubescence, more in the lower half near the antenna; equal in width at upper and lower ends, but slightly broader in the middle, 1st abdominal segment with about 6 small black bristles; abdomen slightly more elongate than the male. Rest description similar to male.

Length. Body : 2.8mm; wings : 2.5mm.

Remarks. This species comes close to *T. calcerata* Hardy from Luzon, Philippines because of resemblance of claspers, but other characters are totally different. Hardy mentioned that *calcerata* is close in its description to *T. epichalca*, but this new species *(dehraduniensis)* do not resemble the *epichalca* in any way. The wing venation, chaetotaxy and other characters are all different from *epichalca*: claspers are also having some differences, they are bare in *calcerata* but with strong bristles in *dehraduniensis*.

Etymology. Name based on locality.

Specimens examined. Holotype ♂, Sahastradhara, near Dehra Dun (U.P.), 27 x.1986, coll. S. K. Sharma. *Allotype* ♀, same data.

Tomosvaryella denticulatus sp. nov.

(Fig. 13)

♂. Small sized; black species. Head 1.30x as broad as thorax, 1.25x as long as broad; compound eyes blackish brown with light brown patches, joined on the front for a distance equal to 7 rows of eye facets, leaving a small upper frontal triangle, which is black and almost equal in length to the joining area of compound eyes; ocellar triangle black; lower frontal triangle black with white pubescence, 2.5x as long as the joining area of compound eyes; face black with white pubescence, width same at both ends and also equal to the lower end of frons; occiput black with white pubescence on dorsal and lateral sides, more on the lower half of the lateral side, dorsal side with small brown bristles. Antenna : 1st segment small, dark brown; 2nd segment dark brown with 2 small bristles on the upper side; 3rd segment light brown with pubescence near the margin, acuminate at apex, about 2x as long as the 2nd segment; arista brown, 1.5x as long as 3rd antennal segment (fig. 13B). Proboscis long, brown, with few hairs. Thorax subshining black with scattered brown, comparatively long hairs; pleurae black with white pubescence; scutellum black with yellowish brown hairs; humeri greyish yellow. Halteres yellow. Wings with slight brown tinge; 4th costal section about 2x as long as 3rd costal section; 5th costal section 2x as long as 3rd and 4th combined; crossvein r-m well before middle of the discal cell; last section of vein M_{1+2} gently curved (fig. 13A). Legs black in the ground colour; coxae, trochanters, and femora black with little pubescence; distal tips of femora yellow; tibiae with proximal 1/3rd and distal tips yellow; rest black; tarsi yellow with brown hairs; claws brown; hind trochanter with two protuberances (fig. 13C). Abdomen subshining black with almost parallel sides; 1st abdominal tergum with 5 brown comparatively long bristles on each side on the lateral margin, other terga with small, black bristles scattered all over the abdomen; 8th abdominal segment more than 0.5x as long as 5th, almost as broad as 5th slightly protruding out on the right side with membranous area at the tip (fig. 13D). Male genitalia with claspers of moderate length, slightly bent inward near the tip and with scattered setae; left one slightly more longer than the right one; cerci broad, with bristles pointing outward (fig. 13E & F); aedeagus trifid, long; ejaculatory apodeme broad; shape of aedeagus, ejaculatory apodeme, aedeagal basal plates as shown in fig. 13G.

Length. Body : 2.0mm; wing : 1.8mm.

♀. Ovipositor with rounded base and small, straight, brown piercer which is as long as base (fig. 13H). Frons black, without any pubescence narrow in the upper and lower regions, slightly broader in the middle; hind trochanter different from the male in not having any tubercle, but with few minute hairs. Rest description similar to male.

Lenght. Body : 2.2mm; wings : 2.0mm.

Remarks. The species is different from all other species of *Tomosvaryella* because of the peculiar shape of male terminalia and the shape of claspers. The wing venation and the hind trochanter can be considered close to *T. nitens* (Brunetti) although not exactly same. The ratio of 5th to 3rd+4th costal sections is 2x in the new species while 1.5x in T. *nitens*. The shape of hind trochanter is variable, in some cases it has two protuberances, while in others only one.

Etymology. Name based on the presence of tubercle on the hind trochanter.

Specimens examined. Holotype ♂, from grasses, Jahankhelan (Distt. Hoshiarpur, Punjab), 9.ix.1985, coll. S. K. Sharma, *Allotype* ♀, from grasses, Amritsar (Punjab), 17.xi.1985, coll. V. K. Kohli. Paratypes 1 ♂ from Silent valley (Kerala), 7.iv.1983, coll. L. S. Arya; 1 ♂, from weeds, Hoshiarpur (Punjab), 8.xi.1984, coll. V. K. Kohli; 3 ♂, from grasses, Beas (Punjab), 16.xi.1985, coll. V. K. Kohli; 1 ♂, from grasses, Ramnagar (U.P.), 21.xi.1986, coll. S. K. Sharma.

Tomosvaryella *epichalca* (Perkins)

(Fig. 14)

•

♂. Large and black. Head 1.25x as broad as thorax, 0.8x as broad as long, 1.2x as high as broad; compound eyes brown with black patches, joined on the front for a distance equal to 4 rows of facets, leaving a small black triangular area below the median ocellus, known as the upper frontal triangle which is black and equal in length to the joining area of compound eyes; lower frontal triangle black with white pubescence and about 2x as long as joining area of compound eyes; face black with white pubescence, width same at both the ends and also equal to the lower end of frons; occiput black with white pubescence on the lateral sides and with few small black bristles on the dorsal side; occiput with maximum width near the upper half of compound eyes. Antenna : 1st segment grey, 2nd segment grey with two bristles on the upper side and one on the lower side; 3rd segment grey with yellowish pube-

* ***Pipunculus epichalus*** Perkins, 1905, Bull. Div. Ent. Hawaii. Sugar Plrs. Exp. Sta., 1 : (4): 150 Type-loc. : Queensland, Australia

Tomosvaryella epichalcus (Perkins) : Hardy, 1964, Aus. J. Zool., 12:115,

Tomosvaryella epichalca Perkins) : Hardy, 1972. Oriental Insects Supp., 2:71.

scence on the lower half and near margin, acuminate at tip, about 2x as long as the 2nd segment; arista dark brown, slightly more than 2x as long as 3rd segment (fig. 14B). Proboscis not visible externally. Thorax black with little pubescence and few scattered brown hairs on the dorsum; pleurae black with white pubescence more near wing base; scutellum shining black with brownish tinge; humeri orange yellow. Halteres too coloured like humeri. Wings with little brownish tinge; 4th costal section about 3.5x as long as 3rd costal section; 5th costal section about 1.2x as long as 3rd and 4th combined; cross-vein r-m in the middle of discal cell; last segment of vein M_{1+2} gently curved (fig. 14A). Legs : coxae, trochanters, femora and tibiae black with little pubescence except for the distal tips of femora and both tips of tibiae yellow; tarsi grey with many rows of brownish black bristles; claws brown. Abdomen black with few brownish patches; 1st abdominal tergum with white pubescence and with 4-5 short inconspicuous bristles on each side on the lateral margin; other segments with scattered, small black setae; 8th abdominal segment less than 0.5x as long as 5th and with a membranous area on the tip (fig. 14C). Male genitalia with asymmetrical yellowish brown claspers having small setae; right one being smaller and with pointed tip while the left one slightly longer and broader at the tip; cerci long with bristles on both inner and outer sides (fig. 14D, E & F); aedeagus long, trifid; shape of aedeagus, aedeagal basal plates, and ejaculatory apodeme etc. as shown in fig. 14G.

Length. Body : 3.4mm; wing : 3.2mm.

♀ Abdomen more shining as compared to male; ovipositor with black base, brown piercer, slightly curved upward and reaching upto the 3rd abdominal segment (fig. 14H). Tarsi not so profusely haired as in male. Rest description similar to male.

Length. Body : 3.0mm; wing : 2.7mm.

Remarks. This species shows lot of variation. Different specimens from different parts of India were studied and it was found that the ratio of 3rd to 4th costal sections varies from 2.5 to 3.8. The ratio of 5th to 3rd & 4th costal sections varies from 1.2 to 1.75. Colour of humeri varies from grey to yellow and of abdomen from metallic to dull black. In some cases antenna is quite longer. In females, ovipositor varies from straight to very much curved upward. Hind trochanter is hairy in some cases.

* *Specimens examined*. 1 ♂, from weeds, Gagret (H.P.), 8.xi.1985, coll. S. K. Sharma; 1 ♀, from Gagret (H.P.), 8.xi.1985, coll. J S. Grewal; many

* It has been reported for the first time from India.

from different localities in Gagret (H.P.), Pantnagar, Kashipur, Bijnaur, Ramnagar, Dehra Dun, Herbertpur (U.P.), Una (H.P.), Hoshiarpur, Ladowal (Distt. Ludhiana, Punjab), Thekkady, Silent Valley and Mukali (Kerala), Kharak camp (H.P.), Koti (H.P.), Guwahati (Assam) etc. from 1982 to 1986 in different months.

Tomosvaryella eusylvatica sp. nov.

(Fig. 15)

♂. Medium sized, black. Head almost equal to thorax in width, as high as long; compound eyes dark brown with few black patches; joined on front for a distance equal to 8 rows of facets, leaving a small, black, triangular area below median ocellus, the upper frontal triangle is 0.5x as long as the joining area of compound eyes; lower frontal triangle black with white pubescence, about 1.5x as long as joining area of compound eyes; face black with little pubescence, width same at both ends, and also equal to lower end of frons; occiput greyish black with pubescence on the upper and lateral sides, densely pollinose on dorsolateral sides, maximum width near middle of compound eyes on lateral sides. Antenna: 1st two segments brown; 2nd segment with white pubescence and 2 small brown bristles on upper side and one on lower side; 3rd segment and arista broken. Proboscis not visible externally. Thorax subshining, black, some portion on anterior left with brownish tinge and few scattered brown minute hairs; pleurae black with white pubescence; scutellum also shining black, with few brown hairs along margin. Humeri yelllow. Halteres also yellow. Wings with little brownish tinge; 4th costal section 1.5x as long as 3rd costal section; 5th costal section 2.0x as long as 3rd and 4th combined; crossvein r-m slightly before middle of discal cell; last section of vein M_{1+2} distinctly curved (fig. 15A). Legs with coxae, trochanters and femora black, except yellow distal tips of femora; hind femora with rows of small brown bristles; rest black and with rows of brown bristles, tarsi yellow with rows of brown bristles; mid coxae with 3 black bristles on each side; hind trochanter with few strong black bristles on lower side (fig. 15B). Abdomen shining black with slight brownish tinge, slightly pollinose, broad in middle; 1st abdominal tergum with about 3-4 brown bristles on each side; 8th abdominal segment less than 0.5x as long as 5th; both these segments with comparatively long, black bristles; membranous area on right side of 8th segment (fig. 15C). Male genitalia with long claspers, slightly bent inward, left one slightly longer; cerci broad and with small brisles on inner side (fig. 15D & E).

Length. Body : 2.46mm; wing : 2.35mm.

♀. Not known.

Remarks. This species is quite close to *T. sylvatica* (Meigen) because of the resemblance of wing venation and chaetotxy but the shape of claspers differs from that of *sylvatica.* Claspers are more slender and curved in the new species (compare fig. 15D with 30E).

Etymology. Named due to its resemblance with *sylvatica.*

Specimen examined. Holotype ♂, from grasses, Srinagar (J & K), 6.v. 1982, coll. S. K. Sharma.

Tomosvaryella genitalis sp. nov.

(Fig. 16)

♂. Medium sized, black. Head about 1.25x as broad as thorax and about 1.25x as long as broad; compound eyes dark brown, joined on the front leaving a very small, black triangular area below the median ocellus known as the upper frontal triangle covered with white pubescence and almost as long as the joining area of compound eyes; ocellar triangle also black; the joining area of compound eyes equal to 7 rows of eye facets; lower frontal triangle with white pubescence, equal in width to the lower end of frons near the antenna, narrowing towards proboscis; occiput black with little pubescence on the lateral sides. Antenna: 1st segment very small, black; 2nd segment black with one bristle on upper side; 3rd segment light brown, with little pubescence on the tip and margin, narrowing towards tip, about 1.5x as long as 2nd segment; arista brownish black, more than 2x as long as 3rd segment (fig. 16B). Proboscis small, brown. Thorax subshining black, with few scattered minute hairs on the dorsum; scutellum shining black, bare. Humeri and halteres greyish yellow. Wings with light brown tinge; 4th costal section about 1.25x as long as 3rd costal section; 5th costal section about 1.75x as long as 3rd and 4th combined; crossvein r-m distinctly beyond middle of discal cell; last section of vein M_{1+2} gently curved (fig. 16A). Legs almost black with distal tips of femora and both proximal and distal tips of tibiae yellow; tarsi yellow with many rows of yellow hairs (mid tarsi with brownish hairs); claws brown, well developed; pulvilli yellow. Abdomen subshining black, 1st tergum with white pubescence and with 3 well developed black bristles on each anterolateral side, other segments with slight pubescence on the dorsolateral sides; 5th and 8th segments with small black bristles scattered all over other segments bare; 8th segment almost as long as 5th. Male genitalia with long asymmetrical claspers, left one slightly longer and bent inward, right one more broader, almost straight with few minute hairs on the outer side; cerci not so broad and with bristles on the outer side (fig. 16C & D); aedeagus tetrafid; the shape of ejaculatory apodeme, aedeagal basal plates etc. as shown in fig. 16E.

Length. Body : 2.35mm; wing : 2.05mm.

♀. Ovipositor with blackish brown piercer which is almost as long as base, very slightly curved upward and reaching upto 3rd abdominal segment (fig. 16F). Frons black with white pubescence more near antenna; slightly more broader in the middle. Rest of description similar to male.

Length. Body : 2.75mm; wing : 2.6mm.

Remarks. This species is different from all other known species in its quite different combination of characters. Its venation, hind trochanter, humeri colour, abdominal characters etc are quite normal. However, its claspers are different from all other species. Its wing venation can be condered close to *T. subvirescens* (Loew) (but not exactly same). The other characters are, however, quite different from *subvirescens*.

Etymology. Named because of peculiar shape of male claspers.

Specimens examined. Holotype ♂, by sweeping over the weeds from Amb (H P.), 23.ix.1985, coll. J S. Grewal. Allotype ♀, from wild bushes, Pantnagar (U.P,), 9.xi 1983, coll. V. K Kohli.

Tomosvaryella indica sp nov.

(Fig. 17)

♂. Large sized, black. Head 1.2x broader than thorax and about 0.8x as long as broad; compound eyes brick red, joined on the front leaving a very small, black, triangle below median ocellus, the upper frontal triangle; ocellar triangle black; lower frontal triangle about 2x as long as joining area of compound eyes, black, with white pubescence; face equal in width at both ends, its width equal to that of lower end of frons, with white pubescence; occiput black with pubescence on the lateral sides: dorsal side with small black bristles along margin of eyes. Antenna: 1st segment small, brownish black; 2nd segment also brownish black with 2 bristles on upper side; 3rd segment dark brown with white pubescence along margin, acute at apex, about 2x as long as 2nd segment; arista brownish black, about 2.5x as long as 3rd segment (fig. 17B). Proboscis not exposed. Thorax black with few scattered minute hairs, pollinose on sides near wing bases; scutellum shining black, bare. Humeri greyish yellow. Halteres brownish yellow. Wing with very light brownish tinge; 4th costal section about 3x as long as 3rd costal section; 5th costal section 1.2x as long as 3rd and 4th combined; cross-vein r-m very slightly beyond middle of discal cell; last section of M_{1+2} distinctly curved (fig 17A). Legs almost black with distal tips of femora, and both tips of tibiae yellow; tarsi dark brown with rows of brownish hairs; claws brown and well developed. Abdomen black, 1st abdominal tergum with about 4 inconspicuous bristles on each side, other segments with small black bristles scattered all over; 8th abdominal segment less than half as long as 5th abdominal segment and with a membranous area at tip of 8th segment (fig. 17C). Male genitalia with long claspers curved downard and bent outward at tip, left clasper comparatively long, broad and with spoon-shaped apex bearing minute hairs; the right clasper with minute hairs on external side and few hairs on internal side; cerci broad and with small hairs on inner as well as outer sides (fig. 17D, E & F); aceagus trifid The shape of ejaculatory apodeme, aedeagus, and aedeagal basal plates, etc. as in fig. 17G.

Length. Body : 3.8mm; wing : 3.4mm.

♀. Agrees with the male except comparetively smaller, thorax slightly more shining and not pollinose; hind trochanter with minute hairs (fig. 17H); tarsi yellowish brown and with many rows of brown bristles; ovipositor with dark brown base and brown piercer, 2x as long as the base & slightly curved upward as shown fig. 17 I.

Remarks. This species is close to *T. robusta* and *T. epichalca*. The wing venation is more close to *robusta*, but the presence of minute bristles on the first abdominal tergum differentiates the new species from it. The genitalia of the new species is different from both these species in length and shape. The ovipositor of female is close to *robusta* but it has hairy hind trochanter and bristles on 1st abdominal tergum as in *epichalca*.

Etymology. Named because of its widespread nature in various parts of India.

Specimens examined. Holotype ♂, by sweeping over weeds, Una (H.P.), 9.xi.1985, coll. S. K. Sharma. Allotype ♀, from grasses, Dehra Dun (U.P.), 24.vi.1983, coll. S. K. Sharma. Paratypes: many specimens from different localities of Gagret (H.P.), Thekkady (Kerala), Jahan Khelen (Distt. Hoshiarpur, Punjab), Solan, Kandaghat (H.P.); Sudhar (Distt. Ludhiana, Punjab); Pinjore (Haryana); Hoshiarpur (Punjab), etc. from 1982 to 1985.

Tomosvaryella kashipurensis sp. nov.
(Fig. 18)

♂. Comparatively large black species. Head 1.25x as broad as thorax, 1.2x as broad as long; compound eyes brown with some blackish spots, joined on the front for a distance equal to 5 rows of eye facets leaving a small black upper frontal triangle which is almost as long as the joining area of compound eyes; lower frontal triangle black with little pubescence near the antenna, more than 2x as long as the joining area of compound eyes, face black with white pubescence, equal in width to the lower end of frons near the antenna, getting narrower towards proboscis; occiput black with white pubescence on the lower half of lateral side; dorsal side with small yellowish hairs. Antenna : 1st segment small, brown; 2nd segment brown with white pubescence and with 2 small brown bristles on the upper side; 3rd segment brown with white pubescence, broad at upper end, acuminate at tip, about 2x as long as 2nd segment; arista dark brown, slightly more than 2x as long as 3rd segment (fig. 18B). Proboscis not visible externally. Thorax black with few scattered brown small hairs; scutellum also black with scattered brown small hairs; pleurae black with white pubescence near the scutellum; humeri yellow. Halteres yellow. Wing with little brownish tinge; 4th costal section about 2.52x as long as 3rd costal section; 5th costal section 1.25 as long as 3rd and 4th combined; crossvein r-m almost in the middle of the discal cell; last section of vein M_1+_2 gently curved (fig 18 A). Legs : coxae, trochanters and femora black with white pubescence except the distal tip of femora which is yellow, tibiae with proximal 1/3 yellow, rest black with white pubesence; fore and mid tarsi yellowish brown with dark brown bristles; claws brown, well developed. Abdomen black having metallic tinge with little pubescence on the hind segments; 1st abdominal segment with 3-4 small incospicuous bristles on each side, other segments with small, scattered brownish bristles; 8th abdominal segment less than 0.5x of 5th and with a membranous area at the tip (fig. 18C). Male genitalia with asymmetrical claspers covered all over with small bristles; left clasper is slightly larger than the right one and both are with blunt tips; cerci long and with many strong bristles on the inner side; aedeagus trifid. The shape of claspers, cerci, aedeagus, aedeagal basal plates as shown in figs. 18D, E, F, G.

Length. Body : 3.2 mm; wing : 3.1 mm.

♀. Ovipositor with rounded base and brown piercer curved upward reaching upto the 2nd abdominal segment (fig. 18H); frons black with white pubescence, equal in width at both the ends, slightly broader in the middle. Rest of description similar to male.

Length. Body : 3.0 mm; wing : 2.9 mm.

Remarks. This species is close to *T. epichalca* (Perkins) because of short inconspicuous bristles and peculiar metallic sheen on the abdomen; the other characters like shape of antenna and legs without any modification are also close to *T. epichalca.* The characters like wing venation, shape of genitalia are, however, dfferent. The ratio of 4th to 3rd costal section is 2.25x in this species while in *T. epichalca* it is 3–3.5x; the ratio of 5th to 3+4th is 1.25x in new species while in *T. epichalca* it is 1.1x. The shape of claspers also differs. The right clasper is pointed at the tip in *epichalca* (fig. 19D) while blunt at the tip in the new species. The claspers are also comparatively shorter than *epichalca.*

Etymology. Name based on the locality.

Specimens examined. Holotype ♂, from weeds, Kashipur (Distt. Nainital U.P.), 21-ix-1986, coll. S. K. Sharma. *Allotype* ♀, same data, coll. Ashwani Kumar. Paratype 1 ♀, same data, coll. S. K. Sharma.

Tomosvaryella limpidipennis (Brunetti)
(Fig. 19)

Pipunculus limpidipennis, Brunetti, Rec. Ind. Mus., 1912, 7 : 491.

Tomosvaryella limpidipennis : Hardy, 1972, Orient. Ins. suppl., 2 : 73. ♂, ♀.

Head with frons of uniform width, greyish, with a silvery white shimmer when seen from above; face below antennae similar; antennae blackish, 3rd joint white with silver shimmer; arista black : eyes (in ♀) with the facets much larger on each side of the frontal space than those behind. Thorax dark aeneous-grey, moderately shining, bare; sides and humeri a little lighter; scutellum aeneous-black, bare, shining. Abdomen concolorous, with a slight olive-green tint, submetallic, bare, unmarked ; venter unicolorous; the last abdominal segment bears in the male a knob-like process, and in the female a long horny process bent under the venter. Legs : femora blackish, base and tips yellowish-brown; tibiae with a broad blackish ring, occupying the middle third or more; tarsi yellowish-brown; no ciliation on middle femora; hind femora shining black on inner side. Wings quite clear; 4th longitudinal vein, after quitting the posterior crossvein, running almost straight to the wing border, without being bent outwards in a bow ; anterior crossvein almost exactly over centre of discal cell; no distinct stigma, but the costal vein is little thickened along the 3rd and 4th costal segments; 3rd and 4th costal segments of about equal length, and taken together only half the length of the 5th segment ; wings barely pale yellowish at base; halteres pale livid yellow.

Length. nearly 2 mm.

Specimens examined. Holotype ♂ (no. 5690/15, partly broken), 4 ix.1907, Calcutta, in Museum collection of Zoological Survey of India; allotype ♀ (no. 4545/15, partly damaged), 5.ix.1907, Calcutta; paratype 1 ♂ (head broken, no. 4544/6), Igatpuri (Western Ghats, India), 1 ♂ (no. 5889/15) Benikhola (Nepal), 17.ii.1908; three specimens missing, only their labels left; all coll, by Annadale in museum collection of Zoological Survey of India, Calcutta.

Tomosvaryella longipygiamis sp. nov.

(Fig. 20)

♂. Medium sized, black. Head about 1.3x as broad as thorax and as long as broad ; compound eyes dark brown, joined on front leaving a small triangular area below median ocellus, known as upper frontal triangle, which is black and about 1/3x as long as the joining area of compound eyes ; ocellar triangle black; joining area of compound eyes as long 3 rows of eye facets; lower frontal triangle black with white pubescence and about 1.15x as long as joining area of compound eyes; face grey with white pubescence equal in width at both ends and equal to lower end of frons; occiput grey with white pubescence on lateral sides and with few brown bristles on dorsal side near ocellar triangle. Antenna : 1st segment small, dark brown ; 2nd segment dark with white pubescence and with 2 minute bristles on upper side; 3rd segment brown with white pubescence on margin, more than 2x as long as 2nd segment and with a bristle like tip; arista dark brown and more than 2x as long as 3rd segment (fig. 20B). Proboscis not visible externally. Thorax subshining, black with few scattered black bristles on dorsum ; pleurae black with little pubescence; scutellum also black with few bristles. Humeri slightly greyish yellow, halteres orange yellow. Wings hyaline; 3rd costal section about 0.5x as long as 4th costal section ; 5th costal section about 2x as long as 3rd and 4th combind ; crossvein r-m almost in middle of discal cell (slightly beyond middle in one specimen);last section of vein M_{1+2} distinctly curved (fig.20A).

Abdomen dull black with slight pollinosity, 1st abdominal tergum with about 5 brown comparatively long bristles on each side, other segments with scattered black bristles ; 8th abdominal segment almost equal to 5th in length and with a membranous area on right side of the tip (fig. 20C); 5th segment with comparatively more bristles than on other segments. Male genitalia with long, yellow, asymmetrical claspers ; left one being slightly longer than right one and both having small yellow setae ; cerci broad in middle with many hairs on inner side (fig. 20D, E) ; ejaculatory apodeme small ; aedeagus quite long, trifid. The shape of ejaculatory apodeme, aedeagus, aedeagal basal plates as shown in fig. 20F.

Length. Boby : 2.79 mm; wing : 2.3 mm.

♀. Not known.

Remarks. This species differs from all other species of *Tomosvaryella* in the presence of long hypopygium which is almost as long as 5th abdominal segment ; but its width is slightly less than the 5th segment. The claspers are also quite long and strong. The wing venation is close to *T. flavicrus* but the r-m crossvein is not at 1/3rd of discal cell but in the middle; the legs are not totally yellow as in *flavicrus.*

Etymology. Name is based on very long hypopygium.

Specimens examined. Holotype ♂ by sweeping over weeds, Srinagar (J. & K.), 12. ix 1985, coll. S. K Sharma. Paratypes 1♂, DehraDun (U.P.), 21. vi. 1983, coll. S. K. Sharma; 2♂, Hoshiarpur (Punjab), 8.xi.1985, coll. V. K. Kohli; 1♂; Kufri (H.P.), 25.ix.1986, coll. J. S. Grewal; 1♂, Mashobra (H.P.), 27.ix.1986, coll. S. K. Sharma; 1♂, Mashobra (H P.) 27.ix.1986, coll. J. S. Grewal.

Tomosvaryella minutus sp. nov.
(Fig. 21)

♂. Small sized, black. Head about 1.2x broader than thorax, as long as broad; compound eyes brown with black patches, joined on the front for a distance equal to 5 rows of eye facets, leaving a small black triangular area below the median ocellus, the upper frontal triangle, which is 0.5x as long as the joining area of compound eyes; ocellar triangle black; lower frontal triangle black with white pubescence and about 2x as long as the joining area of compound eyes; face black with white pubescence equal in width at both ends and also to lower end of frons; occiput black with little pubescence on the lateral sides and with few brown hairs on dorsolateral side on hind margin. Antenna: 1st segment small, brown; 2nd segment brown having 1 small bristle on upper side; 3rd segment broad, brown, acute at apex with pubescence in the lower half near tip, about 1.5x as long as 2nd segment ; arista brown, about 2x as long as 3rd antennal segment (fig. 21B). Proboscis not visible externally. Thorax subshining, black with scattered yellowish hairs, more near humeri ; pleurae black, bare ; scutellum also subshining black and with few scattered hairs. Wings with slight brown tinge ; 4th costal section 1.5x as long as 3rd costal section ; 5th costal section 2x as long as 3rd and 4th combined ; cross-vein r-m in middle of discal cell ; last section of vein M_{1+2} gently curved (fig. 21A). Legs black in ground colour with distal tips of femora and both tips of tibiae yellow, all tibiae with many rows of yellow hairs, tarsi yellowish brown, with brown bristles; claws dark brown Abdomen shining black, barrel-shaped, broad in middle; 1st abdominal tergum with 4 small yellowish brown bristles on each lateral margin, other segments with small scattered, blackbristles ; 8th abdominal segment less than 1/2x as long as 5th. Male genitalia with long asymmetrical claspers; left one slightly longer than right one, with tips bent inside in such a way that they can fit into each other (fig. 21 C & D) ; cerci broad with bristles on inner side; aedeagal basal plates as shown in fig. 21 E.

Length. Body : 1.9 mm ; wing : 1.7 mm.

♀. Ovipositor with globose base and brown piercer turned downward, reaching upto the 2nd abdominal segment (fig. 21 F) ; frons black with little pubescence on the lower half and equal in width at both the ends ; hind trochanter with few brownish hairs. Rest of description similar to male.

Length. Body : 1.9 mm ; wing : 1.8 mm.

Remarks. This species is close to *T. subvirescens* (Loew) because of the similarity of wing venation, but differs from it in the shape of hind trochanter and claspers. The shape of claspers is somewhat close to *T. synadephoides* but it is not exactly same.

Specimens examined. Holotype ♂, by sweeping over grasses, Chandigarh, 24. x. 1985, coll. S. K. Sharma. Allotype ♀, same data. Paratype 1♀, same data.

Tomosvaryella nitens (Brunetti)

(Fig. 22)

Pipunculus nitens **Brunetti, 1912, Rec. Ind. Mus., 7 : 492.**

Tomosvaryella nitens **(Brunetti) ? hardy 1966, Bull. Brit. Mus. (nat. hist), Ent.,17(10) : 477.**

♂. Head with frons and face shining silvery-white ; eyes contiguous for some distance ; antennae black, 3rd joint, except at the base, reddish-yellow ; back of head blackish-grey, rather well puffed out, with silver shimmer at least round the edge. Thorax blackish, with a slight bluish tint, moderately bare ; sides dark-bluish grey, with a little whitish shimmer in certain lights ; scutellum concolorous, with a few hairs ; metanotum with a greyish-white shimmer. Abdomen shining bluish-black, with some short whitish hairs ; 1st segment pale bluish-grey ; genitalia rather small, clubbed, concolorous. Legs : femora black, except at tips, with a little grey shimmer ; rest of legs yellow ; tibae with a broad band (apparently not always complete) occupying nearly their entire length ; tips of tarsi blackish on upper side ; hind femora apparently not shining on inner side ; wings clear ; 3rd costal segment very short ; 4th very slightly yellowish, anterior cross-vein exactly at middle of discal cell (in one specimen) or immediately before it (in the 2nd specimen).

Length. 2 mm.

Specimens examined. Holotype ♂,no. 1929/H1, badly damaged, Maddathorai, Travancore (South India), 19.xi.1908, coll. Annadale, in musem collection, Zoological Survey of India, Calcutta. Paratypes missing from museum collection.

Remarks. Its original description (Brunetti, 1912; 491) is quite similar to *limpidipennis*. Brunetti (1923), therefore, doubted its independent specific status and thought it to be the same as *limpidipennis*. Hardy (1966) also supported this view. He even suggested that *nitens* might represent a subspecies of *subvirescens*. Its systematic status could not be confirmed as its holotype is now in badly damaged condition. The present description has been taken from Brunetti (1923).

Tomosvaryella oryzaetora Koizumi

(Fig. 23)

* ♀. Medium sized, black. Head 1.25x as broad as thorax, 0.75x as long

---

*

Tomosvaryella oryzaetora Koizumi, 1959 Sci Rept. Fac. Agric. Okayama Univ., 13:38. Type-loc. : Okayama city, Japan.

Alloneura oryzaetora (Koizumi). 1960. Sci Rept. Fac. Agric. Okayama Univ , 16:34.

as broad; compound eyes dark brown, not joining on front; frons black with little pubescence on lower half, equal in width at both ends; face black with white pubescence, equal in width at both ends and to lower end of frons; occiput black with white pubescence on lateral and dorsolateral sides, maximum width near upper 1/4th. Antenna : 1st two segments dark brown; 2nd segment with 2 minute bristles on upper side and with little pubescence; 3rd segment brownish on upper side, rest white due to dense pubescence, tapering downward into a bristle-like tip, more than 2x as long as 2nd segment; arista dark brown, about 1.3x as long as 3rd segment (fig. 23B). Proboscis small, brown. Thorax black with little pubescence near margin; pleurae black with white pubescence; scutellum shining black;both thorax & scutellum with smallbrown hairs on dorsal side; humeri black Halters yellow.Wings hyaline; 4th costal section 1.75x as long as 3rd costal section; 5th costal section 1.5x as long as 3rd and 4th combined; crossvein r-m almost at middle of discal cell; last section of vein M_{1+2} slightty curved (fig 23A). Legs with coxae, trochanters, femora and tibiae black with white pubescence except for yellow distal tips of femora and both ends of tibiae; hind tibiae with rows of light yellow hairs; tarsi yellow with rows of brown bristles. Abdomen subshining black with brownish tinge and white pubescence on lateral sides; 1st abdominal tergum with 5 brown comparatively long bristles on each side on lateral margin; other segments with scattered, light brown bristles all over dorsal side. Ovipositor with black base and brown piercer which is straight pointed at tip reaching upto 3rd abdominal segment (fig. 23C).

Length. Body : 2.6mm; wing : 2.6mm.

♂. Not known.

Specimens examined. 1 ♀, P. A. U., Ludhiana, 26.ix.1984, coll. G. S. Sidhu. 2 ♀, weeds, Hoshiarpur (Punjab), 8.xi.1985, coll. J. S. Grewal.

T. ramnagariensis sp. nov.
(Fig. 24)

♂. Medium sized, black. Head about 1.1x as broad as thorax, 1.2x as broad as long; compound eyes dark brown with black patches more near the occiput; joined on the front for a distance equal to 6 rows of eye facets leaving a small black upper frontal triangle black with white pubescence, about 1.5x as long as the joining area of compound eyes; face black with white pubescence, equal in width to the lower end of frons near antenna, getting narrower towards proboscis; occiput greyish black with little pubescence on the lateral and dorsal side and with few brown bristles. Antenna: 1st segment small, brown; 2nd segment also brown with one bristle on the upper side, 3rd segment brown with white pubescence near the tip and the margin, broad at the upper end, tapering towards the tip (fig. 24B); proboscis not visible externally. Thorax dull black with small scattered brown bristles and with little pubescence near humeri and near the margins; scutellum also dull black and with scattered small bristles; humeri greyish yellow. Halteres yellows. Wings hyaline; 4th costal section 1.5x as long as 3rd costal section; 5th costal section about 2x as long as 3rd and 4th combined; cross-vein r-m distinctly beyond the middle of the discal cell; last section of vein M_{1+2} distinctly curved (fig. 24A). Legs: coxae, trochanters, femora and tibiae black with white pubescence except the distal tip of femora and proximal tip of tibiae which are yellow; tarsi yellow with brown bristles; last tarsomere grey in colour; claws brown, well developed; hind trochanter with few yellowish setae at the tip (fig. 24C). Abdomen dull black with scattered yellowish minute hairs; 1st abdominal segment with about 3-4 brown bristles; 8th abdominal segment almost as long as 5th and with a membranous area on the right side of the the tip. Male genitalia with asymmetrical claspers bearing many small bristles which are slightly overlapping each other; left one is slightly longer and with a hook-like structure at the tip while the right one is shorter, more broader and without any hook; cerci long and with row of bristles on the inner side (fig. 24D & E); aedeagus long, trifid; ejaculatory apodeme large and with small bristles. The shapes of claspers, aedeagus, ejaculatory apodeme and aedeagal basal plates as shown in fig. 24F.

Length. Body : 2.2mm; wing : 2.2mm.

♀. With a peculiar brown ovipositor, first going upward and then downward forming a S-shaped structure. Body thickly pollinose; abdomen with comparatively longer bristles as compared to male and abdomen is more elongate than the male; frons black with white pubescence, equal in width at both the ends which is equal to 4 rows of eye facets. Antenna pointing outward (fig. 24G). Rest description similar to male.

Length. Body : 2.5mm; wing : 2.3mm.

Remarks. This species comes close to *T. troangulatus* sp. nov. because of the resemblance in hind trochanter; the ratios of 4th to 3rd and 5th to 3rd+4th costal sections and the shape of antenna.It differs from it in its hind trochanter which is not exactly triangular as in *troangulatus*. The shape of claspers is very different in two species. They are symmetrical and beak-like in *troangulatus* but asymmetrical in this new species. In female the shape of ovipositor is also different; it is straight and small in *troangulatus* but long and curved in this new species.

Specimens examined. Holotype ♂, on weeds just outside the Corbett National Park, Ramnagar (U.P.), 21.xi.1986, coll. S. K. Sharma. Allotype ♀, Ranikhet, 20.xi.1986, coll. S.K. Sharma. *Paratype* ♂, on way to Ranikhat 20.xi.1986, coll. S. K. Sharma.

Tomosvaryella robusta Hardy

(Fig. 25)

♀. Large sized, black. Head 1.25x as broad as thorax, 0.8x as long as broad; compound eyes dark brown with few blackish patches; ocellar triangle black*; frons black with white pubescence on lower 2/3rd portion, as broad as 3 rows of eye facets, slightly more broader in middle, equal in width at both upper and lower ends; face black with white pubescence, width similar at both ends and also equal to lower end of frons; occiput grey with white pubescence on lateral sides; maximum width along upper half of compound eyes on lateral sides. Antenna : 1st and 2nd segments brown; 2nd segment with 2 small brown bristles on upper side and one on lower side; 3rd segment and arista broken. Proboscis not visible externally. Thorax shining black with white pubescence along margin near wing base; scutellum subshining black with white pubescence along anterior margin; pleurae black with white pubescence; humeri yellow. Halteres yellow. Wings with little brownish tinge; 4th costal section about 3.5x as long as 3rd; 5th costal section 1.3x as long as 3rd and 4th combined; cross-vein r-m almost at middle of discal cell; last section of vein M_{1+2} gently curved (fig. 25A). Legs with coxae, trochanters, femora and tibiae black bearing white pubescence except for yellow distal tips of femora and both ends of tibiae; tarsi yellow with rows of yellowish bristles, hind tarsi with brown bristles; claws brown; pulvilli yellow. Abdomen shining black, parallel-sided; 1st abdominal tergum with white pubescence and 2-3 short, inconspicuous bristles on lateral sides; other segments with small, scattered, black bristles. Last segment with little pubescence along margin. Ovipositor having black base and brown piercer which is turned upward reaching upto 3rd abdominal segment (fig. 25B)

Length. Body : 3.4mm; wing ; 3.2mm.

♂. Not known.

---

* *Tomosvaryella robusta* Hardy, 1968, Ent. Meddel., 36;485. Type-loc.:Luzon, Philippines.

Specimens examined. 1♀, on weeds, P.A.U., Ludhiana, 18.x.1983, coll. G. S. Sidhu; 1♀, on weeds, Calcutta, 28.iii.1985, coll. V. K. Kohli.

Remarks. This specimen is different from that of Hardy because of the presence of small inconspicuous bristles on the 1st abdominal segment; otherwise it agrees with Hardy's description. This species has been recorded for the time from India.

Tomosvaryella subhectena sp. nov.
(Fig. 26)

♂. Medium sized, black. Head about 1.25x as broad as thorax, as long as broad; compound eyes dark brown with little pollen, joined on the front for a distance equal to 12 rows of facets, leaving a very small triangular area below the median ocellus known as the upper frontal triangle, which is black and 0.5x as long as the joining area of compound eyes; ocellar triangle black; lower frontal triangle black with white pubescence and about 1.5x as long as the joining area of compound eyes; face black with white pubescence, equal in width to the lower end of frons near antenna, getting narrow towards proboscis; occiput black with white pubescence on the lateral sides; its maximum width is near the middle of compound eyes on the lateral sides. Antenna : first two segments dark brown; 2nd segment with two minute bristles on the upper side and with little pubescence; 3rd brown with white pubescence, acute at apex and about 1.5x as long as 2nd antennal segment; arista dark brown, about 1.5x as long 3rd antennal segment (fig. 26B). Proboscis small, brown. Thorax subshining black, bare, with brownish metallic tinge on dorsum; pleurae black with white pubescence; scutellum also shining black, bare, with metallic tinge; humeri yellow. Halteres yellow. Wings with slight brownish tinge; 4th costal section about 3.5x as long as 3rd costal section; 5th costal section about 1.2x as long as 3rd and 4th combined; cross-vein r-m beyond middle of the discal cell; last section of vein M_{1+2} gently curved (fig. 26A). Legs : coxae, trochanters and femora black with white pubescence, except distal tip of femora yellow; tibiae with both ends yellow; tarsi yellow with brown bristles; claws brown. Abdomen shining black, broad in the middle, with little metallic tinge; first two segments with little pubescence; 1st abdominal tergum with about 4 minute bristles on either side on lateral margin, other terga with few scattered black minute bristles; 8th abdominal segment slightly more than 0.5x as long as 5th. Male genitalia with asymmetrical claspers, right one slightly longer than left one, both with minute bristles; cerci broad and with bristles on inner and outer sides (fig. 26C); ejaculatory apodeme broad at apex. The shape of ejaculatory apodeme, aedeagal basal plates as in fig. 26D.

Length. Body : 2.9mm; wing : 2.7mm.

Remarks. This species is similar to *T. hectena* Hardy (1972) from Thailand because of wing venation, shape of claspers and presence of bristles on 1st abdominal tergum. The only difference is that of claspers, which are mirror image of those in *T. hectena.* In *hectena*, the left one is longer and the right one is shorter while in the new species left one is shorter and right one is longer.

Etymology. Name because of its closeness to *T. hectena.*

Specimens examined. Holotype ♂, from grasses, Solan (H.P.), 19.x.1982, coll. L. S. Arya. Paratype ♂ from Kandaghat (H P.), 22.x.1982, coll. L.S. Arya.

Tomosvasyella subrobusta sp n.

(Fig. 27)

♂. Comparatively longer, black species Head as broad as throax, 1.1x as broad as long; compound eyes dark brown, joined on the front for a distance equal to 6 rows of eye facets, leaving a black upper frontal triangle which is as long as the joining area of compound eyes; lower frontal triangle black with white pubescence more near the antenna; face black with white pubescence, equal in width at both the ends which is equal to the lower end of frons; occiput black with little pubescence on the lower half of the lateral sides and with few scattered small bristles on the upper side. Antenna : 1st segment small, brown; 2nd segment brown with 2 small bristles on the upper side; 3rd segment brown with white pubescence along the margin, acute at apex and about 2x as long as 3rd segment (fig. 27B). Proboscis not visible externally. Thorax black, bare with very little pubescence on dorsal as well as lateral sides; scutellum also black and with little pubescence; humeri greyish yellow. Halteres yellow. Wings hyaline, 4th costal section 3x as long as 3rd costal section; 5th costal section 1.15x as long as 3rd and 4th combined; crossvein r-m almost in the middle of the discal cell; last section of vein M_{1+2} gently curved (fig. 27A). Legs : coxae, trochanters, femora and tibiae black with little pubescence except distal tip of femora and both the tips of tibiae which are yellow; trochanters, femora and tibiae without any conspicuous bristles ; tarsi yellow with rows of brown bristles; tarsi of midleg greyish; claws brown and well developed. Abdomen black with scattered pubescence; 1st abdominal segment with 2 small black bristles on each side, other segments bare; 8th abdominal segment 0.5x as long as 5th abdominal segment & with a membranous area on the right side of the tip (fig. 27C). Male genitalia with slightly asymmetrical claspers, bent downward and with many small bristles on dorsal as well as ventral sides; left clasper is slightly longer than the right one; both claspers with broad, blunt tips; cerci long and with many bristles on inner as well as outerside (fig. 27D, E & F); aedeagus trifid, not so long. The shapes of aedeagus, aedeagal basal plates as shown in the fig. 27G.

Length. Body : 3.25mm; wing : 3.25mm.

Remarks. This species comes in between T. *epichalca* Perkins and *T. robusta* Hardy. It resembles *T. epichalca* in wing venation and chaetotaxy but the shape of claspers is different and close to those of *T. robusta* but not, exactly the same. They resemble in shape, but are slightly longer in the new species.

Etymology. Named because of resemblance to *T. robusta*.

Specimen examined. Holotype ♂,on way to Ranikhet,(U.P.), 20.xi.1986, coll. Ashwani Kumar.

Tomosvaryella subvirescens (Loew)

(Fig. 28)

Pipunculus subvirescens Loew, 1872, *Berl. Ent Zeit.*, **16**:87.

Tomosvaryella subvirescens Hardy, 1956, *Insects of Micronesia*, **13**(1):4–5.

Pipunculus aridis Williston, 1893, *North American Fauna*, **7**:255.

Pipunculus pilosiventris Becker, 1900, *Berl. Ent. Zeit.*, **45**:233.

Pipunculus glabrum Adams, 1905, *Univ. Kansas Sci. Bull.*, **3**(6):165.

Pipunculus albiseta Cresson, 1911, *Am. Ent. Soc. Trans.*, **36**:318.

Pipunculus insularis Cresson, 1911, *Am. Ent. Soc. Trans.*, **36**:317-318.

Pipunculus metallescens Malloch, 1913, *U. S. Nat. Mus. Proc.*, **43**:298.

Pipunculus knowltoni Hardy, 1939, *Kansas Ent. Soc J.*, **12**:20-22.

♂. Medium sized, black. Head about 1.2x as broad as thorax, as long as broad; compound eyes dark brown joined on front for a distance equal to five rows of facets, leaving a very small, black, triangular area below median ocellus, the upper frontal triangle, which is 0.5x as long as joining area of compound eyes; lower frontal triangle with white pubescence, about 2x as long as joining area of compound eyes; face black with white pubescence, equal in width at both ends and equal to lower end of frons; occiput black with white pubescence on lateral sides and with small greyish bristles on dorsal side. Antenna with first two segments dark brown; 2nd segment with two minute bristles on upper side and one on lower side; 3rd segment brown with white pubescence on lower half and near margin, with acuminate tip and about 1.75x as long as 2nd segment; arista dark brown, about 2x as long as 3rd segment (fig. 28B). Proboscis dark brown with small yellowish hairs. Thorax shining black with brownish tinge and many brownish hairs on dorsal side; lateral margins of terga with white pubescence; scutellum also shining black with brown bristles on margin; pleurae black with white pubescence; humeri grey. Halteres yellow. Wings hyaline; 4th costal section about 2x as long as 3rd costal section; 5th costal section 2x as long as 3rd and 4th costal sections combined; crossvein r-m slightly beyond middle of discal cell; last segment of vein M_{1+2} gently curved (fig. 28A). Legs : coxae, trochanters, femora and tibiae black with distal tips of femora and both tips of tibiae yellow; tarsi yellow with brown hairs : claws brown; hind trochanter rhomboidal with brown setae on lower side (fig. 28C); fore femora with two black bristles near proximal end. Abdomen subshining black; 1st abdominal tergum with four black bristles on each side, other segments with small, black bristles all over abdomen; 8th abdominal segment about 0.5x as long as 5th abdominal segment and with a membranous area on right side and with little pubescence (fig. 28D). Male genitalia with asymmetricaly twisted claspers (bearing small hairs all over; cerci small with small bristles all over (fig. 28E & F); aedeagus trifid. The shape of ejaculatory apodeme, aedeagus, aedeagal basal plates as in fig. 28G.

Length. Body : 3.00mm; wing : 2.9mm.

♀. Ovipositor with dark brown base and brown piercer which is almost straight and reaches upto the 2nd abdominal segment (fig. 28 I). Hind trochanters with few minute hairs as shown in fig 28H; frons black with white pubescence more in the lower half, more broader in the upper and narrow in the lower region near antenna. Rest description is similar to male.

Length. Body : 2.5mm; wing : 2.9mm.

Remarks. The female of this species is quite close to the female of *T. troangulatus* because of the shape of ovipositor and the hairy hind trochanter and so they are often confused. But the wing venation is different in the two cases. In *subvirescens* the 5th costal section is 2 or more than two times as long as 3rd and 4th combined, while in *troangulatus* it is 1.75x. The shape of antenna is also different in the two cases; 3rd antennal segment is more tapering near the tip in *troangulatns*, than in *subvirescens*.

Specimens examined. ♂, Jahankhelan (Distt. Hoshiarpur, Punjab), 9 ix. 1985, coll. S. K. Sharma; many specimens from different parts of Thekkady (Kerala), Dehra Dun, Pantnagar, Bilaspur, Kashipur, Afzalgarh and Ranikhet (U.P.), Amritsar, P.A.U., Ludhiana, Phillaur, Habowal (Distt. Ludhiana), Hoshiarpur, Chandigarh, (Punjab), Gagret, Amb. Subathu, Gopipur, Solan (H.P.), Kurukshetra (Haryana) from 1983 to 1986 in different months.

Tomosvaryella surstylae sp. nov.

(Fig. 29)

♂. Medium sized, black species. Head about 1.1x broader than thorax, 1.25x as high as long, as long as broad; compound eyes dark brown joined on the front leaving a very small upper frontal triangle which is black and as long as 4 rows of eye facets; ocellar triangle black; joining area of compound eyes equal to 7 rows of eye facets; lower frontal triangle black with white pubescence and about 2x as long as the joining area of compound eyes; face black with white pubescence and equal in width at both the ends; proboscis small, yellowish brown; occiput subshining black with little pubescence on the lower half, maximum width in the middle of upper half. Antenna: 1st segment small, black; 2nd segment black with little pubescence, with one bristle on the upper side; 3rd segment brownish black, about 2x as long as 2nd segment, broad at the upper end, tapering down to a bristle like apex; arista dark brown, about 2x as long as 3rd segment (fig. 29B). Thorax subshining black with little pubescence on dorsal as well as on lateral sides near wing bases; scutellum shining black with little pubescence; both thorax as well as scutellum without any prominent bristle; humeri yellow. Halteres yellow Wings with slightly brown tinge, 4th costal section about 2.1x as long as 3rd costal section; 5th costal section about 1.5x as long as 3rd and 4th combined; crossvein r-m almost in the middle of the discal cell; last section of vein M_{1+2} about straight (fig. 29A). Legs black except both the tips of femora and tibiae which are yellow; tarsi yellow with rows of brown bristles; claws brown, well developed; pulvilli yellow; hind trochanter with few scattered bristles. Abdomen subshining black with few scattering small black bristles; 1st abdominal segment with 4-5 small black bristles on each side; abdomen having maximum width near segment 3rd; 5th abdominal segment more than 2x as long as 8th segment; 8th segment with a membranous area on the right side of the tip as shown in fig. 29C. Male genitalia with asymmetrical claspers; left one is more pointed and turned downward; right one is having a cup-like structure where the left one is fitted, both bear small bristles on inner as well as outer side. Cerci large and bear bristles on inner as well as outer side. Aedeagus is trifid; ejaculatory apodeme is small. The shape of claspers, aedegal basal plates, aedeagus etc. as shown in fig. 29D —H.

Length. Body : 2.4 mm; wing : 2.5 mm.

♀. Having ovipositor with globose base and piercer long, brown, reaching upto the 2nd abdominal segment (fig. 29 I). Wings slightly shorter than body and with crossvein r-m slightly beyond the middle of discal cell. Frons black with white pubescence on the lower 2/3rd, slightly broader in the middle. Rest of description similar to male.

Length. Body : 2.4 mm; wing ; 2.1 mm.

Remarks. This specics is close to T. *nitens* Brunetti because of the resemblance of wing venation, but without gibbosity on the hind trochanter. The shape of male and female genitalia also differs in both the cases.

Specimens examined. Holotype ♂, on way to Tattapani (H.P.), 27.ix. 1986. coll. S. K. Sharma. Allotype ♀, same data. Paratypes : 4 ♂. 1 ♀, same data, coll. G. B. Singh; 3 ♂, same data, coll. J. S. Grewal; 2 ♂, 1 ♀, same data, coll. S. K. Sharma.

Tomosvaryella *sylvatica* Meigen

(Fig 30)

Pipunculus sylvaticus Meigen, 1824. *System. Beschr.*, 4 : 20.

Tomosvaryella sylvatica (Meigen) Aczel, 1939, Zool. Anz., 125 : 22.

Pipunculus scoparius Cresson, 1911, *Trans. Am. Ent. Soc.*, 36 : 317.

Pipunculus hirticollis Becker, 1910, *Deut. Ent. Zeit. Berlin*, 657.

♂. Medium sized, dull black. Head about 1.1x as broad as thorax, as long as broad; compound eyes brown with black patches, joined on the front for a distance equal to 7 rows of eye facets leaving a very small black upper frontal triangle; ocellar triangle black; lower frontal triangle black with white pubescence, about 2x as long as the joining area of compound eyes; face black with white pubescence equal in width to the lower end of frons near the antenna and slightly narrow near proboscis; occiput black with little pubescence. Antenna : 1st segment small, black; 2nd segment brownish black with one small bristle on the upper side and one on the lower side; 3rd segment brown with pubescence along the margin and near the tip, more than 2x as long as 2nd segment and with tip bent outward; arista dark brown, about 1.5x as long as 3rd segment (fig. 30B). Thorax black with slightly brownish tinge on the dorsum and with few scattered long brown hairs along the anterior margin and near humeri, rest bare; scutellum also blackish and bare; pleurae black with white pubescence; humeri grey. Halteres yellow. Wings with slight brownish tinge: 4th costal section about 1·75x as long as 3rd costal section and 5th costal section is 1·75x as long as 3rd and 4th combined; crossvein r-m almost in the middle, last section of vein M_{1+2} gently curved (fig. 30A). Legs : coxae, trochanters, femora, tibiae and tarsi all black except for the distal tip of tibiae; tarsi with black bristles; claws and pulvilli brown; hind trochanter with few brownish bristles (fig. 30C). Abdomen black with little pubescence and with few scattered small brown bristles on the hind segments; 1st abdominal segment with 2 small black bristles on each side; 8th abdominal segment as long as 5th segment (fig. 30D). Male genitalia with slightly asymmetrical claspers, left one is broad at the tip while the right one is slightly bent and rounded at the tip; cerci small with rows of bristles on the inner side; aedeagus long trifid; shape of claspers, aedeagus, aedeagal basal plates as shown in fig. 30E — H.

Length. Body : 2.35 mm; wing : 2.5 mm.

♀. Ovipositor with black rounded base and brown long piercer curved downward (fig. 30 I); wing venation slightly different from the male, 4th costal section is 2x as long as 3rd costal section and 5th costal section is 1.5x as long as 3rd and 4th combined; crossvein r-m is slightly beyond the middle of the discal cell; frons black with white pubescence in the lower half near antenna, equal in width at both the ends; humeri greyish yellow with yellow bristles. Rest description similar to male.

Length. Body : 2.35 mm; wing : 2.3 mm.

Specimens examined. Holotype ♂, ex weeds, Mashobra (H.P.), 27.ix. 1986 coll. S. K. Sharma; Allotype ♀, same data; Paratypes : 2 ♀, same data, coll. J. S. Grewal; 2 ♀, same data, coll. S. K. Sharma; 3 ♂, 1 ♀, Dehra Dun,

27.x.1986, coll. Ashwani Kumar; 3 ♂, 1 ♀, Dehra Dun, 27.x.1986, coll. S. K. Sharma; 1 ♀, Kulu (H.P.), 12.vi.1986, coll. V. K. Kohli.

Tomosvaryella tattapaniensis sp. nov.

(Fig. 31)

♂. Medium sized, black species. Head 1.4x as broad as thorax; 1.3x as broad as long; compound eyes brown, joined on the front for a distance equal to 8 rows of eye facets leaving a small upper frontal triangle which is black and with little pubescence on the lower half; ocellar triangle black but ocelli are yellow in colour; lower frontal triangle with white pubescence and almost 1.5x as long as joining area of compound eyes; face dull black, without any pubescence, equal in width to the lower end of frons getting narrower towards proboscis, proboscis small, yellowish brown; occiput greyish black with white pubescence on the lower half and with minute hairs on the hind margin, maximum width in the middle of upper half. Antenna : 1st segment small, brown; 2nd segment brown with one small bristle on the upper side; 3rd segment brown with white pubescence, more dense near margin and tip which is acuminate; arista dark brown, about 1.5x as long as 3rd segment (fig. 31B). Thorax black with little pubescence near margins and with small scattered yellowish hairs; pleurae black with white pubescence; scutellum also black with pubescence on the margins and with few scattered bristles; humeri greyish yellow. Halteres yellow. Wing hyaline; 4th costal section about 1.25x as long as 3rd costal section; 5th costal section 2x as long as 3rd and 4th combined; crossvein r-m slightly beyond the middle of the discal cell and last section of vein M_{1+2} gently curved (fig. 31A). Legs : coxae, trochanters, femora and tibiae black with little pubescence except the distal tip of femora and both tips of tibiae which are yellow; tarsi yellowish brown with rows of yellow hairs; claws and pulvilli well developed; claws brown, pulvilli yellow; hind trochanter with a row of small yellow hairs (fig. 31C). Abdomen subshining black, barrel-shaped with scattered brownish bristles; 1st abdominal segment with 4 brownish black bristles on each side; 8th abdominal segment about 0.5x as long as 5th and with a membranous area on the tip. Male genitalia with asymmetrical irregular claspers bent downward and with many bristles; the dorsal, lateral and ventral sides as given in fig. 31D–F. Cerci small with row of bristles on the inner side; aedeagus trifid, long. The shape of aedeagus and aedeagal basal plate as shown in fig. 31G.

Length. Body : 2.5 mm; wings : 2.4 mm.

♀. Ovipositor with black globose base ; piercer brown turned upward reaching upto the 2nd abdominal segment (Fg. 31H). Venation slightly different from male; 5th costal section 1.5x as long as 3rd and 4th combined. Humeri yellow. Rest of description similar to male.

Length. Body : 2.5 mm; wing : 2.2 mm.

Etymology. Name based on the locality.

Remarks. The wing venation of this species is close to *T. subvirescence* but with different hind trochanter which is actually close to *T. sylvatica* in having a row of minute hairs. However, the shape of genitalia of both male and female are different from *T. subvirescence* and *T. sylvatica.*

Specimen examined. Holotype ♂, Tattapani (H.P.), 27.ix.1986, coll. S.K. Sharma. Allotype ♀, Mashobra (H.P.) 27.x.1986. coll. S.K. Sharma.

Tomosvaryella longipositor sp. nov.
(Fig. 32)

♀. **Small, black.** Head about 1.25x as broad as thorax, 0.8x as long as broad; compound eyes brown with black spots, not contiguous; frons equal in width at upper and lower ends and slightly broader in the middle, with white pubescence on the lower half ; ocellar triangle black; face black with white pubescence, equal in width at both ends, and slightly less than lower end of frons; occiput greyish black with white pubescence on the lateral side in the lower half. Antenna: 1st segment small, brownish black ; 2nd segment brown, with one minute bristle on upper side and one on lower side; 3rd segment brown with white pubescence on the lower half and near margin, about 2x as long as 2nd segment, acuminate at apex; arista dark brown, 1.5x as long as 3rd segment (fig. 32B). Proboscis not visible externally. Thorax greyish black with white pubescence and with few scattered brown hairs on dorsum; pleurae black with white pubescence; scutellum greyish black with white pubescence; humeri greyish yellow. Halteres yellow. Wings hyaline; 4th costal section 1.5x as long as 3rd costal section; 5th costal section 1.5x as long as 3rd and 4th combined; crossuein r-m slightly beyond middle of discal cell; last section of vein M_{1+2} slightly curved (fig. 32A). Legs : coxae, fore and middle trochanters black and with little pubescence, hind trochanter yellowish; fore and mid femora black except for distal tips yellow, rest black, all tibiae with proximal 1/3rd and distal tips yellow, black in middle; tarsi yellow with rows of yellow hairs; claws brown. Abdomen black, almost parallel sided, with white pubescence, more on first two segments; 1st abdominal tergum with about 5 small brownish bristles on each side, other segments slightly pollinose. Ovipositor with base black, globose, and piercer brown, very long, straight reaching upto the base of first abdominal segment (fig. 32C).

Length. Body : 2.2 mm; wing : 2.1 mm.

♂. Unknown.

Etymology. Name is based on very long ovipositor.

Remarks. This species differs from all other known species of *Tomosvaryella* Aczel in the presence of a very long ovipositor reaching upto the first abdominal segment. The wing venation is close to *T. nitens* (Brunetti), but the other important characters of *T. nitens* like mound-like gibbosity, shape of ovipositor etc. are not found in this species.

Specimens examined. Holotype ♀, Solan (H P.), 19.x.1982. coll. L. S. Arya. Paratypes : 3 ♀, Kandaghat (H.P.), 22.x.1982, coll. L. S. Arya.

2. GENUS *DORYLOMORPHA* ACZEL

Tomosvaryella (Dorylomorpha) Aczel, 1939, Zool. Anz., 125 : 22. Type species : *Pipunculus rufipes* Meigen, by Original designation.

Dorylomorpha Hardy, 1943, Univ. Kansas Sci. Bull., 29 (1) : 131

The name *Dorylomorpha* was first proposed by Aczel (1939) as a subgenus of *Tomosvaryella* for those species which have r-m crossvein situated near the base of the discal cell. Hardy (1943) considered it as a fullfledged genus although Aczel himself (1940) had also acknowledged its generic status. The following generic description is based on that of Hardy (1943).

This genus includes those species which are without stigma; r-m crossvein at the basal 1/6th to 1/4th of the discal cell; eyes of male dichoptic, distinctly separated on the front. The posterior margin of the compound eyes is curved inward on upper half so that the occiput is broader and more swollen above. The abdomen is elongate and strongly swollen apically, elevated in both sexes especially from lateral view; 3rd antennal segment is acuminately pointed and the 3rd costal section is very short compared to the 4th; basal portion of anal cell and alula greatly narrowed and no axillary incision.

This genus appears to be intermediate between *Tomosvaryella* and *Eudorylas* in having many characters in common with both these genera but the characteristics of the head, wings and abdomen separate it from them.

It is not well represented in India. In all 6 species have been included from India. This number includes 3 new species *(abdoflavus*, *abdochaetus* and *appendiculata)*, one new record *(D. lini* Hardy) and two known ones *(D. quartaria* (Brunetti) and *D. pterae* Kapoor & Grewal*)*. These species have been grouped into two subgenera; the nominative subgenus *Dorylomorhpa* includes 5 species while a new subgenus, *Claraeomorpha* is designated to include the new species, *C. appendiculata*. These subgenera and 6 species are separated by the following key.

KEY TO SPECIES

1. Vein M_{1+2} normal, without appendix. Subgenus *Dorylomorpha* 2
   Vein M_{1+2} with an appendix. Subgenus nov. *Claraeomorpha* (Type species *C. appendiculata* sp. n.)
2. Abdomen on sides and apices of terga yellow; legs all yellow; 3rd antennal segment long acuminate; 8th abdominal segment 1/3rd of 5th in male; male terminalia with dorsoapical membranous area..*abdoflavus* sp. n.
   Abdomen entirely black; other characters different........................3
3. Crossvein r-m at basal 1/6th of discal cell (cell $1M_2$)......................4
   Crossvein r-m not extremely basal, usually beyond 1/4th of discal cell...5
4. 8th tergum equal in length to that of 5th; apical triangular membranous area not visible in dorsal view. India & Philippines ....*lini* Hardy
   8th tergum about half in length to that of 5th; large apical triangular membranous area visible in dorsal view.................*abdochaetus* sp. n.
5. Crossvein r-m situated at basal 1/4th of discal cell. India...*quartaria* (Brunetti)
   Crossvein r-m situated of 2/5th of discal cell; body 3mm long; ♂surstyli more expanded. India..................................*pterae* Kapoor & Grewal

A. CLARAEOMORPHA SUBGENUS NOVUM

The characteristics of the genus *Dorylomorpha* will also apply to its nominative subgenus *Dorylomorpha*. The new subgenus *Claraeomorpha* can be easily distinguished from this subgenus by the presence of an appendix on the vain M_{1+2} as in *Claraeola*. T*ype species : D. (C.) appendiculata* sp. n.

Dorylomorpha (*Claraeomorpha*) *appendiculata* sp. n.

(Fig. 33)

♂. Head ca 1.6x as broad as thorax; eyes separated by a gap ca 0.67x the base of ocellar triangle; only anterior tip of frons covered with silvery white pubescence; face black, as broad as the base of ocellar triangle, covered with silvery white pubescence. Antenna with 1st and 2nd segments black; 2nd with 2 bristles dorsally and one ventrally; 3rd segment yellow, acuminate arista black as long as 3rd segment (fig. 33B). Thorax shining black with brown dust; pleurae thickly covered with white dust, chaetotaxy reduced; humeral plates black with one or two bristles; thorax with thin long bristles on lateral sides; scutellum shining black with a transverse row of yellow, thin, long bristles along margin. Halteres brownish yellow. Wings hyaline; 3rd costal section ca 0.33x as long as 4th; 5th costal section equal to 3rd and 4th combined; crossvein r-m at basal 1/5th of the discal cell; vein M_{1+2} forked near apical margin of wing; vein M_2 short, not reaching the wing margin (fig. 33A). Legs black; coxae and trochanters totally black; femora black but yellow distally; tibiae black medially, 1/3rd proximal and distal tips yellow; tarsi yellowish brown, distal tarsi black, dorsoventrally flattened; pulvilli yellow; claws brownish with black tips. Abdomen cylindrical with yellowish dust; 1st abdominal segment with 6-8 long stout, yellow bristles on each side; 8th segment 0.5x as long as 5th; membranous area large quadrangular, occupying whole of the tip. Male genitalic structures like claspers, aedeagus, aedeagal guide and ejaculatory apodeme as shown in fig. 33C-H.

Length. Body : 4.0 mm; wing : 5.0 mm.

♀. Not known.

Etymology. Named due to the presence of appendix on the vein M_{1+2}.

Specimen examined. Holotype ♂, Mashobra (H.P.), 27.ix.1986, coll. J. S. Grewal.

SUBGENUS *DORYLOMORPHA* ACZEL

Dorylomorpha (*Dorylomorpha*) *abdochaetus* sp. n.

(Fig. 34)

♂. small black. Head hemispherical, ca 1.2x broader than thorax; frons 0.76x narrower than base of ocellar triangle, but lower 3/4 as wide as base of ocellar triangle; upper half dull black, lower one silvery white pubescent; face 2x broader than frons, silvery white pubescent; occiput with whitish dust, swollen. Antenna black; 1st and 2nd segments bare; 3rd segment with yellow pubescence, rostrate; arista black, bare as long as 3rd segment. Thorax black, covered with brownish dust and few yellow hairs; scutellum with two transverse rows of yellow bristles, lower row with long and thicker bristles as compared to those of upper row; mesonotum and plurae with thick whitish dust; humeralplates black. Halteres yellowish-brown. Wings hyaline; 3rd costal section ca 0.33x as long as 4th costal section; 3rd and 4th combined 1.2x as long as 5th costal section; crossvein r-m at basal 1/5th of discal cell; last section of vein M_{1+2} strongly curved. Legs black; fore and mid coxae yellow at apices; hind trochanter shining black; femora black except at distal tips which are yellow; tibiae black medially, 1/3rd apical portion and distal tips yellow; tarsi brown, covered with yellowish hairs; distal tarsomeres black; pulvilli yellow; claws blackish. Abdomen shining black with sparse brown dust; 1st tergum with transverse row of bristles having 6-7 long bristles on the lateral side and smaller bristles on the dorsal side; 8th tergum subequal to 5th in length and with a large apical membranous area. Male genitalic structures like claspers, aedeagus, aedeagal guide and ejaculatory apodeme as shown in fig.34D–L.

Length. Body : 4.0 mm; wing : 4.3 mm.

♀. Agrees with male but frons 1.6x broader than base of ocellar triangle; upper half black, lower half covered with white pubescence; ovipositor small brown, equal to base in length, straight with tip curved upward (fig. 34 M, N); shape of antenna also slightly different (fig. 34B).

Length. Body : 3.20 mm ; wing : 4.00 mm.

Etymology. Named due the presence of bristles on abdomen.

Remarks This species comes close to *D. lini.* Hardy in its wing characteristics but can be easily separated from the latter in the ratio of the length of 8th tergum to that of 5th. There is also present a transverse row of bristles across the 1st abdominal segment which is absent in *lini.* It also differs from the latter in its totally differents male claspers (compare 34 I and 36F).

Specimens examined. Holotype ♂, Mashobra (H.P.), 27.ix 1916, coll. S.K. Sharma. Allotype ♀, same data. Paratypes 12 ♂, 13 ♀, same data.

Dorylomorpha (Dorylomorpha) abdoflavus sp.n.

(Fig. 35)

♂ Black with yellow markings on the lateral side of abdomen. Head hemispherical, ca 1.3x as broad as long; upper portion of frons dull black lower portion silvery white pubescent; face as broad as frons, silvery white pubescent. Antenna brownish yellow; 2nd segment without any bristle;

3rd antennal segment acute at apex, with yellow pubescene; arista yellow at base, flagellum black, about 2x as long as 3rd segment. Thorax shining black; mesopleurae and sternopleurae with silvery white pubesecence; propleurae and metanotum dull black; humeral plates yellow. Halteres yellow. Wings hyaline, 3rd costal section equal to 4th section; 5th costel section equal to 3rd and 4th combined; crossvein r-m near basal 1/3rd of discal cell; last section of vein M_{1+2} curved upward. Legs with coxae, femora, tibiae, tarsi, and pulvilli all yellow; claws black at tips. Abdomen shining black, terga 2-5 with lateral margins yellow; 2nd and 3rd abdominal terga with distal portion narrow and with yellow bands, while 4th and 5th terga with lateral yellow spots; 8th tergum 1/3 x as long as 5th tergum. Male genitalia with large surstyli expanded on outer margin, straight on inner, rather pointed at apex as seen from ventral view: shape of clasers, aedeagus, aedeagal guide and ejaculatory apodeme as shown in fig 35D-H.

Lenght. Body : 5.25 mm; wing : 7.3 mm.

♀. Not known.

Specimen examined. Holotype ♂, Kufri (H.P.), 25.ix.1986, coll J.S. Grewal.

Etymology. Named due to peculiar yellow coloration on abdomen.

Remarks : This species close to *D. translucens* (de Meijere) from Java in its abdominal coloration and in having dorso-apical membranous area in male terminalia, but not so much extended as in *translucens*. It can also be separated from the latter in having 3rd antennal segment acute and 8th abdominal segment 1/3rd of 5th while in *translucens* 3rd antennal segment is rostrate and 8th is 2/3rd of 5th abdominal segment. It also differs from the latter in its totally different male claspers (compare fig.35F of this monograph and fig.1C of Handy (1972).

Dorylomorpha (Dorylomorpha) lini Hardy

(Fig. 36)

Dorylomorpha lini Hardy, 1972, Hawaii Ent. Soc., 21 : 81. Type loc. 13 km north of Puerto Princessa, Palawan, Philippines.

♂. Small black. Head 1.3x as broad as long 1.4x as broad as thorax; compound eyes brown with few black patches, separated on the front for a distance equal to one eye facet, getting broader towards upper and lower sides; frons black with white pubescence in the lower half near antenna; ocellar triangle black, face black with white pubescence, equal in width at both the ends which is equal to that of lower end of frons; occiput dull black with few scattered brown hairs. Antenna : 1st segment small black; 2nd segment also black with one small bristle on the upper side; 3rd segment blackish on the upper 1/3rd, rest yellowish, bristle like at the tip, about 2x as long as 2nd segment; arista brownish black, about 1.5 x as long as 3rd segment, proboscis not visible externally. Thorax black with few scattered yellowish hairs near humeri; scutellum black with few scattered hairs; humeri greyish yellow. Halteres yellow. Wings with little brownish tinge, 4th costal section more than 2x as long as 3rd; 5th costal section 1.3 x as long as 3rd and 4th combined; crossvein r-m at basal 1/6th of discal cell; last section of vein M_{1+2} distinctly curved. Legs : coxae, trochanters and femora black except the distal tips which are yellow; tibiae yellow at both the tips, blackish in middle; tarsi yellow, last tarsomere brown, pulvilli brown well developed, claws with brown tips. Abdomen black, cylindrical, with little pubescence on the 1st segment and on the lateral sides of 2nd segment and on the last segment, 1st segment without any bristle on the lateral side; last segment with few scattered yellowish hairs; 8th segment about 2/3rd as long as 5th. Male genitalia asymmetrical, right clasper partially bilobed, both claspers slightly curved downward; shape of dorsal and lateral views of claspers, aedeagus, aedeagal guide and ejaculatory apodeme as shown in the fig. 36C-J.

Legnth. Body : 2.0 mm; wing : 2.35 mm.

♀ Ovipositor with black base which is as long as piercer; piercer brown, slightly curved upward. 4th costal section about 3 x as long as 3rd costal section, 5th costal 0.95x as long as 3rd and 4th combined. Frons very much broad in the middle, equal to about 6 eye facets, getting narrower towards upper and lowers sides. Abdomen very much narrow, about 0.6 x as broad as head.

Length : Body. 1.8 mm; wing 2.3 mm.

Specimens examined. 2♂, 1♀ Ludhiana, 4-8,x.1985, coll. S. K. Sharma; 2 ♂, Pinjore (Haryana), 26.x.1985, coll. V. K. Kohli; 1 ♀, Hoshiarpur (Punjab), 15.x.1986, coll.. S.K. Sharma; 2 ♀, Hoshiarpur, 8.xi.1985, coll. S.K. Sharma; 2 ♀ same date, coll. V.K. Kohli.

Distribution. Philippines and India.

Remarks. This species is recorded here for the first time from India.

It comes close to *quartaria* (Brunetti) from which it is separated by the position of r-m crossvein which is at basal 1/6 in *lini* and at basal 1/4 in *quartaria*.

D*orylomorpha (*D*orylomorpha)* pterae Kapoor & Grewal

(Fig. 37)

D*orylomorpha pterae* Kapoor & Grewal, 1985, Int. J. Ent. 27 (4) : 399-400

♂. Black, small. Head hemispherical, broader than thorax, eyes narrowly separated on front, median protion of frons slightly wider than median ocellus; upper ½ of frons dull black and lower ½ with silvery pubescence; middle portion of frons somewhat convex longitudinally. Antennae brownish black; 2nd segment dark brown with 1 black bristle dorsally and 1 ventrally; 3rd segment acuminate, with thick yellow pubescence; arista black, bare; face thickly white pubescent; hind margin of compound eyes indented on upper ½ so that occiput much broader on upper portion; genae narrow, black. Thorax shining black; metanotum and pleurae curved with whitish dust; humeral plates yellow. Halteres also yellow. Legs : coxae black with yellow apices; hind trochanter shining black, triangular; femora black but yellow distally; tibiae black medially, 1/3 apical portion and distal tip yellow; tarsi brownish yellow, covered with thick black hairs; pulvilli yellow; claws yellow with black tips. Wings hyaline; 3rd costal section short, approximately 1/4 of 4th section; 5th costal section approximately 1½x of 3rd and 4th sections combined; crossvein r-m near middle of discal cell; last section of M_{1+2} approximately straight. Abdomen shining black with terminal portion somewhat rufous; 8th tergum subequal in length to 5th and 5th 1½x of 8th; well-developed membranous area extending slightly over right side of apex. Male genitalia : surstyli large, black, expanded and convex on outer margin but straight on inner margin (fig. 37D).

Length. Body : 3 mm; wing : 3.5 mm

♀. Unknown.

Specimens examined. Holotype ♂, Subathu (H.P.), 23.x.1982, coll. L. S. Arya. Paratype ♂, same data (Holotype completely damaged according to Dr. Albrecht of Finland to whom it was sent on his request).

Etymology. This species was named for its peculiar wing venation.

Remarks. This species comes close to *D. quartaria* (Brunetti) and shares with it the characters of its small body size, mostly black abdomen and legs.

It differs by the position of crossvein r-m, which is at 2/5th of the discal cell (fig. 37A); and also from others in the structure of the surstyli (fig. 37D) which are more expanded in this species.

Dorylomorpha (Dorylomorpha) quartaria (Brunetti)

Pipunculus quartaria Brunetti, 1912, *Rec. Indian Mus.*, 7:493

Type loc. : India : Calcutta.

Dorylomorpha quartaria : Hardy, 1972, Oriental Inst. Suppl., 2 : 8.

♀. Head shining black, wide, lower part with white shimmer as seen from below; face with white shimmer; proboscis brownish yellow; eyes with the facets contiguous to the region of the antennae very much enlarged; antenna blackish, 3rd joint yellowish-white with long whitish style; arista very long, black; back of head considerbly puffed out, cinereous-grey with a tendency of whitish on postocular orbits, bearing a slight fringe of pale hairs. Thorax dark cinereous grey, slightly shining; sides of thorax a little lighter; scutellum concolorous with dorsum, metanotum light grey. Abdomen blackish grey, practically bare but microscopically pubescent, slightly shining; 1st segment grey; 5th segment widest; ovipositor of moderate length, shining brown with a little hair at its base; venter cinereous-grey, unmarked. Legs mainly black; tips of fore coxae, tips of all femora rather broadly, basal 3rd and tips of tibiae, and apical parts of all tarsi, black; femora not shining and absolutely bare. Wings clear; stigma absent but the 3rd costal space much reduced, and the veins limiting it some what thickened; anterior crossvein placed slightly before 1/4th of the discal cell; 4th longitudinal running nearly straight from its junction with the posterior crossvein upto the 3rd vein, which it almost meets rather sooner than usual, thence running parallel with it to the border for a large distance than in most species; halteres pale brownish yellow.

Length. Body : 1.75mm.

Specimens examined. Holotype ♀, no. 5693/15 (badly damaged), Calcutta 13.xii 1907 in Museum collection of Zoological Survey of India; another specimen in this collection missing, only pin with label bearing no. 1928/HI, Simla (7000ft.), 7 v.1910, coll. N. Annandale.

Since the holotype too is in extremely bad state and paratype too is missing, a detailed description could not be drawn and so the original description of Brunetti (1912) has been reproduced above. Even the original description of Brunetti is so incomplete that it is difficult to identify any of the *Dorylomorpha* specimen on its basis.

3. GENUS *EUDORYLAS* ACZEL

Eudorylas Aczel, 1940, Zool. Anz. 132(7/8) : 151. Type species : *Pipunculus opacus* **Fallen** by original designation.

The species of this genus are easily separated from those of other genera by the absence of the propleural fan of hairs. Although originally described as a genus, workers like Hardy (1943) and others treated it as a subgenus of *Pipunculus* Latr. Due to its distinct generic characteristics, it is treated here as a genus. Before the start of the present work the genus was known by 10 species from India. 21 new species and 3 new records have been added in the present work. This brings the total number of the Indian species under this genus to 34. These species can be easily separated by the following key.

KEY TO THE SPECIES

1. 1st abdominal segment without bristles..2
   1st abdominal segment with bristles...3
2. 8th abdominal segment broader than 5th, ca 2x longer, base of hypopygium polished black, vesica cup sclerotized and deep, basiphallus 0.5x as long as distiphallus.......................................*macropygus* de Meijere.
   8th abdominal segment equal or narrower than 5th, hypopygium entirely brown, pubescent; vesica cup sclerotized but shallow; basiphallus ca 0.1x as long as distiphallus.......................................*roralis* (Kertesz).
3. 8th abdominal segment with a membranous area or cleft extending longitudinally bisecting it completely or partially as seen in dorsal view......4
   8th abdominal segment not as above..15
4. 8th addominal segment completely divided into two halves; surstyli asymmetrical (Mutillatus group)..5
   8th abdominal segment divided incompletely; surstyli symmetrical and sickle-shaped, curved outside (Orientalis group*)........................14
5. Trochanters and femora predominatly black..6
   Trochanters and femora predominantly yellow......................................7

---

* *tuberculatus* sp. n. has not been included in the key as its description is based only on female; *E. luteipes* Brunetti also could not be included because of its incomplete original description.

6. 3rd costal section smaller (0.87x) than 4th; cleft on 8th abdominal segment very much oblique and narrow, traverses from middle of anterior border to right corner of posterior end; surstyli asymmetrical as seen in dorsal view.. *bharatiensis* sp. n.
3rd costal section equal to 4th; cleft on 8th abdominal segment broad and traverses longitudinally; surstyli symmetrical as seen in dorsal view ....*minghlanii* sp. n.

7. 3rd antennal segment acute...8
3rd antennal segment acuminate..10

8. 8th abdominal segment in male as long as 5th...................................9
8th abdominal segment ca 0.5x as long as 5th..............*indiaensis* sp. n.

9. 3rd costal section equal to 4th in length; crossvein r-m a little before middle of discal cell...*ludhianaensis* sp. n.
3rd costal section longer (1.4x) than 4th; crossvein r-m situated at basal 2/5th of discal cell...*corbetti* sp. n.

10. Crossvein r-m at basal 1/3rd of discal cell; 8th abdominal segment smaller than 5th length...11
Crossvein r-m approximately in the middle of discal cell; 8th abdominal segment equal to 5th in length...13

11. Crossvein r-m situated opposite to the point of union of costa and subcosta; ejaculatory apodeme membranous ....*jacksoni* sp. n.
Crossvein r-m situated much beyond the point of union of costa and subcosta; ejaculatory apodeme not membranous...................................12

12. 3rd costal section longer than 4th; costal sections 3rd and 4th combined equal to 5th; 3rd antennal segment brown;..................*eulentiger* sp. n.
3rd costal section smaller than 4th; costal sections 3rd and 4th combined longer than 5th; 3rd antennal segment yellow................*mutillatus* Loew

13. 2nd costal section with an incomplete crossvein dividing the 2nd costal cell; 3rd costal section smaller than 4th.......................*bicostalis* sp. n.
No such crossvein present on 2nd costal section; 3rd costal section longer than 4th...*pennatus* sp. n.

14. Antenna totally black, 3rd segment not drawn into long acuminate apex; a keel-like structure present in membranous area of 8th abdominal segment in male...*antennalis* sp. n.
Antenna not totally black, 3rd segment black with yellow apex, drawn

into long acuminate tip; no keel-like structure in membranous area of 8th abdominal segment in male............................*orientalis* Koizumi

15. 3rd antennal segment acute at apex, not sharply pointed..... 16
3rd antennal segment sharply pointed; acuminate at apex..................21

16. Trochanters black, femora predominantly black; humeri black............17
Trochanters yellow, femora at least broadly yellow at ends...............18

17. Costal sections 3rd and 4th combined smaller than 5th; 8th abdominal segment ca 1/2 or more as long as 5th......................*thekkadiensis* sp.n.
Costal sections 3rd and 4th combined ca 1.4x as long as 5th; 8th abdominal segment ca 1/4th as long as 5th.....................*garhwalensis* sp. n.

18. 3rd costal section longer than 4th...........................*dextrostylus* sp.n.
3rd costal section equal to or shorter than 4th..............................19

19. 3rd costal section equal to 4th; crossvein r-m situated at basal 1/3rd of discal cell...20
3rd costal section 0.5x as long as 4th; crossvein r-m at slightly beyond the middle of discal cell..... ....*biroi* (Kertesz)

20. Middle femora with ciliation of hairs on hinder side.........*major*(Brunetti)
Middle femora without any ciliation of hairs on hinder side.................
....*albucus* Hardy

21. Trochanters yellow, femora may be tinged with brown medially or towards bases but broadly yellow at both ends...............................22
Trochanters black, femora predominantly black, yellow only at extreme apices...24

22. 3rd costal section equal to 4th in length; crossvein r-m situated at basal 2/5th of discal cell...23
3rd costal section 2x as long as 4th; crossvein r-m situated at basal 1/3rd of discal cell...*poantaensis* sp. n.

23. Abdomen with sides of segments 2-4 yellow..............*filicornis*(Brunetti)
Abdomen black, opaque..*pinjorensis* sp. n.

24. 3rd antennal segment produced into a long bristle-like apex, which is ca 2x longer than the rest of the segment..25
3rd antennal segment not as above, the point is not longer than the remainder of the segment...26

25. Costal sections 3rd and 4th combined 1.1x as long as 5th; humeri yellow; scutellum lacking stout scutellar bristles; female with piercer slightly

curved upwards near tip..*scutellaris* sp. n.
Costal sections 3rd and 4th combined distinctly shorter than 5th; scutellum with 4 stout bristles; female with piercer straight........................ ....*acroacanthus* Hardy

26. 8th abdominal segment equal to or smaller than 5th in length and width; surstyli normal..27
8th abdominal segment ca 1.5x as long and ca 1.1x as broad as 5th segment; surstyli bifid ....*uniformis* (Brunetti)

27. Crossvein r-m situated at basal 1/3rd of discal cell.................................28
Crossvein r-m situated at basal 2/5th of discal cell...................................31

28. Male terminalia with large membranous area visible from dorsal side; hind tibia with 1–2 erect bristles on outer surface..............................30
Male terminalia with narrow slit-like membranous area not visible from dorsal side; hind tibia without any bristle..29

29. 3rd costal section ca 1.5x as long as 5th; 3rd and 4th costal sections combined as long as 5th; distal portion of vein M_{1+2} moderately curved ....*extensus* Brunetti
3rd costal section as long as 4th; 3rd and 4th costal sections combined as long as 5th; distal portion of vein M_{1+2} slightly curved.................. ....*euciliatus* sp. n.

30. Area of contiguity between compound eyes ca 15 facets long; humeri and halteres black; 3rd costal section equal to 4th in length; surstyli asymmeterical...*manaliensis* sp. n.
Area of contiguity ca 5-6 facets long; humeri and halteres yellow; 3rd costal section equal to 4th in length; surstyli symmetrical................. ....*javanensis* sp.n

31. Humeri black; 3rd costal section longer than 4th; 8th abdominal segment ca 0.5x as long as 5th in male..*tibiatus* sp. n.
Humeri yellow; 3rd costal section as long as 4th; 8th abdominal segment equal to 5th in length in male.......................................*khaziariensis* sp. n.

Eudorylas acroacanthus Hardy

(Fig. 38)

Pipunculus (Eudorylas) acroacanthus Hardy, 1968, Entomol, Meddel, **36** : 439-440.

♀. Small black. Head ca 1.18x as broad as long and 1.29x as broad as thorax; eyes dark brown; dichoptic; ocellar triangle black with yellow ocelli; frons shining black on upper half, with a lower wedge penetrating lower silvery white pubescent portion medially; broadest in the middle, ca 1.5x as broad as base of ocellar triangle, lower ends of frons narrow, ca 0.8x as long as base of ocellar triangle, face black with silvery white pubescence as broad as base of ocellar triangle; occiput black with grey dust, a few yellow hairs along the posterior margin. Antenna black, 1st segment small black, with 2 small dorsal and 1 large ventral black bristle; 3rd segment black with apex drawn into a long thread-like structure about 2x the length of rest of the segment; arista black, ca 1.25x as long as 3rd segment including acuminate apex (fiig. 38B). Proboscis brown. Thorax black with brown dust, 1.29x as long as broad, scutellum with 4 stout black bristles on posterior margin; metanotum and pleurae black with grey dust, humeri black. Halteres black. Wings (fig. 38A) hyaline; 3rd costal section 2x as long as 4th; 3rd and 4th costal sections combined 0.78x as long as 5th, crossvein r-m a little beyond basal 1/3rd of discal cell; distal portion of vein M_{1+2} greatly curved. Legs black; coxae and trochanters black; femora black but yellow at extreme ends; tarsi brown, last tarsomeres black; claws yellow with black tips; pulvilli yellow, both as long as distal tarsomere; fore and hind tibiae with 1 stout black medial bristle on posterior side; fore tibiae with stout black apical spur. Abdomen black, opaque; 1st abdominal segment with 2-3 stout black bristles on either side; ovipositor with base small, globose ca 0.6x as long as piercer; piercer yellow, cylindrical and straight (fig. 38C).

Length. Body : 3.71 mm; wing : 4.14 mm.

♂. Unknown.

Specimen examined. 1♀, Kurseong (W.B.), 6.iv.1985, coll. S.K. Sharma.

Eudorylas albucus Hrady
(Fig. 39)

Pipunculus (Eudorylas) albucus Hardy, 1968, Entomol. Meddel., 36:441-442.

One female from Ludhiana agrees with the original description of female of *albucus* of Hardy from New Ireland. The differences are only in body size (2.8 mm in present specimen) and in having light brown stigma. The following description of male is from Hardy (1968) while that of female is based on collected material.

♂. Head : eyes joined for distance about equal to the lower portion of front; lower front subshining black; face approximately equal in width to lower portion of front; 2 basal segments of antennae brown, tinged with yellow; 3rd segment and base of arista pale yellow, 3rd is long acuminate (fig. 39B). Thorax brown, pollinose on dorsum, grey on sides; humeri and stems of halteres yellow; knobs of halteres yellow; tinged lightly with brown. Scutellum with short, inconspicuous pale brown setae around margin. Legs : coxae brown tinged faintly with yellow, legs otherwise yellow except for discolourations of brown on dorsobasal portion of femora; a prominent yellow ventral bristle present at middle of each hind tibia, tarsal claws normal in development. Wings (fig. 39A) hyaline, with stigma very dark brown and filling whole of 3rd costal section; 3rd section just slightly shorter than 4th and r-m crossvein near basal 3rd of cell 1st M_2; last section of M_{1+2} gently curved. Abdomen rounded on sides, broadest at junction of segments 3 and 4; terga entirely opaque brown on dorsum with faint indications of grey along apices; lateral margins of terga grey; 8th segment entirely grey brown pollinose, compressed to right, about 2/3rd as long as 5th abdominal segment and with an apical membranous area on right side; 6th tergum not visible in dorsal view. Male genitalia as in fig. 39C and D; claspers long and slender, curved slightly upwards and enlarges at apices.

Length. Body : 5.00 mm; wing : 5.90 mm.

♀. Small dark brown. Head ca 1.22x as broad as long and 1.2x as broad as thorax; eyes dark brown with black patches, ocellar triangle black with ocelli yellow; frons black, lower 2/3rd covered with silvery white pubescence; ca 1.5x as broad in middle as on either end; face black with silvery white pubescence, slightly broader (1.12x) than frons at lower end; occiput black with white dust, swollen Antenna yellow; 1st segment small brown with one small dorsal black bristle; 2nd segment quadrangular, brown with 2 dorsal and 2 ventral small black bristles, 3rd segment yellow, brownish at base, with apex acuminate; arista brown ca 1.5x as long as 3rd antennal segment. Proboscis yellow. Thorax ca 1.25x as long as broad, covered with brown dust, metanotum black, pleurae brown; humeral plates yellow. Halteres yellow. Wing hyaline with brownish tinge; 3rd costal section ca 1.44x as long as 4th; 3rd and 4th costal sections combined ca 1.5x as long as 5th; crossvein r-m at basal 1/3rd of discal cell; last section of vein M_{1+2} slightly curved. Legs brown; coxae black with light brown distal margin; trochanters light brown; femora dark brown medially, yellow at ends, tibiae yellow with medial discolouration of brown; tarsi yellow except the distal tarsomeres which are dark brown; claws yellow with tips black, 1.5x as long as distal tarsomere; pulviili yellow,

1.25x as long as distal tarsomere. Abdomen brown; terga 2–5 entirely opaque, brown with faint indication of grey along apices; 6th segment 0.8x as long as 5th; ovipositor with base globose, black, 1.12x as long as piercer, piercer yellow, flattened dorsoventrally (fig. 39E).

Length. Body : 2.8 mm; wing : 3.15 mm.

Specimen examined. 1♀, Ludhiana, 8.x.1915, ex. paddy, coll. G.S. Sidhu.

Eudorylas antennalis sp. n.

(Fig. 40)

♂. Small black. Head 1.16x as broad as long and 1.25x as broad as thorax; eyes reddish brown with area of contiguity 13 facets long; ocellar triangle black, ocelli brown; upper frontal triange much obliterated, hardly 3 facets long, shining black; lower frontal triangle with silvery white pubescence except the area along ptinial suture, 15 facets long; base 1.25x as broad as base of ocellar triangle; face black with silvery white pubescence, as wide as base of lower frontal triangle; occiput black with white dust and small yellow hairs along posterior margin. Antenna brown; 1st segment small, black; 2nd segment dark brown with 2 dorsal and 1 ventral bristles; 3rd segment brown acuminate; arista black, ca 2x as long as 3rd segment (fig. 40B). Thorax as broad as long, black covered with brown dust; scutellum with white dust and small hairs along margin, mesopleurae brown, rest of pleurae black, humeri yellow. Halteres with base and knob brown, shaft yellow. Wings (fig. 40A) hyaline; 3rd costal section 2.5x as long as 4th; 3rd and 4th costal sections combined ca 0.6x as long as 5th; r-m crossvein slightly before 1/3rd of discal cell; vein M_{1+2} almost straight at distal end. Legs black, coxae and trochanters black, femora yellow only at extreme tips; 2/3rd distal portion of tibiae black with one black spine on outer side medially; last tarsomere black, claws yellow with black tips, pulvilli yellow, small. Abdomen black with apices of segments shining black and distal halves covered with silvery white dust; 1st abdominal segment with 5-7 strong black bristles on each side, 8th segment ca 0.5x as long and ca 0.5x as broad as 5th abdominal segment having a deep, broad apical membranous area reaching almost 5th segment, divides 8th segment into 2 subequal halves. Male genitalia with surstyli slightly asymmetrical; surstyli, aedeagus, ejaculatory apodeme, aedeagal guide as shown fig. 40C to G.

Length. Body : 2.73 mm; wing : 3.1 mm.

♀. Frons broad in the middle ca 1.5x broad as base of ocellar triangle;

3rd antennal segment drawn into acuminate tip; humeri yellow; halteres brown; wing as in male; ovipositor with base swollen, sharply pointed reaching upto the base of 1st abdominal segment.

Length. Body : 3.14 mm; wing : 3.42 mm.

Remarks. This species comes very close to *orientalis* Koizumi sharing with it the characters of 3rd antennal segment, wing with 3rd costal section 2x or more longer than 4th, and general outline of male genitalia; but differs in the characters like male antenna not drawn into long acuminate apex as in *orientalis*, stigma not filling the angle between 3rd costal section and R_1, crossvein r-m at a level little basad to the point of union of subcosta with costa, and a little before 1/3rd of discal cell; surstyli and ejaculatory apodeme short in size as compared to that of *orientalis* Koizumi and presence of a keel on membranous area of 8th segment in male.

Etymology. Name based on the character of 3rd antennal segment which is not drawn into long acuminate apex as in *orientalis.*

Specimens examined. Holotype ♂, Ludhiana (Pb.), 29.ix.1982, ex rice, coll. L. S. Arya. Allotype ♀, Dharampur (H.P.), 26.x.1985, ex weeds, coll. V. K. Kohli; 2 ♀, Sahastradhara, 27.x.1986, ex weeds, coll. A. Kumar; 1♂, Nahan (H.P.), 25.x 1986, coll. S. K. Sharma.

Eudorylas bharatiensis sp. n.

(Fig. 41)

♂. Small, black. Head 1.2x as broad as long, 1.2x as broad as thorax; ocelli brown, ocellar triangle black; upper frontal triangle as long as 2 facets; joining area of compound eyes as long as 18 facets; lower frontal triangle as long as 15 facets, lower half covered with silvery white pubescence, base as broad as the base of ocellar triangle; face black with white pubescence, as broad as base of lower frontal triangle; occiput not swollen. Antennae black; 1st segment black; 2nd brownish black, with 2 dorsal and 1 ventral bristle; 3rd segment dark brown to black, sharply pointed, moderately acuminate; arista black, 1.5x as long as 3rd segment (fig 41B). Thorax black with brown dust, as long as broad; scutellum bare with brown dust; pleurae black, bare, humeri yellow. Halteres dark brown. Wing (fig. 41A) hyaline, stigma filling the 3rd section completely; 3rd costal section 0.87x as long as 4th; 3rd and 4th combined 1.25x as long as 5th; crossvein r-m slightly before basal 2/5th of discal cell; vein M_{1+2} almost straight; subcosta with a very small branch just before joining the costa. Legs black; coxae and trochanters black; femora yellow at distal end only; tibiae yellowish brown with median portion black; tarsi dark brown, distal tarsomeres black; claws yellow with black tips, about 1.5x as long as last tarsomere. Abdomen dull black, covered with brown dust; 1st segment with 4-5 stout black bristles. Male genitalia with right surstylus pointed; surstyli, aedeagus, ejaculatory apodeme, aedeagal guide as shown in fig. 41D-G.

Length. Body : 2.9 mm; wing : 3.9 mm.

♀. Unknown.

Remarks. It is close to *mutillatus* Loew in having 8th segment divided unequally by a cleft which tilts towards right, and in general outline of male genitalic characters. It differs from it in having 3rd antennal segment, humeral plates, halteres and legs black and shape of surstyli differing in dorsal as well as lateral view. The wing venation is also different, in having the 3rd costal section approximately equal to 4th in this species while, in *mutillatus*, it is smaller.

Etymology. Name based on wide distribution of the species in India (Hindi version Bharat).

Specimens examined. Holotype ♂, Dharifatehpur (H.P.), ex weeds, 26.x. 1985, coll. V. K. Kohli. Paratypes 3 ♂, Solan (H. P.), 19.x 1982, ex. grass, coll. L. S. Arya; 1 ♂, 6.iv.1985, Kurseong (West Bengal), coll. S. K. Sharma; 1 ♂, Ramgarh (Bihar), 22.iii.1985, coll. S. K. Sharma; 1 ♂ Dehra Dun, 23. vi. 1983, coll. S. K. Sharma; 1 ♂, Subathu (H. P.), 23.x.1982, coll. L. S. Arya; 1 ♂ Sahastradhara (U. P.), 27.x.1986, coll. S. K. Sharma; 2 ♂, Ranikhet (U. P.), 20.xi.1986, coll. A. Kumar.

Eudorylas bicostalis sp. n.

(Fig. 42)

♂. Medium sized, black. Head ca 1.27x as broad as long and 1.2x as broad as thorax; eyes dark brown, reddish brown along the margin; area of contiguity ca 15 facets long; ocelli dark brown, upper frontal triangle much obliterated, hardly 4 facets long; lower frontal triangle black with silvery white pubescence only near the base; occiput black with white dust. Antenna : 1st segment black, small, with one dorsal black bristle; 2nd quadrangular, black with 2 dorsal and 2 ventral black bristles; 3rd segment broken. Thorax black with brown dust, ca 1.25x as long as broad; scutellum bare;

metanotum and pleurae black with brown dust; humeri yellow. Halteres yellow. Wings (fig. 42A) hyaline with brownish tinge; 2nd costal section with an incomplete crossvein dividing the costal cell; 3rd costal section ca 0.75x as long as 4th; 3rd and 4th combined ca 1.25x as long as 5th; r-m crossvein a little before the middle of discal cell; last section of vein M_{1+2} almost straight. Legs yellow; coxae black with distal margin yellow; trochanters yellow, hind trochanter with small bristles on lower margin; femora black medially, broadly yellow at both ends; tibiae with 2-3 well developed spurs; tibiae and tarsi yellow except the last tarsomeres which are dark brown, flattened; claws yellow with black tips, 1.25x as long as last tarsomere; pulvilli yellow, 0.75x as long as tarsomere. Abdomen black with brown dust; 1st abdominal segment with 6-7 stout black bristles on each side; 8th segment as long as and 0.8x as broad as 5th segment and with a deep cleft dividing it into two subequal parts having an elliptical apical membranous area on the ventral side. Male genitalia with slightly asymmetrical claspers. The shapes of claspers, aedeagus ejaculatory apodeme, 9th tergum, and aedeagal guide as shown in fig. 42D-G.

Length. Body : 3.1 mm; wing : 4.14 mm.

♀. Unknown.

Remarks. This species is close to *mutillatus* Loew in having legs, humeri and halteres yellow, 8th segment with a deep cleft and wing venation; but differs in having a branch on second costal section which divides the costal cell into two subequal parts; crossvein r-m situated a little before the middle of discal cell and in shape of surstyli and ejaculatory apodeme.

Etymology. This species is named on the basis of the character of costa in having a small branch on the second costal section which incompletely divides the costal cell into two subequal parts.

Specimen examined. Holotype ♂, Silent valley (Kerala), 7.iv.1983, ex rice, coll. L. S. Arya.

Eudorylas biroi (Kertesz)

Pipunculus biroi Kertesz, 1903, Ann. hist.-nat. Mus. natn. Hung., 1 : 466 (♂). Type-loc : Colombo, Sri Lanka.

Pipunculus (Eudorylas) biroi : Hardy 1975. In Cat. Dipt. Orient. Reg. Hawaii. Vol. II : 300

♂. ♀. *Head* in ♂ with eyes contiguous for a considerable space; frons brownish, grey-dusted, with an elongate black streak just below the middle, and when viewed from above, with a white shimmer immediately above the antennae; face brilliantly shining white; antennae rather small, first two joints blackish, the 2nd with a few bristles, 3rd joint yellowish-grey, with a white shimmer when viewed from above; the long arista black; proboscis and mouth-parts orange; occiput considerably puffed out, browinsh-grey with a white shimmer in certain lights. In ♀, frons with parallel sides, grey-dusted, shining white just above antennae; the front eye-facets enormously enlarged. *Thorax* olive-grey; shoulders, side margins and hind margin, also the pleurae and metanotum wholly ash-grey; scutellum brownish-grey. *Abdomen* dark ash-grey; a broad dark olive-brown basal band, narrowing at the sides, on each segment, extending in the centre nearly or quite to the next segment; base of abdomen more or less greyish; venter mainly dark grey. Genitalia in ♂ blackish, shining, of moderate size; in ♀ blackish, with a long reddish-brown ovipositor. *Legs* : coxae greyish; femora rather darker grey; trochanters, tips of all femora and base also of hind pair, orange; inner sides of hind femora wholly shining black; tibiae and tarsi orange, tips of latter blackish. *Wings* pale grey, stigma brownish, rather long; anterior cross-vein barely before middle of discal cell : halteres yellow.

Length. 3 mm.

Redescribed from a number of specimens of both sexes; apparently a widely distributed species; type described from Colombo, 28.ii.1902.

As we could not get any specimen of this species from India, the description has been taken as such from Brunetti (1923).

Eudorylas corbetti sp. n.

(Fig. 43)

♂. Small, black. Head as broad as long, eyes dark brown with area of contiguity ca 16 facets long; upper frontal triangle obliterated, black, only 2 facets long; lower frontal triangle black with lower 1/3rd covered with silvery white pubescence, base as broad as base of ocellar triangle, ca 20 facets long; face black covered with white pubescence, as broad as base of ocellar triangle; occiput black with white dust, greatly swollen. Antenna yellow; 1st segment small, black; 2nd segment black, quadrate with 2 dorsal and 1 ventral black bristles; 3rd segment brown with apex acute; arista black ca 2x as long as 3rd antennal segment (fig. 43B). Proboscis yellow. Thorax black, covered with brown dust, 1.33x as long as broad; pleurae black; humeral plates yellow. Halteres yellow. Wings (fig. 43A) hyaline, stigma brown, filling whole of angle between vein R_1 and 3rd costal section; 3rd costal section 1.4x as long as 4th; 3rd and 4th combined ca 1.2x as long as 5th; r-m at basal 2/5th of discal cell; distal end of vein M_{1+2} slightly curved. Legs yellow; coxae black with distal rims yellow; trochanters yellow; femora broadly yellow at apical and distal extremities; tibiae and tarsi yellow, last tarsomere black; claws yellow with black tip, as long as last tarsomere; pulvilli yellow, small, ca 0.7x as long as last tarsomere. Abdomen black, opaque covered with brown dust; 1st segment with 4-5 black bristles on either side; 8th abdominal segment as long as and 0.6x as broad as 5th segment with small rounded apical membranous area. Surslyli very much asymmetrical; shape of surstyli, aedeagus, ejaculatory apodeme, aedeagal guide as shown in fig 43D-G.

Length. Body : 2.8 mm; wing : 3.4 mm.

♀. Small, black, frons 0.75x as broad as base of ocellar triangle, black, covered with white pubescence; face black with silvery white pubescence, as broad as frons; 3rd antennal segment acuminate; 3rd costal section 0.75x as long as 4th; 3rd and 4th combined as long as 5th, crossvein r-m near middle of discal cell, distal end of M_{1+2} slightly curved. Ovipositor with globose black base, ca 0.4x as long as piercer which is brownish yellow, curved upward reaching base of the 3rd abdominal segment (fig. 43H).

Length. Body : 3.4 mm; wing : 3.8 mm.

Remarks. This species resembles *mutillatus* Loew in having 3rd antennal segment and legs yellow and in the wing venation, but differs strikingly in the structure of 8th abdominal segment which is without cleft and apical membranous area is visible from dorsal view. It also differs from *mutillatus* in the shape of its surstyli.

Etymology. Named after type-locality.

Specimens examined. Holotype ♂, Corbett National Park, Ram Nagar (U.P.), ex weeds, 21.ix.1986, coll. S. K. Sharma. Allotype 1 ♀, same data.

Eudorylas dextrostylus sp. n.

(Fig. 44)

♂. Small, black. Head as long as broad; 1.2x as broad as thorax; eyes reddish brown with dark brown patches; area of contiguity 16 facets long; ocellar triangle black, ocelli yellow; upper frontal triangle obliterated, hardly 3 facets long; lower frontal triangle 13 facets long, with base 1.5x as broad as base of ocellar triangle, covered with silvery white pubescence except upper frontal angle which is dull black; face black with silvery white pubesecence, as broad as the base of lower frontal triangle; occiput moderately swollen with a rim of yellow hairs along the margin. Antenna (fig.44B) light brown; 1st segment small black with one small dorsal spine; 2nd segment quadrate, dark brown with 3 dorsal and 1 ventral black bristles; 3rd segment light brown, acute; arista dark brown, ca 2x as long as 3rd segment. Proboscis brown. Thorax black with brown dust; 1.2x as long as broad; mesopleurae brown, rest of pleurae black; humeral plates yellow. Halteres brownish yellow Wings (fig. 44A) hyaline with brownish tinge; 3rd costal section 1.7x as long as 4th; 3rd and 4th sections combined 1.2x as long as 5th section; crossvein r-m slightly before middle of discal cell; last section of vein M_{1+2} slightly curved; stigma filling the 3rd costal section completely. Legs yellow; coxae black with yellow distal margin; trochanters, tibiae, and tarsi yellow; femora broadly yellow at apical end and distal tip black medially; last tarsomere brown, flattened; claws yellow with black tips, as long as last tarsomere; pulvilli yellow. Abdomen shining black with a little brown dust; 1st abdominal segment with 1 or 2 stout black bristle on the either side; 8th segment ca 0.5x as long and 0.6x as broad as 5th; small apical membranous area visible from dorsal side. Surstyli asymmetrical, right surstylus bifid; 9th segment, surstyli, aedeagal guide as shown in fig. 44E-H.

Length. Body : 2.9 mm; wing : 3.5 mm.

♀. Unknown.

Remarks. This species comes close to *scissus* Hardy from *Thailand* in in having 3rd antennal segment and legs yellow and bifid surstyli but differs in having 3rd antennal segment acute not acuminate as in *scissus* and also right surstylus bifid, not both as in the latter.

Etymology. Name based on the character of right surstylus which is bifid in this species.

Specimens examined. Holotype ♂, Pinjore (Haryana), 26.x.1985, coll. J. S. Grewal. Paratype 1 ♂, Datyar (H.P.), 26 x.1985, ex weeds, coll. S. K. Sharma.

Eudorylas euciliatus sp. n.

(Fig 45)

♂. Small black. Head ca 1.16x as broad as long and 1.16x as broad as thorax; eyes dark brown with black patches, area of contiguity ca 17 facets long; ocellar triangle with ocelli brown; upper frontal triangle black, obliterated, hardly 3 facets long; lower frontal triangle black, ca 16 facets long; lower 2/3rd covered with silvery white pubescence, base ca 1.5x as broad as base of ocellar triangle; proboscis yellow; occiput black with white dust, greatly swollen, with yellow hairs along posterior rim. Antenna (fig. 45B) black, 1st segment small, black with 1 black dorsal bristle; 2nd segment quadrate, black with 2 dorsal and 1 ventral bristles; 3rd segment black with greatly acuminate apex, pubescent; arista black, 1.5x as long as 3rd segment. Thorax 1.16x as long as broad, black with brown dust; scutellum with small weak bristles along posterior margin; pleurae all black; metanotum and pleurae with white dust; humeral plates dull yellow. Halteres black. Wings (fig.45A) hyaline with brownish tinge; 3rd costal section as long as 4th; 3rd and 4th combined 1.3x as long as 5th; r-m a little beyond 1/3rd of discal cell; distal portion of vein M_{1+2} slightly curved; stigma dark bown filling almost whole of angle between costa and R_1. Legs black; coxae, trochanters black; femora yellow only at distal extremities, tibiae yellow at both ends, black medially; tarsi brown, last tarsomeres black; claws yellow with black ends, as long as last tarsomere; pulvilli as long as claws. Abdomen black, opaque with brown dust, 1st abdominal segment with 2-3 stout black bristles on each side; 8th segment 0.8x as long and 0.7x as broad as 5th segment. Surstyli asymmetrical; aedeagus, ejaculatory apodeme and aedeagal guide as shown in fig. 45D-G.

Length. Body : 3.7 mm; wing : 4.1 mm.

♀. Frons ca 1.25x as broad in middle as on ends; lower 2/3rd covered with silvery white pubescence, ovipositor with base black, oblong, 0.7x as long as piercer, piercer brown very slightly curved upwards (fig. 45 I); in other char acters agrees with male.

Remarks. This species resembles *E. ciliatus de Meijere* from Java in characters like 3rd antennal segment acuminate and black, legs black, humeri dull yellow and halteres black, shape of 8th segment as seen from dorsal side; but differs in lacking the dense villose on posteroventral surface of hind femur in male and shape of surstyli.

Etymology. The name is based on it close resemblance with *ciliatus.*

Specimens examined. Holotype ♂, Kufri, 25.ix.1986, ex weeds, coll. J.S. Grewal. Allotype ♀, same data except coll. G. B. Singh. Paratypes 2 ♂, 4♀, same data except coll. S.K. Sharma; 1 ♂, Kufri, 25.ix.1986, coll. J.S. Grewal;

1♂, Mashobra, 27.ix.1986, coll. J. S. Grewal; 4 ♀ Carignano, 25.ix.1986, coll. S. K. Sharma; 3 ♀, 1♂, Kufri, 25.ix.1986, coll. G. B. Singh; 2 ♀, Mashobra, 25.ix.1986, coll. G. B. Singh (all localities in Himachal Pradesh); 1 ♀ Mussorrie (U. P.) 26.x.1986, coll. S. K. Sharma.

Eudorylas eulentiger sp. n.

(Fig. 46)

♂. Blackish brown, medium sized. Head ca 1.1x as broad as long and 1.3x as broad as thorax; as long as thorax and scutellum combined; ocellar triangle black; upper frontal triangle obliterated; lower frontal triangle 0.9x as long as area of contiguity (15 facets long); black with white pubescence near the base; base as broad as base of ocellar triange; face black with white pubescence; as broad as base of ocellar triangle; occiput slightly swollen with yellowish white hairs along margin ventrally. Antenna (fig. 46B) brown; 1st and 2nd segments brown, 2nd segment with 1 dorsal black bristle; 3rd segment brown, acuminate; arista black ca 1.25x as long as 3rd segment. Thorax black with brown dust 1.22x as long as broad; pleurae black except propleurae and mesopleurae yellowish brown; humeral plates yellow. Wings (fig. 46A) light brown; 3rd costal section ca 3x as long as 4th; 3rd and 4th section combined equal to 5th; stigma yellow, filling 3rd costal section; r-m crossvein at basal 1/3rd of the cell $1M_2$; vein M_{1+2} slightly curved. Legs yellow, except brown coxae, middle of femur and distal tarsus; claws smaller than the distal tarsi. Abdomen black with brown dust; 1st segment with 4-5 black bristles, 8th segments 1/2x as long as 5th, slightly tilted towards right. Surstyli asymmetrical; surstyli, 9th tergum, aedeagus, ejaculatory apodeme, aedeagal guide as shown in fig. 46D-G.

Length. Body : 3.05 mm; wing : 3.77 mm.

♀. Not known.

Remarks. The peculiar lobe-like surstyli and the position of membranous area brings it close to *P. (E) lentiger* Kertesz from Taiwan although not exactly same. The ratio of 8th to 5th abdominal segment is different, 8th is 1/3rd in *lentiger* while 1/2x in this species. The 3rd antennal segment is obtuse in *lentiger* while acute at tip in this species. Shapes of claspers, ratio of 3rd to 4th costal sections are also different from that of *lentiger*.

Etymology. The species is named so as it fits close to species *lentiger*.

Specimen examined. Holotype ♂, Haldwani (U. P.), 10.xi.1983, ex weeds, coll. A. Kumar.

Eudorylas extensus (Brunetti)
(Fig. 47)

Pipunculus extensus Brunetti, 1923, Fauna Br. India, Dipt. III : 13. (♂, ♀), Type-loc : Pusa, India.

Pipunculus (Eudorylas) extensus : Hardy 1975, In. Cat. Dipt. Orient. Reg. Hawaii., Vol. II : 301.

♂ . ♀ . *Head* in ♂ with eyes contiguous for a moderately long distance, vertex very small; frons and face silvery white when seen from above, an indistinct median black ground-colour stripe on the former; antennae dark, 3rd joint whitish grey-dusted, arista shining black; occiput a little puffed out behind. In ♀, frons as wide as face; 3rd antennal joint rather longer, more pointed, the tip slightly turned up; front facets of eyes enormously enlarged. *Thorax* and scutellum cinereous; pleurae nearly slate-grey: metanotum ash-grey. *Abdomen* ash-grey, with a transverse blackish band on base of each segment reaching to the sides, widened in the centre, but not sufficiently to reach the next segment; sides of abdomen curving considerably under the blackish venter; genitalia rather small. *Legs* all black, except base of tibiae which is dull orange; brownish-yellow pubescence below hind tarsi; inner sides of hind femora shining black; no ciliation behind middle femora. *Wings* nearly clear; stigma very pale and indistinct; anterior cross-vein more nearly at one-third than at the middle of the discal cell. Halteres black.

Length. Body : 3–3.5 mm.

During present survey no specimen of this species could be collected. The description given above is taken as such from Brunetti (1923.)

Eudorylas filicornis (Brunetti)
(Fig. 48)

Pipunculus filicornis Brunetti, 1912, Rec. Indian Mus., 7 : 489 (♀). Type-loc : Kurseong, India.

Pipunculus (Eudorylas) filicornis : Hardy, 1975, In Cat. Dipt. Orient. Reg. Hawaii., Vol. II : 301.

♀. Head with frons and face narrow, still narrower at the the level of the antennae, almost wholly with a greyish-white reflection. Antennae bright yellow; 3rd joint very elongate, pointed, and the tip bearing a long straight black bristle; arista thickened considerably at the yellow base, thence black and long, thus giving the appearance of the antennae bearing two aristas, neo pointing upwards and one downwards. Facets of eyes immediately in front very greatly enlarged; back of head very slightly puffed out grey, with a narrow fringe of pale hairs. Thorax dark aeneous-black, moderately shining, with microscopic pale pubescence; humeral calli yellowish grey-dusted, rather more prominent than usual in this genus; sides dirty yellowish; scutellum livid yellow, microscopically grey-dusted; metanotum dark grey. Abdomen pale yellow, microscopically pale-haired, with a black rather wide, dorsal stripe on the 2nd, 3rd and 4th segments, which has a tendency to form a narrow transverse line at the bases of these segments; 5th and 6th segments wholly black, posterior corners of former slightly yellowish; venter dirty yellow, blackish towards tip. Genitalia large, blackish, globular, shining, with a long shining brown ovipositor bent under the venter. Legs practically entirely yellow; coxae brownish on basal half; tibiae and tarsi microscopically beset with black bristles, on the former longitudinally, on the latter transversely; claws long, pale, yellow, black-tipped; pulvilli apparently large, strong and reddish-yellow; no ciliation behind middle femora; inner sides of hind femora not shing black. (The apical parts of most of the legs are damaged.) Wings clear; stigma pale yellow, stigmatic segment barely longer than 4th costal segment; anterior cross-vein at two-fifth of the discal cell; 4th longitudinal vein curved.

Length. Body : 4 mm.

During present survey no specimen of this species could be collected. The description given above is taken as such from Brunetti (1923).

Eudorylas garhwalensis sp. n.
(Fig. 49)

♂. Medium sized, black. Head large, ca 0.33x the body length; 1.18x as broad as long and 1.25x as broad as thorax; eyes reddish brown with area of contiguity ca 16 facets long; ocellar triangle black, ocelli brown; upper frontal triangle shining black, ca 9 facets long; lower frontal triangle black with silvery white pubescence, 21 facets long, base ca 1.5x as broad as base of ocellar triangle; face black with silvery white pubescence, as broad as base of lower frontal triangle; occiput black with white dust, not swollen. Antenna dark brown; 1st segment small, black with 2 dorsal and 1 ventral black bristles; 2nd segment quadrangular, black with 3 small dorsal and 2 large (ca 0.75x as long as 3rd segment) ventral black bristles; 3rd segment dark brown with round apex; arista black ca 1.5x as long as 3rd segment (fig. 49B). Proboscis yellow. Thorax shining black with brown dust; ca 1.25x as long as broad; scutellum bare; metanotum and pleurae black with white dust; humeral plates black. Halteres black. Wing (fig. 49A) hyaline; stigma brown, filling 0.9th portion of angle between costa and R_1; 3rd and 4th combined ca 1.4x as long as 5th section; r-m crossvein a little before 2/5th of discal cell; distal portion of vein M_{1+2} greatly curved. Legs dark brown; coxae dark brown with distal margin light brown; trochanters dark brown, hind trochanter with thin long bristles on ventral side; femora mostly black, dark brown on both tips; tibiae black on 2/3rd distal part, proximal 1/3rd dark brown, extreme distal tip brown; tarsi brown except the last tarsomere black; claws yellow with black tips, ca 1.5x as long as last tarsomere; pulvilli yellow, small ca 0.75x as long as last tarsomere. Abdomen shining black with brown dust dorsally and white dust laterally; 1st abdominal segment with 8-10 thin, long, black bristles on each side; 2nd segment also with 12-14 small thin bristles while 3rd segment with 6-10 small hair like bristles; 8th segment very small ca 0.22x as long and 0.4x as broad as 5th segment, and with a large apicoventral membranous area with a small ventral keel. Male genitalia with symmetrical surstyli. Surstyli, ejaculatory apodeme, aedeagus and aedeagal guide as shown in fig. 49C-F.

Length. Body : 4.62 mm; wing : 5.31 mm.

♀. One specimen with wings broken. Frons dull black, broader in the middle ca 1.25x as broad as on both ends where it equals base of ocellar triangle in width; lower 1/4th covered with silvery white pubescence; pleurae brownish; ovipositor with globose black base, ca 0.5x as long as piercer; piercer dark brown, long straight reaching upto base of 1st abdominal segment (fig. 49G).

Length. Body : 4.14 mm.

Remarks. This species comes close to *megacephalus* (Kertesz) from Taiwan in sharing characters like head abnormally large equalling 1/3rd of the body length and hind margin of scutellum bare, but differs from latter by possessing 3rd antennal segment with apex round (cf. acuminate in *megacephalus*).

Etymology. Named after its type-locality.

Specimens examined. Holotype ♂, Dehra Dun (U.P.), 24.vi 1983, ex grass, coll. V. K. Kohli. Allotype ♀, Shimla (H.P.), 20.vi.1982, coll. S. K. Sharma. Paratype 1 ♂, data same as that of holotype.

Eudorylas indiaensis sp. n.
(Fig. 50)

♂. Small, black. Head 1.3x as broad as long and 1.3x as broad as thorax; eyes reddish brown with dark brown patches, area of contiguity 15 facets long; ocellar triangle black, ocelli yellow; upper frontal triangle shining black, obliterated, only 2 facets long; lower frontal triangle black, covered with silvery white pubescence, as long as area of contiguity between the eyes, base as broad as base of ocellar triangle; face black with silvery white pubescence, as broad as base of lower frontal triangle; occiput swollen, black with grey dust and small yellow hairs along posterior margin. Antennae (fig. 50B) brown, 1st segment small, black, 2nd segment quadrate, brown with 2 dorsal and 2 ventral small black bristles; 3rd segment brown, acute; arista black ca 1.5x as long as 3rd antennal segment. Thorax black, covered with brown dust ca 1.2x as long as broad; scutellum with small black hairs along the posterior margin, pleurae black, humeral plates yellow. Halteres yellow. Wings (fig. 50A) hyaline, 3rd costal section ca 1.33x as long as 4th; 3rd and 4th combined ca. 1.56x as long as 5th; stigma yellow filling ca 0.8th of the angle of 3rd costal section with R_1; crossvein r-m situated a little before middle of discal cell; last portion of vein M_{1+2} almost straight. Legs yellow; coxae brown with distal tips yellow, trochanters, tibiae and tarsomeres yellow except the last one which is dark brown; femora broadly yellow at the tips, black medially; claws yellow with black tips, as long as last tarsomere, pulvilli small, yellow. Abdomen black with brown dust; 8th segment ca (fig. 50C) 0.5x as long and 0.5x as broad as 5th segment; 1st abdominal segment with 4-5 bristles on each side. Male genitalia with surstyli asymmetrical. Shape of surstyli, ejaculatory apodeme, aedeagus, aedeagal guide as shown in fig. 50D-G.

Length. Body : 2.62 mm; wing : 3.1 mm.

♀. Head broken; crossvein r-m at basal 2/5th. Ovipositor with base black, globose, 0.42x as long as piercer, piercer long yellow, curved upward (fig. 50H). Rest of the description similar to male.

Remarks. This species comes close to *bharatiensis* sp. nov. in the characters of black antenna and 8th abdominal segment having a deep cleft but differs in the wing venation having 3rd costal section longer (1.33x) than 4th whereas in *bharatiensis* 4th is 1.25x longer than 3rd and vein r-m situated just before middle of discal cell (cf. at basal 2/5th in *bharatiensis*), shape of surstyli and size of 9th abdominal segment.

Etymology. Name based on occurrence of this species throughtout India.

Specimens examined. Holotype ♂, Guwahati (Assam), 12.iv.1985, coll. S. K. Sharma. Allotype ♀, Kurseong (W. B.), 6 iv.1985, coll. S. K. Sharma. Paratype 1 ♂, Solan (H. P.), 19.x.1982, coll. L. S. Arya; 1 ♂, Kurseong (W. B.), 6.iv.1985, coll. S. K. Sharma.

Eudorylas jacksoni sp. n.
(Fig. 51)

♂. Small, black. Head 1.18x as broad as long and 1.2x as broad as thorax; compound eyes reddish brown with dark patches, area of contiguity equal to ca 15 facets; ocellar triangle black, ocelli yellow; upper frontal triangle black, 3 facets long; lower frontal triangle black with silvery white pubescence, ca 16 facets long, base as broad as ocellar triangle; face black with silvery white pubescence, as broad as base of lower frontal triangle; occiput black with white dust, not swollen. Antenna (fig 51B) yellow; 1st segment small, black with one dorsal bristle; 2nd segment black, quadrangular with 3 dorsal and 2 ventral black bristles; 3rd segment yellow with acuminate apex; arista black, 2x as long as 3rd segment. Proboscis yellow. Thorax black with brown dust, 1.1x as long as broad, metanotum and pleurae black with white dust; humeral plates yellow. Halteres yellow. Wings (fig. 51A) hyaline, 3rd costal section 0.86x as long as 4th; both combined 1.2x as long as 5th; crossvein r-m a little beyond basal 1/3rd of discal cell and just below the point of union of subcosta and costa; last section of vein M_{1+2} slightly curved. Legs yellow; coxae black with yellow distal margin; trochanters yellow; femora black medially, broadly yellow at tips; tibiae and tarsi yellow except the last one which is black; claws yellow with black tip, 1.25x as long as last tarsomere; pulvilli yellow, 0 75x as long as last tarsomere. Abdomen black with brown dust; 1st abdominal segment with 2-3 stout black bristles on each side; 8th segment with a deep cleft dividing into 2 subequal parts, 0.7x as long and 0.7x as broad as 5th segment. Male genitalia with surstyli asymmetrical; ejaculatory apodeme membranous. The shape of surstyli, ejaculatory apodeme, aedeagus, aedeagal guide as shown in fig. 51C-F.

Length. Body : 2.8 mm; wing : 3.8 mm.

♀. Fits in the description of male except frons with sides parallel grey pubescent and shape of antenna (fig. 51G); abdomen cylindrical with brown dust; ovipositor with base dark brown, globose, 0.87x as long as piercer; piercer yellow, strongly curved upward fig. 51H.

Length. Body : 3.00 mm; wing : 3.95 mm.

Remarks. This species is close to *mutillatus* Loew and shares characters like yellow acuminate antennae, & 8th abdominal segment with a deep cleft dividing into two subequal parts; but differs in position of crossvein with respect to costal vein (in this species it is situated at the point of union of costa and subcosta, while in *mutillatus* it is between the points of union of subcosta and R_1 with the costa), r-m situated at basal 1/3 of discal cell in this species while at basal 2/5th in case of *mutillatus*. This species also differs from *mutillatus* in having small membranous ejaculatory apodeme while in the latter it is well developed and chitinized.

Etymology. The species is named after Dr. R. D. Jackson. (Director, FERRO, American Embassy, New Delhi).

Specimens examined. Holotype ♂, Pinjore (Haryana), 26.x1985, ex weeds, coll V. C. Kapoor. Allotype 1♀, Chandigarh, 24.x.1985, ex grass, coll. S. K. Sharma. Paratypes 1♀, 1♂ from Dharifatehpur (H.P.), ex weeds, 20.iv.1985, coll. S. K. Sharma; 1♂ Pinjore (Haryana), 26.x.1985, coll. V. K. Kohli; 1♂ Dehra Dun (U.P.), 21.vi.1283, ex grass, coll. S. K. Sharma.

Eudorylas javanensis (de Meijere)
(Fig. 52)

Pipunculus javanensis de Meijere, 1907, Tijds V. Ent., 50 : 262.

Dorilas (Eudorylas) tsuboii Koizumi, 1959, *Sci. Rep. Fac. Agric.* Okayama University, 13 ; 40.

Pipunculus (Eudorylas) javanensis : Hardy 1968, Entomol. Meddel., 36 : 451-53.

Two female specimens from Dehra Dun fit the description of Hardy (1968) from Bismarck Islands. The species is widespread in Oriental region. The following description of male is from Hardy (1968) while that of female is based on the collected material.

♂. Small, black. Junction of compound eyes very short, about equal in length to 5 or 6 rows of eye facets; upper portion of front almost as long as lower one, entirely subshining black; lower front dull grey, pubescent on upper half, silvery on lower portion; face about equal in width to lower portion of front. Antennae brown (fig. 52A), tinged with yellow, 3rd segment acuminate, rather densely silvery grey, pubescent. Thorax brown, pollinose on dorsum, grey on sides; humeri yellow; hairs in row on hind margin of scutellum, short and inconspcuous. Halteres yellow. Legs : coxae dark brown to black, covered with grey pubescence; femora predominantly dark brown to black, grey pubescent, yellow on narrow apices; tibiae yellow, discoloured with brown medially; tarsi yellow, except for the brown apical tarsomeres; ventral bristles at apices of front and middle tibiae short, rather inconspicuous; 1 or 2 prominent black setae present on the anterior surface of each hind tibia. Wings subhyaline, stigma pale brown and not fully filling whole of 3rd costal section; 3rd costal section 1/3rd to 1/2 longer than 4th and these 2 sections combined distinctly longer than 5th; crossvein r-m just beyond the basal 3rd of discal cell and last section of vein M_{1+2} gently curved. First tergum of abdomen with 5 or 6 strong black bristles on each side and entirely grey; 2nd predominantly grey, brown pollinose at apex; terga 3-5 mostly brown pollinose, nearly equal in length to 5th segment and with a large apical membranous area; as seen from the ventral view, the membranous area covers apex of 8th segment. Claspers rather broad, slightly pointed at inner apices (fig. 52B-C).

Length. Body : 3.2 mm; wing : 3.5 mm.

♀. Small black. Head 1.17x as broad as long and 1.32x as broad as thorax; eyes dark brown; ocellar triangle black with ocelli yellow; frons black, opaque, lower 1/6th portion covered with silvery white pubescence; sides of frons almost parallel; face black with silvery white pubescence, as broad as frons; occiput black with grey dust, swollen. Antenna yellow; 1st antennal segment small, black, with 1 small dorsal black bristle, 2nd segment black, quadrangular with 2 small dorsal and 2 large ventral black bristles; 3rd antennal segment yellow to light brown with apex acuminate; arista black, 2x as long as 3rd segment. Proboscis light brown. Thorax black with brown dust 1.28x as long as broad; metanotum and pleurae black with grey dust, humeri brown. Halteres with base and knob dark brown and shaft yellow. Wing hyaline, 3rd costal section ca 0.8x as long as 4th; 3rd and 4th costal sections combined 0.7x as long as 5th; crossvein r-m at basal 1/3rd of the discal cell; distal end of vein M_{1+2} moderately curved. Legs black; coxae and trochanters black; femora black, yellow at extreme ends; tibiae black medially, broadly yellow at proximal end and narrowly at distal end; tarsi yellow except black distal tarsomeres; claws and pulvilli yellow, ca 1.5x as long as distal tarsomeres. Abdomen black, opaque with brown dust; 1st abdominal segment with 3-4 stout black bristles on either side; ovipositor with base shining black, oblong, 0.85x as long as piercer; piercer yellow, strongly curved upward and reaches upto base of 2nd segment (fig. 5 D).

Length. Body : 3.41 mm; wing : 3.84 mm.

Specimens examined. 2 ♀, Dehra Dun (U. P.), 21, 24.vi.1983, ex grass, coll. S. K. Sharma.

Eudorylas khaziarensis sp. n.
(Fig. 53)

♂. Black, small. Head ca 1.29x as broad as long, 1.16x as broad as thorax; eyes brown with area of contiguity ca 15 facets long; ocellar triangle black with ocelli yellow; upper frontal triangle shining black, obliterated, hardly 3 facets long; lower frontal triangle black with silvery white pubescence, ca 20 facets long, base ca 1.5x as broad as base of ocellar triangle; face black with silvery white pubescence, as broad as base of lower frontal triangle; occiput black with grey dust dorsally and white dust on lateral sides, swollen. Antenna dark brown (fig. 53B), 1st antennal segment black with two small black dorsal bristles; 2nd segment quadrangular, black, with one small dorsal bristle; 3rd segment dark brown with yellow pubescence, apex yellow, acuminate; arista black, twice as long as 3rd antennal segment. Proboscis yellow. Thorax black with grey dust; ca 1.19x as long as broad; scutellum bare; metanotum and pleurae black with white dust; humeral plate mushroom colour. Haltere with base black, shaft yellow and knob brown. Wings (fig. 53A) hyaline with brownish tinge, stigma pale brown, completely filling 3rd costal section; 3rd costal section as long as 4th; 3rd and 4th combined ca 1.4x as long as 5th; r-m crossvein at basal 2/5th of discal cell; distal end of vein M_{1+2} slightly curved. Legs black; coxae and trochanters black; femora black except at distal tips; tibiae black, yellow only at extreme tips; tarsi dark brown, last tarsomere black; claws yellow with black tip, ca 1.25x as long as last tarsomere; pulvilli yellow as long as last tarsomere. Abdomen black with brown dust, 1st abdominal segment with 4-6 stout black bristles on either side; 8th abdominal seegment as long and 0.8x as broad as 5th segment. Male genitalia with slightly asymmetrical surstyli. Surstyli, aedeagus, ejaculatory apodeme as shown in fig 53C-E.

Length. Body : 2.62 mm; wing : 3.3 mm.

Remarks. This species comes close to *javanensis* de Meijere by sharing characters like large apical membranous area; 3rd antennal segment brown and acuminate, but differs in wing venation i.e. 3rd costal section is one half longer than 4th; r-m crossvein at 2/5th basal of discal cell in former and at basal 1/3rd in latter; it also differs in male genitalic characters like shape of surstyli, aedeagus and ejaculatory apodeme.

Etymology. Named after its type-locality.

Specimens examined. Holotype ♂, Khaziar (H.P.), 15.ix.1981, coll. S.K. Sharma. Paratype 1 ♂, Shimla (H P.), 20.vi.1982, coll. S. K. Sharma.

Eudorylas ludhianaensis sp. n.
(Fig. 54)

♂. Medium sized, black. Head ca 1.2x as broad as long and 1.2x as broad as thorax; eyes reddish brown with area of contiguity ca 18 facets long; ocelli yellow; upper frontal triangle much reduced, shining black, ca 7 facets long; lower frontal triangle black, lower 1/3rd with silvery white pubescence, base as broad as base of ocellar triangle; face black with silvery white pubescence, as broad as base of ocellar triangle; occiput black with white dust, swollen, fine hairs present on posterior rim. Antenna (fig. 54B) yellow; 1st antennal segment small black; 2nd quadrangular, brown with 3 dorsal and 2 ventral black bristles; 3rd antennal segment yellow, acute at apex; arista blaek 2x as long as rest of 3rd segment. Proboscis yellow. Thorax black with brown dust, ca 1.35x as long as broad; scutellum bare; metanotum and pleurae black; humeral plates yellow. Halteres yellow. Wings (fig. 54A) hyaline with brownish tinge, 3rd costal section equal to 4th; 3rd and 4th combined 1.2x as long as 5th; crossvein r-m a little before middle of discal cell; distal portion of M_{1+2} slightly curved. Legs yellow; coxae black with distal margin yellow; trochanters yellow; femora black dorsomedially, broadly yellow at both ends; tibiae and tarsi yellow except distal tarsomeres which are black and flattened; claws yellow with tips black, ca 1.5x as long as distal tarsomere; pulvilli brownish as long as distal tarsomere. Abdomen black with brown dust; 1st segment with 3–4 black stout bristles on either side; 8th abdominal segment as long as and 0.7x as broad as 5th segment, with a cleft which divides 8th segment in two subequal parts; apical membranous area not visible from dorsal side (fig. 54C). Male genitalia with surstyli quite broad; aedeagus, ejaculatory apodeme, aedeagal guide and 9th segment as shown in fig. 54D-G.

Length. Body : 4.27 mm; wing : 4.83 mm.

♀. Unknown.

Remarks. This species comes near *mutillatus* Loew in the characters like, antenna, legs, humeri and halters yellow and having a cleft dividing 8th abdominal segment; but differs in wing venation having 3rd costal section equal to the 4th and r-m situated little before middle of the discal cell; the main character in which this species differs from *mutillatus* is that of male genitalia in having the surstyli more broader and larger in size as compared to that of *mutillatus*.

Etymology. This species is named after the type-locality.

Specimen examined. Holotype ♂, Punjab Agric. Univ., Ludhiana, 22. ix.1985, ex weeds, coll. J. S. Grewal.

Eudorylas luteipes (Brunetti)

Pipunculus luteipes Brunetti, 1923, Fauna Br. India, Dipt. III : 18 (♀). Type-loc : Pusa, India.

Pipunculus (Eudorylas) luteipes Brunetti : Hardy, 1975, In Cat. Dipt. Orient. Reg., Hawaii, Vol. II : 302.

♀. Head with frons rather broad, slightly widening from vertex downward, distinctly though not greatly contracted throughout that portion in contact with the exceptionally enlarged eye-facets, blackish grey, but the whole frons with silvery-white shimmer if viewed from above; face wholly, brilliantly shining white. Antennae black; 3rd joint considerably elongate, with long pointed tip, bright yellow, with a white shimmer if viewed from above. Mouth parts withdrawn; occiput moderately puffed out, blackish grey, white-dusted laterally. Thorax and scutellum moderately black, dusted with olive brown. Abdomen ash-grey; 1st segment with a basal olive brown band; 2nd segment wholly ash-grey; 3rd, 4th and 5th with olive-brown bands basally, the colour not or barely reaching the side margins and then only basally, but extending posteriorly nearly or quite to the next segment. Genitalia very large, fully as wide as last segment, with a deep groove on upper side of the globular basal piece; ovipositor reddish-brown. Legs wholly rather pale yellow to the tips of the tarsi, but the minute black bristles on the joints of the tarsi give them a slightly darkened appearance; claws much lengthened, pulvilli pale yellow, very greatly enlarged. Wings pale grey; stigma pale brownish, ill defined; anterior cross-vein distinctly before middle of discal cell; halteres pale yellow.

Length. Body : 2·5 mm.

During the presnt survey no specimen of this species could be collected, so the above description is taken as such from Brunetti (1923).

Eudorylas macropygus (de Meijere)
(Fig. 55)

Pipunculus macropygus de Meijere, 1914, Tijds. V. Ent., 57 : 167.

Pipunculus (Eudorylas) macropygus : Hardy, 1968, Entomol Meddel., 36 : 453-54.

Pipunculus chalybeus Brunetti, 1923, Fauna Brit. India. Dipt., 3 : 15.

♂. Small, black. Head 1.33x as broad as thorax, eyes reddish brown with area of contiguity 8 facets long; ocellar triangle black with ocelli yellow; upper frontal triangle shining black, obliterated, ca 10 facets long; lower frontal triangle black with silvery white pubescence, ca 22 facets long, base ca 1.5x as broad as base of lower frontal triangle; occiput black with white dust on lateral and ventral sides, with few scattered yellow bristles on posterior margin. Antenna (fig. 55B) black; 1st segment small, black; 2nd segment quadrangular black with 2 dorsal and 1 ventral small black bristle; 3rd segment black with apex acuminate and with yel'ow pubescence; arista black, about 1.5x as long as 3rd antennal segment. Proboscis yellow. Thorax black with sparse brown dust on mesonotum; pleurae black with white dust; humeri black. Halteres black with shaft yellow. Wings (fig. 55A) hyaline with slight brownish tinge; 3rd costal section as long as 4th; 3rd and 4th combined 1.36x as long as 5th; crossvein r-m a little before basal 1/3rd of discal cell; last section of vein M_{1+2} slightly curved; stigma dark brown occupying 0.86x of angle between costa and R_1. Legs black with coxae and trochanters black; femora black with extreme distal tip yellow; tibiae black with brown and distal tips yellow; tarsi brown, distal tarsomere dark brown; claws yellow with black tips; pulvilli yellow, both as long as distal tarsomere Abdomen black with white dust; 1st abdominal segment without any bristle, other segments also bare; 8th segment 1.67x as long as and 1.3x as broad as 5th segment (fig. 55C); 9th segment visible dorsally. Surstyli asymmetrical; surstyli aedeagus, aedeagal guide and ejaculatory apodeme as shown in fig 55D-G.

Length. Body : 3.15 mm; wing : 3.45 mm.

♀. Resembles male in most of the characters. Frons black, upper 1/3rd black and lower 1/3rd with silvery white pubescence, broadest in the middle, 1.25x as broad as the tips; face with silvery white pubescence, as broad as lower end of frons. Antenna with 3rd segment dark brown and apex yellow; arista 1.5x as long as 3rd antennal segment. Ovipositor with black globose base, as long as piercer; piercer light brown, thin and straight (fig. 55H).

Length. Body : 3.26 mm; wing : 3.4 mm.

Specimens examined. About 240 specimens from different localities of India.

Eudorylas major (Brunetti)
(Fig. 56)

Pipunculus major Brunetti, 1923, Fauna Br. India. Dipt., III : 10. (♂, ♀). Type-loc : Pusa, India.

Pipunculus (Eudorylas) major : Hardy, 1975, In Cat. Dipt. Orient. Reg. Hawaii., 2 : 296-306.

♂ . ♀. Head with eyes touching in ♂ for less than half the distance from the rather large elongate vertex to the antennae; frons and face silvery-white when seen from above; antennae light brown, with a little white shimmer when seen from above, arista black; back of head only moderately puffed out, greyish round margin. Frons in ♀ as wide as face. Thorax dull blackish, with traces of a thin cinereous-brown covering of tomentum; a little greyish about the shoulders; sides and pleurae more or less ash-grey; scutellum dull black; metanotum ash-grey. Abdomen in ♂ with 1st segment ash-grey, dirty black at base; 2nd, 3rd and 4th segments dark slate-grey, with a shining black basal band filling about half the segment and extending to the sides while latter are ash-grey, except at the base of each; 5th segment nearly as long as 4th, mainly light grey or ash-grey, broadly black at base; genitalia very small, mainly concealed. In ♀, light grey, nearly ash-grey; 1st segment as in ♂; 2nd, 3rd and 4th with a narrow ill defined black basal band; 5th segment not much longer than 4th; basal segment of genitalia appearing like a 6th abdominal segment and of the same coloration. Legs black, tips of femora rather broadly, base and tips of tibiae very broadly, orange; middle tarsi orange, except the last joint, which is black; fore and hind tarsi brown on basal half, black on apical half. All femora with minute bristles on apical half of under side; inner side of hind femora very shining black; middle femora with a ciliation of hairs on hinder side. Wings (fig. 56) clear, iridescent; stigma pale brown, rather weak; anterior cross-vein more nearly at one-third than middle of discal cell. Halteres brownish.

Length. Body : 4.00 mm.

As during present survey no specimen of this species could be collected, the description has been taken from Brunetti (1923).

Eudorylas manaliensis sp. nov.

(Fig. 57)

♂. Small, black. Head as broad as long and ca 1.18x as broad as thorax; eyes reddish brown with area of contiguity ca 17 facets long; ocellar triangle black with ocelli brown; upper frontal triangle obliterated, black, hardly 3 facets long; lower frontal triangle ca 15 facets long, black, lower 1/3rd covered with silvery white pubescence, base ca 1.2x as broad as base of ocellar triangle, face black, covered with silvery white pubescence, as broad as base of lower frontal triangle; occiput black with brown dust, swollen. Antenna black; 1st segment small, black; 2nd segment quadrangular, black with 2 dorsal and 2 ventral black bristles; 3rd segment black with apex acuminate; arista black ca 1.5x as long as 3rd segment (fig. 57B). Proboscis yellow. Thorax black with brown dust ca 1.18x as long as broad, scutellum bare, metanotum and pleurae black with white dust; humeral plates black. Halteres black. Wings (fig. 57A) hyaline with brownish tinge, stigma pale brown filling 3rd costal section; 3rd costal section equal to 4th; 3rd and 4th combined ca 1.12x as long as 5th; r-m crossvein at basal 1/3rd of discal cell, distal portion of vein M_{1+2} greatly curved. Legs black, coxae and trochanters black; femora black, yellow only at distal tips; tibiae black except yellow at both ends; tarsi dark brown to black; claws brown with black tips, ca 2x as long as distal tarsomere; pulvilli yellow, ca 1.5x as long as distal tarsomeres. Abdomen black with brown dust, 1st segment with 3–4 black stout bristles on each side; 8th abdominal segment as long as 5th segment; large apical membranous area scarcely visible. Surstyli asymmetrical; surstyli, 9th segment, aedaegus, ejaculatory apodeme and aedeagal guide as shown in fig. 57C-G.

Length. Body : 2.55 mm; wing : 4.00 mm.

♀. Unknown.

Specimen examined. Holotype ♂, Manali (H.P.), 9.vi.1986, ex weeds, coll. S. K. Sharma.

Remarks. This species comes close to *javanensis* de Meijere in having large apical membranous area on 8th abdominal segment, 3rd antennal segment acuminate and black legs, but deffers from it by having area of contiguity between compound eyes ca 15 facets long (cf. 5-6 facets in *javanensis*), humeri and halteres black (yellow in *javanensis*); 3rd costal section equal to 4th (0.5x longer than 4th in *javanensis*) and shape of surstyli is quite different in this species.

Etymology. The name is based on the type locality.

Eudorylas minghlanii sp. n.

(Fig. 58)

♂. Small, black. Head as long as broad; eyes brown with dark patches, area of contiguity ca 17 facets long; ocellar triangle black with ocelli yellow; upper frontal triangle obliterated, ca 3-4 facets long; lower frontal triangle black, covered with silvery white pubescence, except for the extreme of upper angle; base as broad as base of ocellar triangle; face black with silvery white pubescence; as broad as base of ocellar triangle; occiput black covered with white dust, slightly swollen. Antenna black, 1st segment small, black with one dorsal black bristle; 2nd segment black, quadrate with 2 dorsal and 1 ventral black bristles; 3rd antennal segment black, acuminate, arista black, ca 2x as long as the 3rd segment (fig. 58B). Proboscis yellow. Thorax black covered with brown dust, 1.25x as long as broad; pleurae black, humeral plates yellow. Halteres also yellow. Wings (fig. 58A) hyaline with brownish tinge; stigma brown filling almost whole of the angle between R_1 and 3rd costal section; 3rd costal section equal to 4th; 3rd and 4th costal sections combined 1.35x as long as 5th section; r-m crossvein at basal 2/5th of discal cell; distal portion of vein M_{1+2} almost straight. Legs black; coxae and trochanters black; femora black except at the extreme distal tips; tibiae black except at 1/4th apical and distal tip; tarsi dark brown, last tarsomere black, flattened; claws yellow with black tips, ca 1.5x as long as last tarsomere; pulvilli large yellow, as long as claws. Abdomen black, opaque; 3-4 long black bristles on either side of 1st abdominal segment; 8th segment ca 0.5x as long and 0.5x as broad as 5th abodminal segment. Male genitalia with asymmetrical surstyli;surstyli, ejaculatory apodeme, aedeagal guide as shown in fig. 58C-G.

Length. Body : 3.4 mm; wing : 3.6 mm.

♀. Unknown.

Etymology. Species is named after Mr. S. L. Minghlani (FERRO, American Eambassy, New Delhi) due to his active cooperation during the course of this project.

Remarks. This species comes near *antennalis* sp. n. in having black antenna and legs, and 8th abdominal segment with a cleft; but differs in wing venation, 3rd costal section equal to 4th costal section; cleft of 8th segment much broader and in shape of surstyli.

Specimens examined. Holotype ♂, Tattapani (H.P.), 27.ix.1986, on grass, coll. J. S. Grewal. Paratype 1 ♂, same data but coll. G. S. Sidhu.

Eudorylas mutillatus Loew
(Fig. 59)

Pipunculus mutillatus Loew, 1857 Ofvers. K. Svenska Vet. Acad. Forh. 14 : 374 (♂). Type-locality : Cafraria.

Pipunculus hepaticolor of de Meijere, 1907, not Becker, misidentification.

Pipunculus aequalis Becker, 1924, Ent. Mitt., 13 : 16 ♂. Type-loc. : Taiwan.

Pipnculus matema Curran, 1936, Proc. Calif Acad. Sci. (4), 22 : 22 (♂). Type loc. : Matema Island, Samta Cruz Group.

Pipunculus (Eudorylas) hiatus Hardy, 1956, Insects Micronesia, 13 : 5 (♂). Type-loc. : Yap, Caroline Islands.

Pipunculus (Eudorylas) distocruciator Hardy, 1966, Bull Br. Mus. Nat. Hist. (Ent.), 17 : 441 (♂, ♀). Type-loc. : Sangu, E. Nepal.

Pipunculus (Eudorylas) cruciator of Koizumi, 1959, not Perkins misidentification.

Pipunculus (Eudorylas) mutillatus Loew : Hardy, 1968, Ent. Meddel., 36:456. *

♂. Medium sized, black. Head ca 1.15x as broad as long and 1.2x as broad as thorax; eyes reddish brown with area of contiguity ca 15 facets long; ocellar triangle black with ocelli yellow; upper frontal triangle black, much obliterated, hardly 7 facets long, lower frontal triangle black, covered with silvery white pubescence, ca 18 facets long, base 1.25x as broad as base of ocellar triangle; face black with silvery white pubescence, as broad as base of lower frontal triangle; occiput black with white dust, swollen, having small yellow hairs on posterior rim. Antenna yellow (fig. 59B), 1st antennal segment small, black with one dorsal black bristle; 2nd sgment quadragular, black, with 2 dorsal and 3 ventral black bristles; 3rd segment yellow with apex acuminate, arista black, ca 1.5x as long as 3rd segment. Proboscis yellow. Thorax 0.33x as long as broad, black with brown dust; scutellum bare; metanotum and pleurae black with white dust; humeri yellow. Halteres yellow. Wing hyaline (fig. 59A) with brownish tinge; stigma filling 0.8th angle between costa and R_1; 3rd costal section ca 0.78th of 4th section; both combined 1.42x as long as 5th; crossvein r-m a little beyond basal 1/3rd of discal cell; vein M_{1+2} slightly curved. Legs yellow; coxae black, distal

* ***Pipunculus (Eudorylas) ranikhetiensis*** Kapoor et al., 1977, Bull. Ent., 18: 74-77. Type loc. : Ranikhet (Kumaon Hills, U.P.)

Pipunculus (Eudorylas) kumaonensis Kapoor et al., 1977, Bull Ent., 18:74-77. Rahkneit-(Kumaon Hills, U.P.)

margin yellow; trochanters yellow; femora black medially, broadly yellow at both ends; tibiae and tarsi yellow except last tarsomere which is dark brown; claws yellow with brown tips; as long as last tarsomere; pulvilli yellow, as long as claws. Abdomen black with brownish grey dust; 1st abdominal segment with 3-4 stout black bristles; 8th segment 0.75x as long as and 0.7x as broad as 5th, with a deep cleft on the right side dividing it into two subequal parts. **Male genitalia with asymmetrical surstyli; left one pointed and right one with rounded tip; 9th segment, surstyli, aedeagus, ejaculatory apodeme and; aedeagal guide as shown in fig. 59C-G.**

Length. Body 4.1 mm; wing : 4.8 mm.

♀. Frons black with little pubescenc on the lower half, 1.25x as broad in the middle as on the ends. Crossvein r-m a little beyond the basal 2/5th of discal cell. Ovipositor (fig. 59H) with black, globose base about 0.8x as long as piercer; piercer yellow, curved upward reaching upto the middle of 3rd segment. Rest similar to male.

Length. Body : 3.6 mm: wing. 4.5 mm.

Specimens examined. 1 ♂ Ladian (Ludhiana), 25.xi.1984, coll. S. K. Sharma; 22 ♀ and 28 ♂ from different localities of Distt. Ludhiana, Chandigarh, Pinjore (Haryana), Mukali, Thekkady, Silent valley (Kerala), Una (H.P.), Ranikhet, Dehra Dun (U.P.), Kandaghat, Mashobra (H.P.), Guwahati (Assam), Kurseong (West Bengal), Ramgarh (Bihar), Karignano, (H.P.), Gagret (H.P.), Jahan Khelan (Hoshiarpur) by J. S. Grewal, S. K. Sharma, L. S. Arya, V. K. Kohli and A. Kumar from 1983-1986.

Distribution. Burma, Taiwan, India, Nepal, Philippines Africa, Japan, Pacific, and Palaearctic Asia.

Eudorylas orientalis Koizumi

(Fig. 60)

Dorilas (Eudorylas) orientalis Koizumi, 1959, Sci. Rep. Fac. Agric. Okayama Univ., 13 : 43.

Eudorylas orientalis Koizumi, 1960, Sci. Rep. Fac. Agric. Okayama Univ., 16 : 41.

Pipunculus (*Eudorylas*) *orientalis* (Koizumi) Hardy, 1968, Ent. Meddal. 36 : 459.

♂. Small, black. Head 1.2x as broad as long, 1.2x as broad as thorax;

eyes reddish brown with area of contiguity 14 facets long; upper frontal triangle obliterated, hardly 4 facets long; lower frontal triangle black, 16 facets long, base as broad as base of ocellar triangle, lower half covered with silvery white pubescence; ocellar triangle black; face black covered with thick silvery white pubescence, as broad as the base of ocellar triangle; occiput black, not swollen, with few yellow hairs along posterior rim. Antennae black (fig. 60B), 1st segment small, black with one dorsal bristle, 2nd segment black, quadrate with 1 or 2 small black bristles; 3rd segment dark brown with yellow pubescence, apex yellow acuminate; arista dark brown, 1.5x as long as 3rd antennal segment. Thorax shining black covered with brown dust, 1.2x as long as broad; pleurae all black, scutellum without any bristle, humeri yellow. Halteres also yellow. Wing hyaline (fig. 60A) with brownish tinge; 3rd costal section 2x as long as 4th, 3rd and 4th combined 0.75x as long as 5th, r-m crossvein situated at basal 1/3rd of discal cell; distal portion of vein M_{1+2} straight. Legs black; coxae, trochanters black, femora narrowly yellow at extreme ends, tibiae black with 1/3rd anterior yellow; tarsi brownish yellow except distal tarsomere dark brown; claws yellow with black tips, as long as last tarsomere; pulvilli yellow, small, 0.7x as long as claws. Abdomen black, covered with white dust; 1st abdominal segment with 2-3 black bristles on each side; 8th segment 0.7x as long and 0.7x as broad as 5th segment; large round apical membranous area on right side of 8th segment. Male genitalia with surstyli symmetrical. Ejaculatory apodeme, aedeagus, aedeagal guide as shown in fig. 60C-H.

Length. Body : 2.73 mm; wing : 3.18 mm.

♀. Upper 2/3rd of frons polished black; lower 1/3rd black covered with silvery white pubescence; broadest (ca 1.7x) near middle, lower end as broad as base of ocellar triangle; 3rd antennal segment light brown, acuminate; 3rd costal section ca 1 63x as long as 4th; r-m crossvein situated a little before the middle of discal cell; ovipositor with base globose, black ca 0.9x as long as piercer, thin slender, yellow and straight (fig. 60 I).

Length. Body : 2.95 mm; wing : 3.27 mm.

Remarks. 3 males and 2 females of this species, all have antenna slightly acuminate as compared to one described from the oriental region by Hardy (1971) in which the apex of 3rd antennal segment is long and acuminate; otherwise they tally with already published description of this species.

Distribution. Widespread in oriental region, Bismark Islands and Japan.

Specimens examined. 1 ♂, Sunet (Ludhiana, Punjab), ex rice, 6.x.1982, coll. J. S. Grewal; 2 ♂, Dehra Dun, (U.P.) ex grass, 22,24.vi.1983, coll. S. K. Sharma; 2 ♀, Pinjore (Haryana), ex weeds, 26.x.1985, coll. S. K. Sharma.

Eudorylas pennatus sp. n.

(Fig. 61)

♂. Small, black. Head 1.6x as broad as long and 1.6x as broad as thorax; eyes brown with dark patches and area of contiguity ca 14 facets long; ocellar triangle black with ocelli yellow; upper frontal triangle black, ca 7 facets long; lower frontal triangle black, lower half covered with silvery white pubescence, base as broad as base of ocellar triangle; occiput black with silvery white dust, not swollen. Antenna yellow (fig. 61B); 1st segment small, black with 1 dorsal and 1 ventral black bristle; 2nd segment black quadrate with 1 dorsal and 1 ventral black bristle; 3rd segment yellow, slightly acuminate; arista dark brown, ca 1.5x as long as 3rd antennal segment. Proboscis yellow. Thorax black, covered with brown dust; ca 1.16x as long as broad; scutellum bare; pleurae all black; humeral plates yellow. Halteres also yellow. Wings hyaline with brownish tinge (fig. 61A), 3rd costal section 1.16x as long as 4th; 3rd and 4th combined 1.2x as long as 5th section; crossvein r-m a little before middle of discal cell; distal portion of vein M_{1+2} almost straight. Legs yellow : coxae black with distal rim yellow, trochanters yellow; femora broadly yellow at both ends; tibiae and tarsi yellow, last tarsomere black, claws yellow with black tips, ca 1.5x as long as last tarsomere, pulvilli yellow as long as last tarsomere. Abdomen black with white and brown dust; 1st abdominal segment with 3-4 black stout bristles on each side; 8th segment as long as and 0.8x as broad as 8th abdominal segment; male genitalia with surstyli asymmetrical; aedeagal guide with a peculiar spine. Shape of surstyli, aedeagus, aedeagal guide, ejaculatory apodeme as shown in fig. 61C-G.

Length. Body : 3.8 mm; wing : 4.14 mm.

♀. Agrees with male except with r-m crossvein at basal 2/5th of discal cell; ovipositor with base black, oval in shape, 0.74x as long as piercer, piercer yellow and curved upwards (fig. 61H).

Length. Body : 3 mm; wing : 3.8 mm.

Remarks. This species comes close to *mutillatus* Loew in the characters like antenna and legs yellow and 8th segment with a cleft; but differs from

it in wing having a dark streak closing the stigma, shape of surstyli and a peculiar spine on aedeagal guide.

Etymology. **Species is named after the character of pennis i.e. the aedeagal guide possessing a peculiar spine.**

Specimens examined. Holotype ♂, Dehra Dun (H. P.), 21.vi 1983, ex grass, coll. V. K. Kohli. Allotype ♀, Ram Nagar (U. P.), 21.ix.1986, ex weeds, coll. S. K. Sharma. Paratypes 2 ♂, Ranchi (Bihar), 20.iii.1985, ex weeds, coll. S. K. Sharma.

Eudorylas pinjorensis sp. n.

(Fig. 62)

♂. Medium-sized, black. Head 1.15x as broad as long; 1.26x as broad as thorax; eyes reddish brown with dark brown patches; area of contiguity 17 facets long; ocelli yellow; ocellar triangle black; upper frontal triangle greatly obliterated, hardly three facets long; lower frontal triangle 13 facets long with base 1.5x as broad as base of ocellar triangle; lower half of ocellar triangle with silvery white pubescence; face black, as broad as base of lower frontal triangle, covered with silvery white pubescence; occiput slightly swollen. Antenna dark brown to black (fig. 62A), 1st segment black, small; 2nd segment dark brown, quadrate, with 2 small dorsal and one long (3x as long as dorsal ones) ventral black bristles; 3rd segment dark brown, acuminate; arista black, about 1.5x as long as 3rd antennal segment. Proboscis yellow. Thorax black, covered with brown dust; 1.3x as long as broad, scutellum with a pair of black bristles; mesopleura yellow while rest of pleurae black; humeral plates yellow. Halteres also yellow. Wings (fig. 62A) hyaline, 3rd costal section about 3x as long as 4th; 3rd and 4th combined as long as 5th; r-m crossvein at about basal 2/5th of discal cell; distal portion of M_{1+2} straight; stigma completely filling the angle of 3rd costal section. Legs yellow; coxae black with distal margin yellow; trochanters yellowish brown; femora black, except the narrow tips which are yellow; tibiae and tarsi yellow; last tarsomere black; hind tibiae with a medial stout black bristle on outer side. Abdomen black, opaque, covered with brownish dust; 1st segment with white pubescence and 4 stout black bristles on either side, 8th segment as long as 5th and with a dorsomedial hump; slit-like membranous area placed obliquely on distal tip, surstyli asymmetrical, bilobed, right one oar-shaped, aedeagal guide spiny. The ejaculatory apodeme, aedeagus and aedeagal guide as shown in fig. 62C-G.

Length. Body : 3.25 mm; wing : 3.25 mm.

♀. Unknown.

Remarks. This species comes close to *setosilobus* Hardy from Viet Nam in having characters like 3rd antennal segment acuminate, legs prominently yellow and surstyli bifid but differs in the characters of 3rd antennal segment black, r-m crossvein at 2/5th basad of cell $1M_2$ and shape of surstyli.

Etymology. Name based on type-locality.

Specimens examined. Holotype ♂, Pinjore (Haryana), 26.x.1985, coll. J.S. Grewal. Paratype 1 ♂, same data.

Eudorylas poantaensis sp. n.
(Fig. 63)

♂. Small, black. Head ca 1.2x as broad as long and 1.2x as broad as thorax; eyes brown with reddish brown patches, area of contiguity ca 17 facets long; ocellar triangle black, ocelli yellow; upper frontal triangle obliterated and ca 5 facets long, black; lower frontal triangle 16 facets long, black with silvery white pubescence on lower 2/3rd; base 1.5x as broad as base of ocellar triangle, face black with silvery white pubescence; as broad as base of lower frontal triangle; occiput black with white pubescence, not swollen; proboscis brown Antenna yellow (fig.63B); 1st segment small black; 2nd segment quadrangular, brown with 1 dorsal and 1 ventral black bristle; 3rd segment yellow with apex slightly acuminate; arista black ca 1.5x as long as 3rd segment (fig.63). Thorax ca 1.3x as long as broad, black with brown dust; scutellum bare; metanotum and pleurae black wi h brown dust; humeral plates yellow. Halteres with base and knob black, shaft yellow. Wings (fig. 63A) hyaline with brownish tinge; 3rd costal section 2x as long as 4th; 3rd & 4th combined 1.3x as long as 5th; crossvein r-m at basal 1/3rd of discal cell, vein M_{1+2} slight curved at distal end. Legs yellow; coxae black with distal portion yellow; trochanters yellow; femora yellow except black medially; tibiae and tarsi yellow; last tarsomere black; claws yellow with black tips, as long as last tarsomere; pulvilli yellow, ca 0.5x as long as distal tarsomere. Abdomen black with grey dust; 1st segment with 3-4 stout black bristles on each side; 8th segment ca 0.7x as long and 0.8x as broad as 5th segment; small apical membranous area hardly visible from dorsal side. Surstyli asymmetrical. Surstyli, aedeagus, ejaculatory apodeme and aedeagal guide as shown in fig. 63C-F.

Length. Body : 3.25 mm; wing : 3.8 mm.

♀. Unknown.

Remarks. This species comes close to *eulentiger* sp. n. and shares with it the characters like 3rd costal section at least twice as long as 4th, legs yellow and shape of ejaculatory apodeme; but differs in having black pleurae, halteres and abdomen, different shape of surstyli, aedeagal guide and size of ejaculatory apodeme.

Etymology. Named after type-locality.

*

Eudorylas roralis (Kertesz)
(Fig. 64)

Dorilas roralis Kertesz, 1915, Ann. Mus. Nat. Hung., 13 : 389.

Pipunculus (*Eudorylas*) *roralis* ; Hardy, 1968, Entomol. Meddel., 36:461-62.

♂. Small, black. Head ca 1.17x as broad as long and 1.3x as broad as thorax; eyes brown with dark patches, area of contiguity ca 10 facets long; ocellar triangle black with ocelli yellow; upper frontal triangle polished black, ca 12 facets long; lower frontal triangle black with silvery white pubescence, only upper portion ca 3 facets long without pubescence; base of lower frontal triangle as broad as base of ocellar triangle, ca 21 facets long; face black with silvery white pubescence, ca 1.5x as broad as base of lower frontal triangle; occiput black with white dust, a few yellow hairs on posterior margin. Antenna brown (fig. 64B); 1st segment black; 2nd segment dark brown, quadrangular, with 2 dorsal and 1 ventral small black bristles; 3rd segment brown with yellow acuminate tip; arista dark brown, ca 1.5x as long as 3rd antennal segment. Proboscis yellow. Thorax black with brown dust; ca 1.37x as long as broad; metanotum and pleurae black with white dust, humeri black. Halteres also black. Wings hyaline with brown tinge (fig. 64A); 3rd costal section ca 0.75x as long as 4th; 3rd and 4th combined ca 1.25x as long as 5th; r-m crossvein a little before basal 1/3rd of discal cell; last section of vein M_{1+2} slightly curved; stigma dark brown, filling whole of angle between costa and vein R_1. Legs black, coxae and trochanters black, hind trochanter with tuft of black bristles ventrally; femora black with distal tips yellow; tibiae black with proximal and distal tips yellow; tarsi brown except distal tarsomere dark brown; claws brown, pulvilli yellow, both as long as distal tarsomere. Abdomen black; 1st and 2nd segments with white dust; segments 3–5 with brown dust; 1st abdominal segment without black

---

* Specimen examined : Holotype ♂, Poanta Sahib (U. P.), 25. ×. 1986, coll. S. K. Sharma

bristles on either side; 8th abdominal segment 1.22x as long and 0.9x as broad as 5th abdominal segment; surstyli slightly asymmetrical. Surstyli, aedeagus, ejaculatory apodeme and aedeagal guide as shown in fig. 64C-G.

Length. Body : 2.89 mm; wing : 3.51 mm.

♀. Frons black, lower half covered with silvery white pubescence, upper half shining black. Ventral bristle at the apex of front tibia elongated. Haltere yellowish with extreme tip black. Ovipositor with base black, slightly oblong, 1.33x as long as piercer; piercer yellow, thin and straight (fig. 64H).

Length. Body : 2.58 mm; wing : 3.42 mm.

Specimens examined. 20♂, 35♀ from different localities in India.

Eudorylas scutellatus sp. n.

(Fig. 65)

♂. Small, black. Head ca 1.2x as broad as long and 1.2x as broad as thorax; eyes reddish brown with dark patches; area of contiguity ca 14 facets long; ocellar triangle black, ocelli brown; upper frontal triangle black obliterated, hardly 4 facets long, black; lower frontal triangle black with silvery white pubescence, ca 14 facets long, base 1.25x as broad as base of ocellar triangle; face black with silvery white pubescence, 1.5x as broad as base of ocellar triangle; occiput black with white dust, swollen Proboscis yellow. Antenna black (fig. 65B), 1st segment small, black with 1 dorsal black bristle; 2nd segment quadrangular, black with 2 dorsal and 1 ventral black bristles; 3rd segment black with apex greatly acuminate, apex ca 2x as long as rest of 3rd segment; arista black ca 1.2x as long as 3rd segment. Thorax black with brown dust, ca 1.3x as long as broad; scutellum with few fine hairs along posterior border, metanotum and pleurae black with grey dust; humeral plates yellow. Halteres dark brown at base and knob while shaft yellow. Wings hyaline with brownish tinge (fig. 65A); 3rd costal section equal to 4th; 3rd and 4th combined ca 1.2x as long as 5th; crossvein r-m at 1/3rd basal of discal cell; distal portion of vein M_{1+2} slightly curved; stigma brown, filling whole of the angle between costa and R_1 Legs black; coxae and trochanters black; femora brown at extremities; tibiae dark brown at ends and black medially, fore tibiae with one and mid tibiae with two large apical spines; tarsi dark brown with distal tarsomeres black; claws yellow with black tips, ca 1.5x as long as distal tarsomeres; pulvilli yellow, as long as distal tarsomeres. Abdomen black, opaque, covered with dark brown dust, 3 stout black bristles on either side of 1st abdominal segment, 8th segment as long as and 0.8x as broad as 5th segment; apical slit-like membranous area tilted towards right; surstyli asymmetrical. Surstyli, aedeagus, ejaculatory apodeme and aedeagal guide as shown in fig. 65C-G.

Length. Body : 2.6 mm; wing : 3.5 mm.

♀. Agrees with male except frons ca 1.25x as broad in the middle as at ends, black, lower half covered with silvery white pubescence; apex of 3rd antennal segment more than 2x as long as rest of 3rd segment; ovipositor with base black, globose, 0.8x as long as piercer; piercer brown, thin and slightly curved upward near tip (fig. 65H).

Length. Body : 2.9 mm; wing : 3.73 mm.

Remarks. This species resembles *E. acroacanthus* Hardy (1968) described from a female from New Ireland. The female of new species is close to the latter in having long bristle-like apex ca 2x as long as rest of 3rd antennal segment and legs black; but differs in having frons with lower half covered with silvery white pubescence (cf lower 1/3rd in case of *acroacanthus)*, humeri yellow (cf. black); no bristle on scutellum as compared to that of *acroacanthus* which has 4 stout black bristles, approximately equal in size to bristle on lateral margins of 1st abdominal tergum; costal sections 3rd and 4th combined ca 1.1x as long as 5th section and not distinctly shorter as in *acroacanthus*; ovipositor with base 0.8x as long as piercer, not 0.5x as in *acroacanthus*.

Etymology. The name of this species is based on the character of scutellum which has no bristles as compared to that of *acroacanthus*.

Specimens examined. Holotype ♂, Ranikhet (U.P.), 20.xi.1986, ex grass, coll. A. Kumar. Allotype ♀, Kufri (H. P.), 25.ix.1986, ex weeds, coll. G. S. Sidhu. Paratypes 1 ♂, 1 ♀ Mashobra (H. P.), 27 ix.1986, ex weeds, coll. J. S. Grewal; 1 ♂, Ranikhet, 20.xi.1986, coll. A Kumar.

Eudorylas thekkadiensis sp. n.

(Fig. 66)

♂. Small, black. Head as broad as long and 1.3x as broad as thorax; ocelli yellow; ocellar triangle black; eye reddish brown, area of contiguity ca 12 facets long; upper frontal triangle 16 facets long, black with white dust; lower frontal triangle ca 1.5x as long as upper frontal triangle, black, covered with silvery white pubescence; base as broad as the base of ocellar triangle; face black with silvery white pubescence, as broad as the base of lower frontal triangle; occiput swollen, black, covered with silvery white dust, small yellow hairs along posterior margin of rim. Antenna yellow (fig. 66B), 1st segment small, black; 2nd segment dark brown with 1 minute dorsal and 2 long ventral black bristles; 3rd segment yellow, acute; arista 1.5x as long as 3rd segment. Thorax 1.4x as long as broad; black, covered with brown dust; scutellum with a few small hairs along posterior margin; mesopleura yellow while rest of pleurae black; humeral plates yellow. Halteres yellow. Wings hyaline (fig. 66A); stigma brown, filling almost whole of angle between 3rd costal section and vein R_1; 3rd costal section ca 1.6x as long as 4th; 3rd and 4th costal sections combined 0.8x as long as 5th; crossvein r-m at basal 2/5th of discal cell; distal portion of vein M_{1+2} slightly curved. Legs black, coxae, trochanters black; femora black except the narrow tips; tibiae with broad apical and narrow distal ends yellow, black medially; tarsi yellow except black outer side; claws yellow with tips broadly black; pulvilli small, yellow. Abdomen black, covered with brown dust; 1st segment with 4-5 stout black bristles on either side; posterior half of 1st and anterior half of 2nd segment covered with silvery white dust; 8th segment ca 0.7x as broad as 5th segment; apical membranous area not visible from dorsal side but appears as a notch on left side of abdomen; claspers broad, pointed at inner apices. Ninth segment, surstyli, aedeagus, ejaculatory apodeme and aedeagal guide as shown in fig. 66C-G.

Length. Body : 3.4 mm; wing : 3.8 mm.

♀. Wing with 3rd costal section equal to 4th; 3rd and 4th sections combined 0.7x as long as 5th; r-m crossvein a little beyond 1/3rd of discal cell. Base of ovipositor brown, oblong, ca 0.8x as long as piercer, piercer yellow, greatly curved upward reaching middle of 2nd abdominal sternum (fig. 66H).

Length. Body : 2.8 mm; wing : 3.2 mm.

Remarks. The male of this species resembles that of *E. javanensis* de Meijere in the characters of large apical membranous area on 8th segment and black legs but differs in having 3rd antennal segment acute and yellow; 3rd and 4th costal sections smaller than 5th section, r-m crossvein at basal 2/5th of discal cell, vein M_{1+2} straight and in the shape of surstyli.

Etymology. This species is named after its type-locality.

Specimens examined. Holotype ♂, Thekkady (Kerala), 24.ii.1984, coll. J. S. Grewal. Allotype ♀, same data except coll. S. K. Sharma. Paratype 2 ♂, same data as holotype; 3 ♂, Ramgarh (Bihar), 22.iii.1985, coll. S. K. Sharma; 2 ♀, Ranchi (Bihar), 22.iii.1985, coll. V. K. Kohli; 1 ♂, Ranikhet (U. P.), 20.xi.1986, coll. A. Kumar; 1 ♂, Motichoor near Rishikesh (U. P.), 8.x.1985, coll. S. K. Sharma.

Eudorylas tibiatus sp. n.

(Fig. 67)

♂. Small, black. Head ca 1.2x as broad as long and 1.3x as broad as thorax; eyes reddish brown with black patches, area of contiguity 8 facets long; ocellar triangle black with ocelli brown; upper frontal triangle obliterated, 3-4 facets long, black; lower frontal triangle black with silvery white pubescence, ca 17 facets long, base 1.5x as broad as base of ocellar triangle; face black with silvery white pubescence, as broad as base of lower frontal triangle; occiput black with white dust, slightly swollen. Proboscis dark brown. Antenna black (fig. 67B); 1st segment small black with 1 minute dorsal black bristle; 2nd segment quadrangular, black with 3 small dorsal and 1 ventral black bristles; 3rd antennal segment black, apex acuminate; arista black, ca 2x as long as 3rd segment. Thorax 1.3x as long as broad, blackish brown dust, scutellum bare; metanotum bare; metanotum and pleurae black with grey dust; humeral plates black. Halteres also black. Wing hyaline with brownish tinge (fig. 67A); 3rd costal section ca 1.16x as long as 4th; 3rd and 4th combined ca 1.18x as long as 5th; crossvein r-m at 2/5th basad of discal cell; distal portion of M_{1+2} slightly curved. Legs black except for distal tips of femora and apical tips of tibiae which are yellow; claws black, as long as last tarsomeres; pulvilli yellow, small, ca 0.7x as long as last tarsomeres. Abdomen black with brown dust; 1st abdominal segment with 2-3 black bristles on either side; 8th segment ca 0.5x as long and 0.6x as broad as 5th segment with membranous area apical but not visible from dorsal side; surstyli slightly asymmetrical. Surstyli, aedeagus, ejculatory apodeme and aedeagal guide as shown in fig. 67C-G.

Length. Body : 2.8 mm; wing : 3.5 mm.

♀. Unknown.

Remarks. This species comes close to *E. holosericeus* Becker from Taiwan in the characters of 3rd antennal segment, humeri and halteres black; legs totally black, and 8th abdominal segment smaller than 5th; but differs in lacking conspicuous hairs on scutellum, and also lacking prominent erect black posterior bristles on basal half of middle tibia. It also differs from it in the shape of surstyli which in present species are greatly flattened.

Etymology. Named after the character of mid tibiae which lack prominent erect black posterior bristles on basal half.

Specimen examined. Holotype ♂, Mashobra (H. P.), 27.ix.1986, ex weeds, coll. J. S. Grewal.

Eudorylas tuberculatus sp nov.

(Fig. 68)

♀. Small, black. Head 1.16x as broad as long, 1.1x as broad as thorax; eyes reddish brown; ocellar triangle black with ocelli yellow; frons with upper half polished black; lower half black with silvery white pubescence; frons broader at upper 2/5th, about 1.5x as broad as base of ocellar triangle; face black with silvery white pubescence, 0.9x as broad as lower end of frons; occiput black with grey dust, scattered yellow bristles on lateral, ventral and posterior margins. Antenna yellow (fig. 68B); 1st segment small, brown; 2nd segment dark brown, quadrangular with 1 dorsally placed small black bristle; 3rd antennal segment yellow, strongly acuminate, apex 2x as long as rest of 3rd segment; arista dark brown, as long as 3rd antennal segment. Proboscis yellow. Thorax polished black with sparse brown dust, 1.27x as long as broad; scutellum with 1 pair of stout black bristles along with small black hairs on posterior margin; metanotum and pleurae black with grey dust; humeral plates yellow. Halteres also yellow. Wings hyaline with slight brownish tinge (fig. 68A); 3rd costal section 1.5x as long as 4th; 3rd and 4th combined 0.83x as long as 5th; r-m crossvein a little before middle of discal cell; last section of vein M_{1+2} slightly curved; stigma filling 0.8x angle of 3rd costal section. Legs yellow, coxae black; trochanters yellow; femora black medially and yellow at apices; tibiae yellow to light brown; claws and pulvilli yellow, as long as distal tarsomere. Abdomen black, opaque, with brown dust; 1st segment with 3-4 black stout bristles; ovipositor typical, base black, 0.57x as long as piercer with 2 ventral knob-like processes on either side (fig. 68C, D); piercer yellow, straight, tapering, reaching upto the base of 2nd abdominal segment.

Length. Body : 3.14mm; wing : 3.29 mm.

♂. Unknown.

Specimen examined. Holotype 1 ♀, Dharampur (H.P.), 26.x.1983, ex weeds. coll. S. K. Sharma.

Remarks. This species comes close to *E. orientalis* (Koizumi) in having 3rd antennal segment long acuminate; frons similar in shape; base of ovipositor globular and piercer about 2x as long as base; but differs in having antenna and legs chiefly yellow rather than black; crossvein r-m in the middle of discal cell (at 1/3rd in *orientalis*). The main difference is the presence of two prominent processes on either side of ovipositor.

Eudorylas uniformis (*Brunetti*)

(Fig. 69)

Pipunculus uniformis Brunetti, 1915, Rec. Indian Mus , 13:82 (♂). Type-loc : Shimla, India.

Pipunculus (*Eudorylas*) *uniformis* : Hardy, 1972, Orient. Insects Supp., 2:68.

♂. Small, black. Head 1.2x as broad as thorax; eyes reddish brown with area of contiguity ca 16 facets long; ocellar triangle black, ocelli brown; upper frontal triangle ca 4 facets long, black, lower frontal triangle 16 facets long, black, lower 3/4th covered with silvery white pubescence; base 1 25x as broad as base of ocellar triangle; face black with silvery white pubescence, as broad as base of lower frontal triangle; proboscis yellow; occiput swollen, black with white dust, small hairs on posterior rim. Antenna black (fig. 69B); 1st segment small, black; 2nd segment quadrate, black with 2 dorsal and 1 ventral black bristles; 3rd antennal segment black with apex yellow, acuminate; arista black, ca 1.25x as long as 3rd antennal segment. Thorax black with brown dust, 1.2x as long as broad; metanotum, pleurae black with white dust; humeral plates yellow Halteres dark brown. Wings hyaline with brownish tinge (fig. 69A); 3rd costal section equal in length to 4th; 3rd and 4th combined 1.3x as long as 5th; r-m a little before 1/3rd of discal cell; last section of vein M_{1+2} slightly curved. Legs black, coxae, trochanters black, femora blackish yellow only at distal extremities; tibiae black except for extremities; tarsi dark brown, last tarsomere black; claws brown with black tips, ca 1.5x as long as last tarsomere; pulvilli yellow, as long as last tarsomere. Abdomen black with brown dust, 1st abdominal segment with 4-5 stout black bristles on either side; 8th segment 1.5x as long and 1.1x as broad as 5th segment. Surstyli asymmetrical; ejaculatory apodeme extremely peculiar. Surstyli, aedeagus, aedeagal guide and ejaculatory apodeme shown as in fig. 69C-I.

Length. Body : 3.1 mm; wing : 3.6 mm.

♀. Agrees with male except frons broadest in middle, ca 1.5x as broad as at ends; 3rd antennal segment with apex sharply acuminate (fig. 69 J), claws enlarged ca 2x as long as distal tarsomeres; pulvilli yellow, enlarged, ca 1.5x as long as distal tarsomere; ovipositor with base black, globose, ca 0.8x as long as piercer; piercer thin, yellow, slightly curved upwards (fig. 69K).

Length. Body : 2.75 mm; wing : 3.1 mm.

Remarks. The specimens observed show differences in the characters like stigma not filling the whole of 3rd costal segment, r-m situated a little before basal 1/3 of discal cell and in the shape of surstyli (both of which in *uniformis* are bifid but in this species left surstylus is bifid and that too not so prominently) but other characters tally with the original description of *uniformis*; therefore these specimens have been placed under this species at the moment.

Distribution. Burma, India.

Specimens examined. 7♂, 7♀, Kufri, 25.ix.1986, coll. S K. Sharma; 2♂, 4♀, Mashobra, 27.ix. 1986, coll. S.K. Sharma; 3♂, 1♀, Carignano, 25.ix.1986, coll. S. K. Sharma; 2♂, 4♀, Kufri, 25.ix 1986, coll. G. S. Sidhu; 1♂, 1♀, Mashobra, 27.ix 1986, coll. G.S. Sidhu; 3♂, 1♀, Kufri, 25.ix.1986, ex weeds, coll. J.S. Grewal; 1♂, 1♀, Carignano, 25.ix.1986, coll. J. S. Grewal; 2♀, Mashobra, 27.ix.1986, coll. J. S. Grewal. 1♂ Tattapani, 22.ix.1986, coll. J. S. Grewal; 1♂ Carignano 11 ix.1976, coll. M.L. Agarwal (all localities in Himachal Pardesh). 1♀, 1♂ Ranikhet (U.P.), 20.xi.1986, coll. S.K. Sharma.

4. GENUS *PIPUNCULUS* LATREILLE

Dorilas Meigen, 1800, Nouv. Class. Mouches : 31. Type species : *Pipunculus campestris* Latreille, by subsequent designation of Coquillett (1910 : 535). Suppressed by ICZN, 1963, opinion 678 : 339

Pipunculus Latreille, 1802, Hist. Nat. Crust. Ins., 3 : 463. Type species : *campestris* Latreille, by monotypy.

The representatives of the genus *Pipunculus* can be easily separated on the basis of the following characters :

Ocellar bristles absent; head nearly spherical; occiput prominent; 3rd costal section with brown colouring (stigma) and usually equal or longer than 4th; usually rather sparsely haired species.

It is represented by 4 subgenera in India. These are *Pipunculus* Latreille, *Cephalosphaera* Enderlein, *Claraeosphaera* Kapoor and Grewal and *Cephalops* Fallen.

i. SUBGENUS *CEPHALOPS* FALLEN

Cephalops Fallen, 1810, Sp. Ent. nov. Dipt. : 10. Type species: *aeneus* Fallen, by monotypy *pratorum* (Fallen).

Collinias Aczel, 1940, Zool Anz., 132 : 151. Type species : *Pipunculus heterostigmus* Perkins, by original designation.

Hardy (1964) synonymised *Cephalops* Fallen with *Pipunculus (Pipunculus)*. Coe (1966), agreeing with Collin (1956), treated *Cephalops* as a distinct genus differing from *Pipunculus* in having the setae on dorsum restricted to uniserial dorsocentral rows rather than having the setae scattered uniformly over the dorsum. Hardy (1972_c) examined these characteristics and treated *Cephalops* as a subgenus only. Hardy (1972_c) gave the following characters for this subgenus.

Mesonotum predominantly bare with scattered setae along sides, behind humeri, and usually a single row down each dorsocentral line. Some species have rather numerous setae along sides and over anterior corners, and a few with 2-3 irregular rows of setae down each dorsocentral line. The entire median portion, between the dorsocentrals, is bare. The abdomen is usually shining or polished but may sometimes be entirely opaque.

The subgenus was so far known by only 3 species in India. Of these we could collect only *flavocinctus* Brunetti, while the other two (*nigronitens* Brunetti and *subaeneus* Brunetti) could not be collected and their descriptions have been reproduced here from Brunetti (1923). Here, 7 new species and 3 new records have been described which bring the total number of species in this subgenus to 13. Two additional species based on female specimens have not been named. All the 13 species of this subgenus are separated by following key.

KEY TO SPECIES

1. 3rd costal section equal to or shorter than 4th 2
   3rd costal section longer than 4th 8

2. Trochanters and femora predominantly yellow 3
   Trochanters and femora predominantly black 5

3. 3rd and 4th costal sections combined equal to or shorter than 5th......4
   3rd and 4th costal combined distinctly longer than 5th..........................
   ....*chandiensis* sp. n.

4. 3rd antennal segment with acute apex; humeri black; 3rd and 4th costal sections combined shorter (0.78x) than 5th..............*kashmirensis* sp. n.
   3rd antennal segment with apex obtuse; humeri yellow; 3rd and 4th costal sections combined equal to 5th. Nepal............*dominitens* Hardy

5. 3rd antennal segment with apex acute or obtuse..............................6
   3rd antennal segment with apex acuminate.........*mashobraensis* sp. nov.

6. 3rd costal section equal to 4th; 3rd antennal segment with apex obtuse; r-m crossvein situated at basal 1/3rd of discal cell; 8th abdominal segment 0.5x as long as 5th.....................................*subdolosus* sp. n.
   3rd costal section shorter than 4th; 3rd antennal segment with apex acute; r-m crossvein situated at basal 1/4th of discal cell; 8th abdominal segment equal to 5th in length..................................*kumaonensis* sp. n.

7. 3rd and 4th costal sections combined longer (1.73-1.80x) than 5th......8
   3rd and 4th costal sections combined shorter (0 81-0.83x) than 5th...10

8. Abdomen with at least sides of segment 2-4 yellow...........................9
   Abdomen polished black. Hainan Islands, India......*subaeneus* Brunetti

9. 3rd antennal segment yellow with apex obtuse; halteres black; r-m crossvein situated at basal 1/3rd of discal cell; surstyli asymmetrical...........
   ....*spenceri* Hardy
   3rd antennal segment black with apex acute; halteres yellow; r-m crossvein situated at basal 2/5th of discal cell; surstyli symmetrical...........
   ....*kurseongiensis* sp. nov.

10. Trochanters and femora predominantly yellow...............................11
    Trochanters and femora predominantly black. India..........................
    ....*flavocinctus* Brunetti

11. Crossvein r m situated at basal 2/5th of discal cell...........................12
    Crossvein r-m situated at basal 1/3rd of discal cell. India..................
    ....*nigronitens* Brunetti

12. Propleural fan with 15-18 stout yellow bristles; 3rd antennal segment dark brown...*eufraternus* sp. n.
    Propleural fan with 6-8 long yellow bristles; 3rd antennal segment yellow. Philippines, India.......................................*palawanensis* Hardy.

Pipunculus (*Cephalops*) *annulifemur* (Brunetti)

Pipunculus annulifemur Brunetti, 1923, Fauna Br. India, Dipt., 3 : 17, ♂. Type-loc. : Bangalore, S. India.

Pipunculus (*Cephalops*) *annulifemur* : Hardy 1975. Cat. Dipt. Orient. Reg., 2 : 304.

Since no specimen of this species could be collected, its description has been reproduced from Brunetti (1923).

♂. Head : eyes dark red; vertical triangle black, frons dull black, lower part with a somewhat quadrate greyish dust-spot; face dull black, lower half appearing grey when viewed from above. Antennae dull yellowish; 3rd joint distinctly pointed, moderately long and almost sub-triangular. Occiput moderately produced behind eye-margins, black, with a little grey dust. Thorax moderately shining black, middle of dorsum with yellow-brown dust and a little pale pubescence; pleurae blackish with some greyish dust. Abdomen shining black; a very little yellowish pubescence toward sides; genitalia with a yellowish tinge. Legs mainly yellow; coxae black, also a broad median band on femora (possibly incomplete in individuals); tarsi darker towards tips. All the femora slightly shining and with a row of very small bristles on about the apical half of the underside. Wings clear; stigma very pale yellow; anterior crossvein at about two-fifth of the discal cell. Halteres yellowish.

Length. Body : 2.5 mm; wing : 3.5 mm.

Described from 2 ♂ in the British Museum, London. Bangalore, Karnataka, about 3000 ft., coll. Brunetti.

Pipunculus (*Cephalops*) *chandiensis* sp. nov.
(Fig. 70)

♂. Black, small. Head 1.25x as broad as long and 1.3x as broad as thorax; compound eyes brown with black patches, joined on the front for a distance equal to 17 facets; ocellar triangle black; upper frontal triangle very much reduced, black, 3 facets long; lower frontal triangle black, 18 facets long; face black, equal in width at both the ends which is equal to the lower end of frons; lower half of face with white pubescence; occiput slightly swollen, small yellow hair on dorsal and lateral side. Antenna (fig. 70B) with 1st and 2nd segments black, 1st segment with one black bristle on dorsal side; 2nd with 4 bristles on dorsal and 2 very long bristles on vental side;

3rd segment black with yellow pubescence, acute at apex; arista black 1.5x as long as 3rd segment. Proboscis black. Thorax black with brownish dust and small yellow scattered hairs; pleurae black with brownish dust; scutellum black with sparse white dust; metanotum with white dust; humeri brownish. Halteres yellow. Wings hyaline (fig. 70A); 3rd costal section equal to 4th costal section; 3rd and 4th costal sections combind 1.66x as long as 5th; crossvein r-m slightly beyond the basal 1/4th of discal cell; last section of vein M_{1+2} slightly curved. Legs yellow; coxae black with distal tip brown; femora black except apical and distal tips; mid femur with yellow hairs on outer side while hind femur with hair on both sides; distal tarsomere black, pulvilli large, yellow; claws yellow with black tips, 2x the distal tarsomere in length; hind femora with 3 strong black bristles on ventral side; femora with yellow hairs on the postero-lateral side; hind tibia with 3 long median bristles. Abdomen, black, 1st segment with grey pubescence; segments 2-5 with brownish pubescence; 1st segment with 8-9 yellow thin bristles on each side; other segments with small scattered yellow hairs; 8th segment about 0.5x as long as 5th abdominal segment and with dorso-apical membranous area bearing a ridge-like structure in the middle. Male genitalia with slightly asymmetrical surstyli; aedeagus long, trifid; ejaculatory apodeme fan-shaped. Shapes of ejaculatory apodeme, surstyli, aedeagus and aedeagal guide as shown in fig. 70D-H.

Length. Body : 3.66 mm; wing : 4.66 mm.

♀. Small, black. Head broken, humeri and halteres yellow; crossvein r-m at basal 1/3rd of discal cell; abdomen with segment 3-5 shining black, ovipositor with base globose, black, ca 0.7x as long as piercer, piercer brownish, slightly curved upwards (fig. 70 I); rest of description same as that of male.

Length. Body (without head) : 2.90 mm; wing : 4.48 mm.

Remarks. This species fits near *P. (C.) microdes* Perkins (Oriental and Australian in distribution) in having antenna, humeral plates and femora almost black; 5th abdominal tergum almost all polished black, 3 and 4 terga polished black at apices. It is also close to *P. (C.) kashmirensis* sp. n. in having small yellow hairs on the thorax, abdomen and femora. It differs from the former in the presence of hairs on body and femora, 3rd costal section equal to 4th, and drastically in the detailed structure of male genitalia. It also differs from the latter by having 3-5 small yellow inconspicous hairs in propleural fan; 3rd and 4th costal sections combined ca 0.8x as long as 5th; hairs on mesonotum, femora and abdomen comparatively smaller and fewer and in shape of the 8th abdomial segment and surstyli.

Etymology. Named after type-locality.

Specimens examined. Holotype ♂, Chandigarh (U. T.), 24.x.1985, coll. J. S. Grewal. Allotype ♀, Pinjore (Haryana), 26.x.1985, coll. J. S. Grewal. Paratype 1 ♂, same data, coll. S. K. Sharma.

Pipunculus (Cephalops) deminitens Hardy

(Fig. 71)

Pipunculus (Pipunculus) deminitens Hardy, 1966, Bull. Br. Mus. Nat. Hist. (Ent.), 17 : 443 (♂). Type-loc. : Sangu, E. Nepal.

Pipunculus (Cephalops) deminitens : Hardy, 1975, Cat. Dipt. Orient. Reg., 2 : 298.

♂. Black, small. Head hemispherical, 1.3x as broad as long and 1.3x as broad as thorax; compound eyes dark brown, joined on the front for a distance equal to 15 facets; ocellar triangle black, ocelli yellow; upper frontal triangle black, 0.6x as long as joining area of compound eyes; lower frontal triangle black with white pubescence, 1.7x as long as the joining area of compound eyes; face black with white pubescence, equal in width at both the ends, which is equal to the lower end of frons; occiput swollen, black with white dust, more on the lateral side; lateral side also with few small yellow bristles. Antenna black (fig. 71B), 1st segment small, black; 2nd segment with 3 dorsal and 4 ventral black bristles; 3rd segment black with dense yellow pubescence, obtuse at apex, about 1.5x as long as 2nd; arista black, bare, 2x as long as 3rd antennal segment; proboscis yellow. Thorax and scutellum shining black, bare; pleurae black with little yellow dust; propleural fan with 11 stout bristles, humeri yellow. Halteres yellow with blackish knobs. Wings hyaline with one black spot just below the point of union of vein R_{2+3} and R_{4+5} (fig. 71A); 3rd costal section 2x as long as 4th; 3rd and 4th sections combined as long as 5th; crossvein r-m at basal 2/7th of the discal cell; last section of vein M_{1+2} gently curved Legs all yellow except coxae which are black, having distal tips yellow; tarsi slightly blackish; last tarsomeres black; claws yellow, black at the tip; hind tibia with one median stout black bristle. Abdomen shining black with sparse brownish dust; 1st abdominal segment with 4 stout black bristles, 8th segment with apical membranous area. Male genitalia with asymmetrical claspers; aedeagus trifid, ejaculatory apodeme cylindrical. The shape of claspers, aedeagus, aedeagal guide, ejaculatory apodeme as shown in fig. 71C-F.

Length. Body : 3.75 mm; wing : 4.8 mm.

♀. 3rd antennal segment yellow with acute apex (fig. 71G); frons equal in width at both the ends, crossvein r-m at about 2/5th of the discal cell; halteres with yellow knobs; ovipositor with base black; piercer brownish yellow reaching upto the base of 3rd segment, thin straight, tip slightly curved upward (fig. 71H); rest of description similar to male.

Length. Body : 3 4 mm; wing : 4.54 mm.

Remarks. This species was described by Hardy (1966 b) from Nepal. It has been reported here for the first time from India.

Specimens examined. 1 ♂, Ponchal (H. P.), 8.vi.1986, ex. weeds, coll. S. K. Sharma; 1 ♀, Solan (H. P.), 14.x.1982, ex. grass, coll. L. S. Arya; 1 ♀, Silent Valley (Kerala), 7.iv.1983, ex rice fields, coll. L. S. Arya; 3 ♀, Chandigarh (U. T., India), 24 x.1985, coll. S. K. Sharma; 1 ♀, Pinjore (Haryana), 26.x 1985, coll. V. K. Kohli; 4 ♀, Subathu (H. P.), 23,24.x 1982, coll. L. S. Arya; 3 ♀, Dehra Dun (U. P.), 27.x 1986, coll. S. K. Sharma.

Pipunculus (Cephalops) eufraternus sp. nov.
(Fig. 72)

♂. Black, small. Head 1.2x as broad as long and 1.16x as broad as thorax; ocellar triangle black, ocelli brown, upper frontal triangle greatly obliterated, only 2 facets long, shining black; lower frontal triangle black, covered with silvery white pubescence, 15 facets long, base as broad as base of ocellar triangle; eyes reddish brown, area of contiguity about 18 facets long; face black with silvery white pubescence, as broad as the base of lower frontal triangle; occiput swollen, covered with white dust; few black hairs along the posterior ventral margin. Antenna brown (fig. 72B), 1st segment small, black with one dorsal black bristle, 2nd segment black with 4 dorsal and 3 long ventral black bristles; 3rd segment brown, apex acute; arista black ca 1.5x as long as 3rd segment. Proboscis yellow. Thorax black with brown dust, 1.2x as long as broad, scutellum with a row of small hairs along the posterior margin; propleural fan with 15-18 long yellow bristles, pleurae all black covered with white dust; humeral plates black. Halteres yellowish brown. Wing hyaline with brownish tinge (fig. 72A); 3rd costal section ca 1.72x as long as 4th; 3rd and 4th costal sections combined ca 0.83x as long as 5th; crossvein r-m at about 2/5th basad of discal cell; distal portion of vein M_{1+2} much curved. Legs yellow; coxae black with distal end yellow; trochanters, tibiae and tarsi yellow; femora dark brown medially, broadly yellow at both ends; hind tibia with two stout black bristles on outer surface near the middle; last tarsomere black, flattened; claws yellow with black tips, ca 0.75x as long as last tarsomere; pulvilli yellow, much reduced. Abdomen shining black, with a little brown dust on 2nd segment; 1st abdominal segment white pubescent, with 5–7 black bristles of different sizes on each side; 8th segment about 0.5x as long and 0.75x as broad as 5th, with dorsoapical membranous area (fig. 72D); surstyli asymmetrical, broad. Surstyli, aedeagus, ejaculatory apodeme and aedeagal guide as shown in fig. 72E-H.

Length. Body : 3.50 mm; wing : 4.10 mm.

♀. Frons black, 0.8th lower portion with silvery white pubescence; upper end as broad as base of ocellar triangle; lower end 1.5x as broad as upper end; 3rd antennal segment acute; wing hyaline, 3rd costal section 0.73x as long as 4th; 3rd and 4th costal sections combined 0.78x as long as 5th; r-m crossvein at 2/5th basad of discal cell; vein M_{1+2} slightly curved at distal end; legs yellow, abdomen black with grey dust; ovipositor with base oblong, black, ca 1.25x as long as piercer; piercer thin, brown, straight (fig. 72 I).

Length. Body : 2.73 mm; wing : 3.72 mm.

Remarks. This species comes close to *P. (C.) fraternus* (Kertesz) from Taiwan in sharing characters like black humeri, halteres brown, scutellum with few setae on hind margin, legs broadly yellow with medially dark femora, large membranous area on the tip of the 8th segment and in general outline of surstyli; but differs in hind tibiae having 2-3 stout black bristles and in wing venation (3rd costal section is equal to 4th in *fraternus* while it is 1.72x in this species, 3rd and 4th costal sections combined are equal to 5th in *fraternus* while in this species these are 0.85x); structure of membranous area on 8th segment and in detailed structure of surstyli.

Etymology. Named due to its closeness to *fraternus* (Kertesz).

Specimens examined. Holotype ♂, Chandigarh (U.T.), 24.x.1985, coll. S K. Sharma. Allotype ♀, Siagaon (U. P.), 26.x. 1986, coll. S. K. Sharma. Paratypes 2 ♂, same data as that of allotype; 2 ♂, Ranikhet (U. P.), 20 xi.1986, coll. S. K. Sharma; 1 ♂, Moti Nagar near Haldwani (U. P.), 19.xi 1986, coll S K. Sharma.

Pipunculus (Cephalops) flavocinctus Brunetti

(Fig 73)

Pipunculus flavocinctus Brunetti, 1912, Rec. Indian Mus , 7 : 438 (♂ ; as *flevocinctus*). Type-loc. : Kurseong, Darjeeling, India.

Pipunculus (*Cephalops*) *flavocinctus* : Hardy, 1975, Cat. Dipt. Orient. Reg., 2 : 298.

♀. Small, black. Head ca 1.2x as broad as long and 1.2x as broad as thorax; ocellar triangle black; frons entirely silvery white pubescent, broadest medially; antennal end as broad as the base of ocellar triangle; face black, silvery white pubescent,ca 0.25x as broad as the lower portion of frons; occiput swollen posteriorly, covered with fine black bristles. Antennae black (fig. 73B), 1st segment small, black; 2nd segment quadrangular, with 2 small dorsal and 1 ventral long black bristles; 3rd antennal segment small, black, with apex acute; arista black. Thorax black, covered with silvery white pubescence, dorsocentral row of bristles along the length; scutellum with a transverse row of small yellowish bristles; propleural fan with 8-10 long black bristles; propleurae, mesopleurae, sternopleurae and metapleurae black with silvery white pubescence; humeri black. Halteres dark brown. Wings (fig. 73A) hyaline, 3rd costal section 1.3x as long as 4th costal section; 3rd and 4th costal sections combined 0.77x as long as 5th; crossvein r-m at basal 1/3rd of the discal cell; distal portion of vein M_{1+2} strongly curved and almost joining the distal end of R_{4+5}; anal lobe well developed, axillary lobe rudimentary. Legs yellow, coxae black with distal end yellow; trochanters yellow, mid and hind trochanters with 1 black bristle; femora black, broadly yellow at basal tip and extreme distal tip; tibia yellowish with median portion black; tarsi yellow; distal tarsomeres black, flattened; claws yellow with tip black; pulvilli large and yellow. Abdomen shining black, cylindrical; 2nd and 3rd segments yellow, 4th segment yellow laterally; 1st abdominal segment with 2-3 large and many small yellowish hair like bristles; other segments with little pubescence. Ovipositor with black globular base; piercer yellow, strongly curved upward reaching upto the base of 3rd abdominal segment (fig. 73C-D).

Length. Body : 3.05; wing : 4.1 mm.

Specimen examined. 1 ♀, Manali (H. P.), 9.vi.1986, ex weeds, coll. S. K. Sharma.

Since we could not collect any male specimen of this species and the holotype ♂ (No. 1931–H_1) in the museum collection of Zoological Survey of India, is now in extremely bad condition, the following description of male has been reproduced from Brunetti (1923).

♂. Head with eyes contiguous for a considerable distance; back of head, frons and face wholly black; antennae with 1st and 2nd joints black, 3rd brownish-yellow, whitish towards tip when seen from above; proboscis slightly brownish-yellow; occiput moderately puffed out. Thorax black, mainly dull, bare, but dorsum a little shining; sides inclined towards blackish grey; scutellum and metanotum apparantly concolorous. Abdomen black, barely shining; posterior margin of 1st segment, the whole of the 2nd, 3rd and 4th, and towards the sides of the 5th segment brownish-yellow, the colour extending over the sides across the venter; genitalia black. Legs yellow; coxae (except tips), femora (except broadly at base and narrowly at tips) black; middle femora with ciliation of hairs behind; hind femora shining on inner side on the black part. Wings clear, 3rd costal segment brown, the colour filling the apical 3-4, 3rd segment about equal to the 4th in length, and much shorter than the 2nd; anterior crossvein just before middle of discal cell; 4th longitudinal vein gently angled after quitting discal cell; anal cell ending at a moderate distance before the margin. Halteres pale yellow.

Length. Body : 2.50 mm.

Described from a type-specimen in the Indian Museum taken by Dr. Annandale at Kurseong, Darjeeling District, 28.vi 1910.

Pipunculus (*Cephalops*) *kashmerensis* sp. n.

(Fig. 74)

♂. Small, black. Head 1.1x as broad as long and 1.33x as broad as thorax; eyes reddish brown with dark patches; area of contiguity 14 facets long; ocellar triangle black with brown ocelli; upper frontal triangle obliterated, about 4-5 facets long, shining black; lower frontal triangle black with silvery white pubescence, about 21 facets long; base 1.5x as broad as base of ocellar triangle; face black with silvery white pubescence, as broad as base of lower frontal triangle; occiput black with white dust, small yellow hairs along the posterior margin. Antenna black (fig. 74B), 1st segment small, black with 1 dorsal and 1 ventral black thin bristle; 2nd segment quadrangular, brownish black with 3 small dorsal and 3 long ventral bristles; 3rd antennal segment black with yellow pubescence, apex acute; arista black, twice as long as 3rd segment. Proboscis yellow. Thorax 1.33x as long as broad, black with brown dust, yellow hairs scattered all over mesonotum, concentrated behind humeral plates; scutellum also having scattered hairs on posterior margin; metanotum and pleurae black with white dust; propleural fan with 7-10 long yellow bristles; humeral plates black. Haltere yellow with base black. Wings hyaline with brownish tinge (fig. 74A); 3rd costal section equal to 4th; 3rd and 4th combined 0.78x as long as 5th; crossvein r-m slightly beyond basal 1/4th of discal cell, last section of vein M_{1+2} moderately curved; stigma light brown filling whole of the angle between costa and R_1. Legs yellow, coxae black with distal margin yellow, trochanters yellow; femora black medially but yellow at ends, bearing yellow hairs on posterior side and few on the anterior side; bristles on the posterior side of mid femora more dense and longer; tibiae and tarsi yellow except distal tarsomeres which are black and flattened; hind tibia with 3 small black bristles; claws yellow with black tip, as long as distal tarsomere; pulvilli yellow, 0.75x as long as last tarsomere. Abdomen black with brown dust, yellow hairs present on dorsal as well as on lateral side of terga, segments 2-5 having black terga; 1st segment with 5-6 comparatively longer yellow hairs; 8th segment about as long and broad as 5th; surstyli slightly asymmetrical. Surstyli, aedeagus. ejaculatory apodeme and aedeagal guide as shown in fig. 74C-F.

Length. Body : 3.5 mm; wing : 4.05 mm.

♀. Unknown.

Remarks. This species resembles *microdes* Perkins from Oriental and Australian regions, in characters like antenna, humeral plates and black femora; 5th abdominal tergum almost all polished black and 3rd and 4th targa with polished black apices, but differs in characters like wing venation, 3rd costal section equal to 4th, and not longer as in later species; 3rd and 4th sections combined 0 78x as long as 5th and not longer than 5th; by having yellow hairs on femora; and also in the shape of 8th abdominal segment and surstyli.

Pipunculus (Cephalops) kumaonensis sp. nov.

(Fig. 75)

♂. Black, small. Head as long as broad; 1.2x as broad as thorax; eyes reddish black with area of contiguity 15 facets long; ocellar triangle and ocelli black; upper frontal triangle obliterated, about 6 facets long, shining black; lower frontal triangle black with golden yellow pubescence, 21 facets long, base 1.5x as broad as base of ocellar triangle; face black with silvery white pubescence, as broad as base of lower frontal triangle; occiput black with white dust, slightly swollen. Antenna black (fig. 75B); 1st antennal segment black, small with 1 dorsal and 1 ventral black bristle; 2nd segment black, quadrangular with 2 small dorsal and 2 long ventral black bristles; 3rd segment black with silvery white pubescence; apex acute; arista black, about 2.5x as long as 3rd antennal segment. Proboscis yellow. Thorax black with brown pubescence; mesonotum and scutellum having scattered yellow hairs in dorsocentral rows and those behind humeri comparatively longer;propleural fan with 6-9 long yellow hairs; humeri black. Halteres yellow black at base. Wings hyaline (fig. 75A); 3rd costal section 0.8x as long as 4th; 3rd and 4th costal sections combined 1.27x as long as 5th; crossvein r-m at basal 1/4 of discal cell; last section of vein M_{1+2} slightly curved. Legs black; coxae and trochanters black; femora black with extreme end yellowish; tibiae black with both tips yellow; tarsi brown with distal ones black, elongated; claws yellow with black tips, 1.25x as long as last tarsomere; pulvilli brownish, 0.75x as long as last tarsomere; femora with long yellow dense hairs on posterior and a few on anterior side; mid-femora with even more dense hairs and 8-9 stout black bristles on posterior face at distal end, hind tibia with 2-3 black bristles in the middle of the outer surface. Abdomen black with brown dust and yellow hairs scattered all over, opaque; 1st segment with 5-6 long yellow bristles on each side; other segments with comparatively larger bristles on the lateral sides than on the dorsal side; 8th segment as long and as broad as 5th; when keel also taken into consideration it is 1.5x as long as 5th (fig. 75C-D); surstyli broad and asymmetrical. Surstyli, aedeagus, aedeagal guide, ejaculatory apodeme as shown in fiig. 75E-H.

Length. Body : 3.64 mm; wing : 3.88 mm.

♀ Resembles male in most of the characters, 3rd antennal segment yellow, acuminate; humeral plates black; halteres yellow; 3rd costal section ca 0.8x as long as 4th; 3rd and 4th combined equal to 5th section; crossvein r-m at basal 1/3 of discal cell; legs yellow, coxae black with distal margin yellow, trochanters yellow, femora almost all black except the extreme ends; fore and hind femora with a few while mid femora with dense yellow hairs on posterior face; femora and mid tibiae yellow, hind tibiae black medially, with 2 medial, stout black bristles; tarsi yellow except the distal tarsomeres black, claws yellow with black tips, 2x as long as distal tarsomeres, pulvilli yellow, broad, as long as distal tarsomere; ovipositor with base globose, black, ca 0.71x as long as piercer, piercer yellow, almost straight reaching upto the base of 1st abdominal segment (fig 75 I).

Length. Body : 3.79 mm; wing : 4.83 mm.

Specimens examined. Holotype ♂, Ranikhet (U.P.), 20.xi. 1986., coll. S. K. Sharma. Allotype ♀, same data.

Etymology. Named after type locality.

Remarks. This species fits near *dolosus* Hardy (from Borneo, Burma & Vietnam) and *subdolosus* sp. n. It resembles the former in characters like antenna,humeri and legs mostly black and in having large apical membranous area but differs in having 3rd antennal segment with acute apex (obtuse in *dolosus*), in wing venation, presence of long yellow hairs on femora, shape of 8th abdominal segment and surstyli which in the present species are comparatively broader. With the latter species, it shares characters like antennae, humeri and legs black, yellow hairs on femora but dfffers in having acute apex of 3rd antennal segment and in having abdomen opaque, 5th tergum not polished black and shape of surstyli.

Pipunculus (*Cephalops*) *kurseongiensis* sp. nov.

(Fig. 76)

♂. Black, small. Head ca 1.1x as broad as long and 1.2x as broad as thorax, eyes reddish brown with dark brown patches; area of contiguity ca 18 facets long; ocellar triangle black, ocelli brown; upper frontal triangle almost completely obliterated, only one facet long, black; lower frontal triangle ca 27 facets long, black with silvery white pubescence, base ca 1.5x as broad as base of ocellar triangle; face black covered with silvery white pubescence, narrow in the middle, ca 0.5x as broad as base of lower frontal triangle; occiput black with white dust, swollen, small yellow bristles along posterior margin. Antenna black (fig. 76B), 1st segment small, black with one small dorsal black bristle; 2nd segment quadrangular black, with 2-3 dorsal and ventral black bristles, 3rd antennal segment black with acute apex; arista black, ca 3x as long as 3rd segment. Proboscis yellow. Thorax black with brown dust, ca 1.2x as long as broad; small hairs behind humeral plates and rows of dorsocentral bristles quite prominent; propleural fan comprised of 8-10 thin yellow hairs, scutellum with a transverse row of small bristles along hind margin; metanotum and pleurae black with white dust; humeral plates black. Halteres yellow. Wings hyaline with brownish tinge (fig. 76A), 3rd costal section ca 1.39x as long as 4th; 3rd and 4th costal sections combined ca 1.8x as long as 5th; crossvein r-m at 2/5 basad of discal cell, last portion of vein M_{1+2} slightly curved; stigma yellowish brown filling ca 0.76th of the angle between costa and vein R_1. Legs yellow; coxae black with distal margin yellow; trochanters light brown; femora dark brown medially, yellow at both ends; tibiae yellow, brownish at 1/3rd distal end, hind tibiae with 2 stout black spines on outer surface in the middle; tarsi yellow except the distal tarsomeres which are black; claws yellow with brown tips, ca 1.25x as long as distal tarsomere; pulvilli yellow, as long as last tarsomere. Abdomen with 2-4 segments yellow to brown with brown dust, 1st abdominal segment with 1 or 2 thin black bristles on either side; 8th abdominal segment ca 0.7x as long and 0.8x as broad as 5th segment; surstyli symmetrical, long. Surstyli, aedeagus, ejaculatory apodeme and aedeagal guide as shown in fig. 76C-F.

Length. Body : 3.23 mm; wing 3.64 mm.

♀. Unknown.

Remarks. This species comes close to *P.* (*C.*) *excellens* (Kertesz) and shares character like legs especially femora yellow or with not more than median discolouration of brown; abdomen largely yellow especially on the sides of first four terga, and in having 3rd costal section distinctly longer than 4th. It differs from *excellens* in having small body size, ca 3.23 mm as compared to 6.7 mm in *excellens*; 3rd antennal segment acute and not with rounded apex as in *excellens* and in shape of 8th segment and surstyli.

Etymology. Named after type locality.

Specimens examind. Holotype ♂, Kurseong (W. Bengal), 6.iv.1985, coll. S. K. Sharma. Paratype 1 ♂, Dehra Dun (U. P.), 29.x.1986, coll. S. K. Sharma.

Pipunculus (*Cephalops*) *mashobraensis* sp. n.

(Fig. 77)

♂. Small, black. Head as broad as long and 1.5x as broad as thorax; eyes pale brown with dark patches, area of contiguity ca 16 facets long; ocellar triangle black with ocelli dark brown; upper frontal triangle shining black, obliterated, ca 4 facets long; lower frontal triangle black with lower half covered with silvery white pubescence, ca 16 facets long, base 1.5x as broad as base of ocellar triangle; face black with silvery white pubescence, as broad as base of lower frontal triangle; occiput black with white dust, small yellow hairs on posterior margin; proboscis yellow Antenna black (fig. 77B), 1st segment small, black, hardly visible; 2nd segment black, quadrangular with two small stout dorsal and two small thin ventral black bristles; 3rd segment black, acuminate; arista black, ca 1.5x as long as 3rd segment. Thorax black with brown dust, a few yellow setae on each side just behind humeral plates; dorsocentral rows and rows along lateral margin comprised of several setae; scutellum with row of small thin hairs along posterior margin; metanotum and pleurae black with white dust; propleural fan consists of 6-8 yellow incospicuous hairs; humeral plates black. Halteres with black base, yellow shaft and brown knob. Wings hyaline (fig. 77A); 3rd costal section ca 0.33x as long as 4th section; 3rd and 4th costal sections combined as long as 5th section; crossvein r-m a little behind 1/3 basad of discal cell; posterior portion of vein M_{1+2} greatly curved; stigma light brown filling ca 0.74th of angle between costa and vein R_1. Legs black; coxae, trochanters and tarsi all black; femora black except yellow at distal extreme tips and tibiae yellow at proximal tips; hind tibiae black with bristles on middle outer surface; claws black with yellow base, ca 1.5x as long as distal tarsomere; pulvilli yellow, small, ca 0.5x as long as claws. Abdomen black, opaque, with dense brown dust, 1st abdominal segment with 6-7 black bristles on each side; 8th segment about as long as 5th segment, but if extended apical membranous area is taken into account, 8th segment becomes ca 2x as long as 5th segment (fig. 77C); surstyli thin cylindrical, slightly asymmetrical (fig. 77D). Surstyli, aedeagus, ejaculatory apodeme and aedeagal guide as shown in fig. 77D-H.

Length. Body : 3.14 mm; wing : 3.60 mm.

♀. Unknown.

Remarks. This species fits near *P.* (*C.*) *exsertus* Hardy (1966) from Nepal, resembling the latter in characters like femora prominently black and membranous area of male hypopygium projected posteriorly but differs drastically in characters like 3rd antennal segment acuminate (not acute as in case of *exsertus*); 3rd costal section smaller (ca 0.33x) than 4th, and 3rd & 4th sections combined equal to 5th (cf. in *exsertus*, 3rd costal section longer than 4th; 3rd and 4th sections combined slightly longer than 5th); and in having legs totally black (cf. in *exsertus*, trochanters, tibiae and tarsi all yellow). It also differs in the shape of surstyli.

Etymology. Named after type locality.

Specimen examined. Holotype ♂, Mashobra (H.P.), ex weeds, 27.ix.1986, coll. J. S. Gerwal.

Pipunculus (Cephalops) nigronitens Brunetti

Pipunculus nigronitens Brunetti, 1912, Rec. Ind. Mus., 7 : 490.

Pipunculus (*Cephalops*) *nigronitens :* Hardy, 1975, Cat. Dipt. Orient. Reg., 2 : 299.

♂. Head with vertex shining black, slightly elongated; frons and face blackish, but if viewed from above the former appears greyish with a slight bluish tinge, and the latter nearly snow-white; occiput slightly puffed out behind; antennae wholly black but if seen from above the tip of the 2nd joint and the apical part of the 3rd are more or less grey-dusted; arista black, thickened at base; proboscis light brown. Thorax and scutellum shining black, bare; sides grey-dusted, the colour carried across the metanotum; humeri brownish-yellow. Abdomen shining black, 1st segment conspicuously grey-dusted; genitalia black, shining; venter black, but less shining than the dorsum. Legs nearly wholly yellow; coxae black; tips of tarsi blackish-brown. No ciliation behind middle femora; hind femora not shining on under side. Wings clear; third costal segment wholly brownish-yellow; longer than 4th segment; anterior cross-vein placed just before 1/3rd of the discal cell; 4th longitudinal vein forming a wide curve before posterior cross-vein, and distinctly bisinuate beyond; first posterior cell rather narrowly open; halteres dirty yellow, the clubs blackish.

Length. Body : 3.00 mm.

Described from a single ♂ in the Indian Museum, taken by Brunetti at Darjeeling, 29.v.1910.

Since no specimen of this species could be collected, the above description has been taken as such from Brunetti (1923).

Pipunculus (*Cephalops*) *palawanensis* Hardy
(Fig. 78)

Pipunculus (*Cephalops*) *palawanensis* Hardy, 1972, Oriental Insect. Supp., 2 : 26-27.

4 ♀ specimens from Subathu (H. P.) fit in the description of this species. The only difference is of the piercer which is shorter and thicker. It is reported for the first time from India. Since no male specimen could be collected during the present survey, its description has been taken from Hardy (1972) while that of female is based on collected material.

♀. Small, black. Head 1.34x as broad as long and 1.34x as broad as thorax; eyes brown, ocellar triangle black with ocelli brown; frons black, opaque, broadest in the middle, ca 2x the base of ocellar triangle; at lower end as broad as base of ocellar triangle; face black covered with silvery white pubescence, as broad as lower end of frons; occiput black with white dust; slightly swollen. Antenna yellow; 1st antennal segment small, black, with one small thin dorsal black bristle; 2nd segment black, quadrangular with 3 small dorsal and 3 long ventral black bristles; 3rd antennal segment yellow with apex acute; arista black, 2x as long as 3rd antennal segment; proboscis yellow. Thorax black with brown dust, 1.3x as long as broad; metanotum and pleurae black with brown dust; propleural fan with 6-8 long yellow hairs; humeri black. Halteres yellow. Wings hyaline; 3rd costal section 1.33x as long as 4th; 3rd and 4th combined ca 0.81x as long as 5th; crossvein r-m a little beyond basal 2/5th of discal cell; distal portion of vein M_{1+2} moderately curved; stigma light brown, filling whole of the angle between 3rd costal section and vein R_1. Legs yellow; coxae black with distal margin yellow; trochanter, femora, tibia and tarsi all yellow; distal tarsomeres dark brown; claws and pulvilli yellow, both as long as the distal tarsomere; hind tibiae with yellow medial stout bristle on posterior side. Abdomen black; subshining, 1st abdominal segment with 3-4 small black bristles; ovipositor with base black, about as long as piercer; piercer yellow straight, reaching upto the base of the abdomen (fig. 78D).

Length. Body : 2.96 mm; wing : 3.67 mm.

♂. Head normal in shape and size, with the junction of compound eyes about equal in length to frontal triangle; front and face densely grey pubescent and approximately equal in width; first two antennal segments brown, 3rd pale yellow and subacute at apex (fig. 78A), 1st and 2nd antennal segments each with a prominent dorsal bristle. Thorax black, brown pollinose on dorsum, grey on sides; sparsely setose with a line of short pale setae extending down each dorsocentral row;scutellum with inconspicuous short pale setae on disc and on margin; humeri brown over median portion, yellow on the margin; propleural fan consisting of 8-10 long pale hairs. Legs entirely yellow except for the brown coxae, sometimes with a faint tinge of brown on upper median portion of each femur and with apical tarsomere sometimes tinged with brown; posteriodorsal cilia on femora short, inconspicuous and all femora with distinct ventral spicules; hind trochanters with a few short, pale, yellow ventral hairs; no posterior bristles or apicoventral spines on front or middle tibiae and no strong erect anterior bristle-like setae on hind tibiae; tarsal claws and pulvilli normal in development, equal or slightly shorter than last tarsomere. Wings subhyaline, stigma brown and filling all of 3rd costal section; in the type, 3rd section slightly longer than the 4th and the two sections combined very slightly longer than the 5th section; r-m crossvein near basal 2/5th of cell 1st M_2 and the last section of vein M_{1+2} very slightly curved; vein Cu_{1+}1stA about half as long as the m crossvein; anal cell and alula well developed; length of 3rd costal section varies slightly, in some paratypes it is equal to 4th section and the two sections combined equal to 5th. Abdomen : 1st tergum mostly gray pollinose; with 6-8 black bristles on each side, 2nd tergum subopaque black; 3rd and 4th terga polished black except for very narrow opaque black basal margins and 5th tergum entirely polished black; terminal segment approximately 3/4th as long as 5th and with a large apical membranous area (fig. 78B); as seen from ventral view the membranous area broadly bisects 8th tergum. The epandrium is about as wide as long and the surstyli comparatively short and broad, each with a short point on inner apex (fig. 78C).

Length. Body : 3.75 mm; wing : 4.75 mm.

Specimens examined. 4 ♀, Subathu, 23.x 1982, ex. grass, coll. L. S. Arya; 1 ♀, Solan (H. P.), 19.x.1982, coll. L. S. Arya.

Pipunculus (Cephalops) spenceri Hardy
(Fig. 79)

Pipunculus (Cephalops) spenceri Hardy, 1972, Orient. Insects Suppl., 2 : 29 (♂). Type loc. : Fyan, Viet Nam.

♂. Black with 2 to 4 abdominal segments yellow. Head 1·1x as broad as long and 1.37x as broad as thorax. Eyes reddish brown with black patches; area of contiguity 17 facets long; ocellar triangle black with ocelli yellow; upper frontal triangle obliterated, 1 facet long, black; lower frontal triangle black, lower 1/3rd with silvery white pubescence. 21 facets long, base 1.5x as broad as base of ocellar triangle; face black with silvery white pubescence; occiput black with white dust, slightly swollen with small hairs along the posterior rim. Antenna yellow (fig. 79B); 1st segment brown with 1 small dorsal black bristle; 2nd segment quadrangular, brown with 3 dorsal and 3 comparatively longer ventral bristles; 3rd antennal segment yellow, obtuse; arista brown to black, yellow at base, about 3x as long as 3rd segment.

Thorax black with dark brown dust, small bristles on either side near humeri, metanotum and pleurae black with grey to white dust, humeri black. Halteres with base black, shaft yellow and knob brown. Wing hyaline with brownish tinge (fig. 79A), 3rd costal section ca 1.42x longer than 4th (in some specimens it is only 1.1x to 1.2x longer than 4th); 3rd and 4th costal sections combined 1.73x as long as 5th; crossvein r-m at 1/3rd basad of discal cell (in some specimens it is situated at 2/5th of discal cell); last portion of vein M_{1+2} strongly curved; stigma dark brown filling distal 0.79th of angle between costa and vein R_1. Legs yellow; coxae black with distal 1/3rd yellow; trochanters, tibiae and tarsi yellow; femora yellow with slightly brownish band covering 1/3rd of distal end just before the apices, distal tarsomere; pulvilli yellow, small ca 0.5x as long as distal tarsomere. Abdomen yellow; 1st, 5th and 8th segments black; 2-4th yellow; 1st abdominal segment with 4-5 stout black bristles on each side; 8th segment ca 0.5x as long and 0.75x as broad as 5th segment; large oval apical membranous area with a small keel (fig. 79C-D); surstyli asymmetrical, right one being longer than the left. Surstyli, aedeagus, ejaculatory apodeme, aedeagal guide as shown in fig. 79E-H.

Length. Body : 2.97 mm; wing : 3.41 mm.

♀. Black with 2-4 abdominal segments yellow; frons narrower at upper end, ca 2x as broad as lower ocellus, broader on lower end, ca 1.5x as broad as base of ocellar triangle; broadest (2x as broad as base of ocellar triangle) at point 11 facets above the lower end; 3rd antennal segment yellow but not as much obtuse as in male (fig. 79 J); wings hyaline with brownish tinge (fig. 79 I); 3rd costal section equal to 4th; 3rd and 4th costal sections combind 1.44x as long as 5th; r-m crossvein at 1/3rd basad of discal cell; distal portion of vein M_{1+2} strongly curved; legs yellow; abdomen with 2-4 segments yellow, brownish on dorsal side; 1st abdominal segment with 2 thin long, black bristles on each side; ovipositor with base black, globose, 0.75x as long as piercer, piercer yellow, thin (fig. 79K).

Length. Body : 2.97 mm; wing : 3.00 mm.

Remarks. This species was described by Hardy (1972 b), from Viet Nam by male only. It is recorded here for the first time from India.

Specimens examined. 2 ♂, Thekkady (Kerala), 29.ii.1984, coll J. S. Grewal; Pinjore (Haryana), 26.x.1985, coll. J. S. Grewal; 1 ♂, 1 ♀, Kashipur (U.P.), 21.xi.1986, coll. S.K. Sharma; 1 ♀, Ramnagar (U.P.), 21.xi.1986, coll. S. K. Sharma.

Pipunculus (Cephalops) subaeneus Brunetti
(Fig. 80)

Pipunculus subaeneus Brunetti, 1923, *Fn. Brit. India*, Dipt., 3 : 12, fig. 3.
Type-loc. : Khasi Hills, Assam, India. Type male in British Museum (Natural History).

Pipunculus (*Cephalops*) *subaeneus* : Hardy, 1972, Or. Ins. Suppl., 2 : 31-33.

♂. First two antennal segments brown, 3rd segment yellow and short, acute to obtuse at apex (fig. 80A), face rather strongly narrowed medially, at narrowest point about half as wide as front above antennae. Thorax shining black, rather lightly brown pollinose over dorsum; humeri yellow, with brown to black knobs; mesonotum and scutellum sparsely setose, with a few inconspicuous hairs down each dorsocentral row and a few short marginal hairs on scutellum; propleural fan rather inconspicuous, made up of fine yellow hairs. Legs : femora dark brown to black except for yellow apices and bases of tibiae broadly yellow, also yellow at apices and with the median portions dark brown to black; no erect setae on anterior or posterior surfaces of tibiae and apical spines lacking; tarsal spurs and pulvilli normal. Wings hyaline, stigma filling about apical 4/5 of 3rd costal section and 3rd costal section just slightly longer than 4th; sections 3rd and 4th combined about 1/2 longer than 5th section; crossvein r-m situated near basal 2/5 of cell 1st M_2 and vein M_{1+2} short, only about half of m-cu crossvein. Abdomen predominantly polished black except for the grey pollinose, 1st tergum and for light dusting of pollen over basal portion of second; 5-6 prominent black bristles on each side of tergum; terminal portion of abdomen slightly compressed to right and with a small apical membranous area on right side; 8th segment just slightly longer than 5th, as seen from dorsal view; from ventral view the membranous area is confined to apex of 8th segment (fig 80B); epandrium is approximately as long as wide and sharply pointed at apices. The surstyli are broad at bases, narrowed apically (fig. 80C).

Length. Body : 3.4 mm; wing : 4.0 mm.

Remarks. Since we could not collect this species, the present description of male has been taken from Hardy (1972_b) based on two specimens from India : Chabua, Assam, 11.iii.1944 (D. E. Hardy), collected on bamboo. The original description by Brunetti was too incomplete to be followed.

Pipunculus (*Cephalops*) *subdolosus* sp. n.
(Fig. 81)

♂. Small, black. Head 1.15x as long as broad and 1.3x as broad as thorax; eyes reddish brown with dark patches, area of contiguity 15 facets long; ocellar triangle black, ocelli dark brown; upper frontal triangle obliterated, shining black, ca 3 facets long; lower frontal triangle 19 facets long, black with yellowish pubescence, base 1.5x as broad as base of ocellar triangle; face black with silvery white pubescence, as broad as base of lower frontal triangle; occiput black with white dust, slightly swollen with small yellowish hairs along the posterior margin. Antenna black (fig. 81B); 1st segment small, black with 1 dorsal and 1 ventral black bristle; 2nd segment quadrangular and black with 4 dorsal and 3 long ventral black bristles; 3rd antennal segment black with obtuse apex; arista black, about 2·5x as long as 3rd antennal segment. Proboscis yellow. Thorax black with brownish dust, 1.4x as long as broad, densely covered with scattered yellow hairs over mesonotum; hairs of dorsocentral line comparatively long; scutellum also with small hairs on dorsal as well as on posterior margin; metanotum and pleurae black with white dust; propleural fan with 7-9 long yellow bristles; humeral plates black. Halteres light brown with base black. Wings hyaline with slight brown tinge (fig. 81A); 3rd costal section equal to 4th; 3rd and 4th combined 1.25x as long as 5th; crossvein r-m at basal 1/3 of discal cell; last section of vein M_{1+2} greatly curved. Legs black, coxae and trochanters black, femora black with tips yellow, all having a row of yellow hairs but in mid femur hairs are more dense and longer; tibiae black with proximal distal tips dark brown; hind tibia with 3 large bristles on the anterior surface in the middle; tarsi black except the proximal tip brown; claws brown with black tips 2x as long as distal tarsomere; pulvilli yellow, about 1.5x as long as distal tarsomere. Abdomen black with 1st and 2nd segments opaque, covered with brown dust; segments 3rd and 4th with distal margins shining black, 5th with distal 2/3 shining black; 8th segment about 0.5x as long and 0.7x as broad as 5th segment; large apical membranous area with a keel (fig. 81C); whole of the abdomen covered with scattered yellow hairs but 1st segment with 6-7 long hairs on each side; surstyli symmetrical. Surstyli, aedeagus, and ejaculatory apodeme as shown in fig. 81D-F.

Length. Body : 3.6 mm; wing : 4.27 mm.

♀. Frons black, covered with silvery white pubescence, broadest in the middle, about 1.25x as broad as base of ocellar triangle; halteres brownish black; crossvein r-m between basal 1/4 and 1/3 of discal cell; ovipositor with base globose and as long as piercer; piercer strong, dark brown, curved upward in the middle and downward at the tip; tip reaching the 2nd abdominal segment (fig. 81G); rest similar to male.

Length. Body : 3.6 mm; wing : 4.55 mm.

Remarks. This species resembles *P.* (*C.*) *dolosus* Hardy (1971) from Burma by having 3rd antennal segment obtuse, humeri and legs black, 8th abdominal segment with apical membranous area having a keel like structure and almost similar wing venation; but differs in characters like having 3 erect posterior bristles in the middle of hind tibia, long yellow hairs on femora; 5th abdominal tergum almost all polished black, 3rd and 4th terga polished black on apices and in the shape of surstyli.

Etymology. Named due to its closeness to *dolosus* Hardy.

Specimens examined. Holotype ♂, Bhowali near NainiTal (U. P.), 20 xi.1986, coll. S. K. Sharma. Allotype ♀, Kufri (H. P.), ex. weeds, 25.ix. 1986, coll. J. S. Grewal. Paratype 1 ♂, Mashobra (H. P.), ex weeds, 27.ix.1986, coll. J. S. Grewal.

Pipunculus (Cephalops) sp. nov. near *microdes*

(Fig. 82)

♀. Medium sized, black. Head ca 1.2x as broad as long and ca 1.3x as broad as thorax; eyes reddish brown; ocellar triangle black, ocelli brown; frons black with silvery white pubescence, broader in the middle, ca 1 5x as broad as upper end, lower end of frons ca 1.3x as broad as upper end; face black with silvery white pubescence, as broad as lower end of frons; occiput black with white dust, small fine yellow hairs on lateral and ventral surface. Antenna yellow (fig. 82B), 1st segment small, black with 2 dorsal and 1 ventral small black bristles; 2nd segment quadrangular, brown with 4 dorsal and 3 ventral long black bristles, ca 1.5 to 2x as long as dorsal ones; 3rd segment yellow, with apex slightly acuminate; arista dark brown, ca 2x as long as 3rd antennal segment. Proboscis brown. Thorax black on dorsal side with grey dust, yellow on lateral side with golden yellow coloured dust; small yellow hairs scattered all over mesonotum and scutellum; hairs behind the humeri and those forming dorsocentral rows comparatively longer; metanotum and pteropleurae black with grey dust; propleura, mesopleura, sternopleura yellow with golden dust; propleural fan with 10-12 long yellow hairs; humeri yellow. Halteres yellow. Wings hyaline with brownish tinge (fig. 82A); 3rd costal section ca 0.8x as long as 4th; 3rd and 4th costal sections combined ca 0.9x as long as 5th; crossvein r-m situated a little beyond basal 1/3rd of discal cell; distal portion of vein M_{1+2} greatly curved. Stigma very faint brown, filling whole of angle between costa and vein R_1. Legs yellow; coxae black with distal margin yellow; fore and hind femora with few yellow hairs and mid femora with a complete longitudinal row of yellow hairs on posterior surface; trochanters and tibiae yellow; femora almost all black, but yellow at tips; tarsi yellow except the distal tarsomeres which are dark brown; claws yellow with black tips, ca 1.5x as long as distal tarsomere; pulvilli large, yellow, as long as claws. Abdomen black with small hairs scattered all over, 1st two segments opaque covered with white dust, segments 3-6 polished black dorsally, but opaque and covered with white dust laterally; 1st abdominal segment with 6-8 long yellow bristles. Ovipositor with oblong base, dark brown, as long as piercer; piercer light brown, curved downwards, reaching the base of 1st abdominal segment (fig. 82C).

Length. Body : 5.0 mm; wing : 5.9 mm.

♂. Unknown.

Remarks. This species comes near *P. (C.) microdes* Perkins by sharing characters like femora almost all black and terga 3-5 shining black; but differs in characters like yellow antenna with acuminate apex; humeral plates, halteres, pleurae (except pteropleura) yellow; piercer curved, not straight as in latter. This species has not been assigned a name due to non-availability of its male specimen.

Specimen examined. 1 ♀, Khazziar (H. P.), 15.ix.1981, coll. M. L. Agarwal.

Pipunculus (Cephalops) sp. nov. near *philippinensis* Brunetti

(Fig. 83)

♀. Medium sized, black. Head ca 1.25x as broad as long, and 1.2x as broad as thorax; eyes reddish brown; ocellar triangle black with ocelli yellow; frons black with 1/6 upper portion polished black, rest covered with silvery white pubescence and small yellow hairs scattered all over, broadest in the middle, ca 2.5x as broad as base of ocellar triangle, lower end ca 2x as broad as base of ocellar triangle; face black with silvery white pubescence; occiput black with white dust, yellow hairs along posterior margin. Antennae black (fig. 83B), 1st segment small with 1 dorsal and 1 ventral black bristles; 2nd segment quadrangular, with 2 dorsal and 3 ventral long black bristles; 3rd segment with rounded apex; arista black, ca 2.5x as long as 3rd segment. Proboscis yellow. Thorax polished black with a little grey dust and few small yellow hairs behind humeri and 4-6 small hairs along dorsocentral rows; scutellum with 6-8 long thin black bristles along posterior margin; metanotum and pleurae all black; propleural fan with 6-8 thin yellow hairs; humeral plates yellow. Halteres yellow. Wings hyaline with brownish tinge (fig. 83A); 3rd costal section ca 0.7x as long as 4th; 3rd and 4th sections combined as long as 5th; crossvein r-m a little beyond 1/4 of discal cell; distal portion of vein M_{1+2} greatly curved. Legs yellow, coxae black with distal ends broadly yellow; trochanters, femora, tibiae and tarsi all black except distal tarsomeres flattened and black; hind tibiae with 2 stout black bristles medially on outer surface; claws yellow with black tips, 2x as long as distal tarsomeres; pulvilli large, yellow, as long as claws. Abdomen black subshining with white dust, 1st segment with 4-6 large stout black bristles. Ovipositor with oval base black, ca 1.45x as long as piercer; piercer yellow, tapering, thin, straight, slightly curved upwards at tip (fig. 83C).

Length. Body : 3.71 mm; wing : 5.03 mm.

♂. Unknown.

Remarks. According to key given by Hardy (1968), the present species fits near *philippinensis* Brunetti but differs from the later in characters like 3rd costal section shorter than 4th (rather than 2x longer in *philippinensis*), r-m crossvein situated a little beyond basal 1/4th of discal cell (rather than at a basal 1/3rd in the latter) and in smaller body size (3.71 mm as compared to 5.5 mm of the latter species).

Specimen examined. 1 ♀, Mashobra (H. P.), 27.ix.1986, ex weeds, coll. J. S. Grewal.

ii. SUBGENUS *CEPHALOSPHAERA* ENDERLEIN

Cephalosphaera Enderlein in Brohmer, Ehrmann and Ulmer, 1936, Die Tierwelt Mitteleuropas, Insekt. (III) 6 : 129. Type species : *Pipunculus furcatus* Egger, by monotypy.

Ancephalops Aczel, 1940, Zool. Anz., 132 : 151. Type sp. : *Pipunculus amboinalis* Walker, by original designation.

This subgenus is clearly distinguished by the presence of an appendix in vein M_{1+2} beyond m-crossvein (also in subgenus *Claraeola* Aczel). The presence of propleural fan readily separates it from *Claraeola* in which it is absent. The subgenus was known by only one species, *prolatus*(Kertesz)(new name for *appendiculatus* Brunetti, 1923) from India; another new species is described below.

Pipunculus (*Cephalosphaera*) *motichoorensis* sp. nov.

(Fig. 84)

The female specimen from Motichoor (U. P.), fits near *amboinalis* Walker from Moluccas (also known from ♀), sharing with it the characters like 3rd antennal segment acuminate, legs black and 3rd costal section equal to 4th. It differs from it in having crossvein r-m at basal 2/5th of discal cell (cf. beyond middle of discal cell in *amboinalis)*; piercer curved upwards while in *amboinalis* piercer first bends upwards and then downwards near distal end.

♀. Small, black. Head ca 1.13x as broad as long and 1.2x as broad as thorax; eyes dark brown; frons, ocellar triangle black with ocelli yellow; frons black with white pubescence, broader in the middle, ca 1.25x as broad as the base of ocellar triangle; lower end as broad as ocellar triangle; face black with silvery white pubescence; occiput black slightly swollen, with silvery white dust, small yellow hairs along posterior morgin. Antenna yellow to light brown (fig. 84B); 1st segment black, small; 2nd segment, black, quadrangular with 2 small dorsal and 2 long ventral black bristles; 3rd antennal segment brown at base, apex yellow, acuminate; arista black, ca 2x as long as 3rd segment. Proboscis yellow. Thorax black with white or grey dust, ca 1.27x as long as broad, small yellow hairs just behind the humeral plates; metanotum and pleurae black; propleural fan with 3-4 small inconspicuous yellow hairs; humeral plates yellow. Halteres yellow. Wings hyaline (fig. 84A); 3rd costal section equal to 4th; 3rd and 4th costal sections combined 0.74x as long as 5th; crossvein r-m a little before 2/5th of the discal cell; vein M_{1+2} with an appendix at a distance ca 0.67x the m-crossvein from point of m crossvein, rest of vein M_{1+2} slightly curved; stigma yellow, filling ca 0.8x of the angle between 3rd costal section and vein R_1. Legs black; coxae and trochanters black, femora predominantly black, yellow only at apices; tibiae black medially, broadly yellow at proximal and distal ends; tarsi yellow, distal tarsomeres black; claws yellow with black tips, ca

1.25x as long as distal tarsomeres; pulvilli yellow, as long as distal tarsomeres. Abdomen black, opaque; 1st abdominal segment with 4-6 thick, stout black bristles on each side. Ovipositor with base oblong, polished black, as long as piercer; piercer yellow, strongly curved upwards approaching the base of 1st abdominal segment (fig. 84C).

Length. Body : 2.95 mm; wing : 3.60 mm.

♂. Unknown.

Etymology. Named after its type locality.

Specimen examined. Holotype ♀, Motichoor (U. P.), 28.x.1986, coll. S. K. Sharma.

Pipunculus (*Cephalosphaera*) *prolatus* (Kertesz)

Pipunculus (*Cephalosphaera*) *prolatus* Kertesz, 1915, Annls. hist-nat. Mus. natn. hung., 13 : 387. (*Dorylas* : n. name for *appendiculatus* Brunetti).

Pipunculus appendiculatus Brunetti, 1912, Rec. Ind. Mus., 7 : 485. (♀; preocc. Cresson, 1911).

Since no specimen of this species could be collected and its type specimen (no. 697/9) in the museum collection of Zoological Survey of India, Calcutta, is in extremely bad condition, its description has been reproduced from Brunetti (1923).

♀. Head (wanting). Thorax bluish-grey, with light brown reflections, but with no distinct marks; humeri distinct, rather large, brownish; sides of thorax dark bluish-grey with whitish reflections when seen from behind; scutellum bluish-grey, tinged with pale brown; metanotum bluish-grey with whitish reflections. Abdomen bluish ash-grey; rather more than the basal half of each segment rich velvet-black, which extends hindwards in the centre until it nearly meets the next segment; these black bands extend over the sides and right across the ventral surface so that the venter is practically a replica of the dorsum; last segment (6th) all bluish-grey, bent under the venter and carrying a moderately long reddish-brown shining process bearing a bunch of hairs near the tip. Legs dark blackish-brown; extreme base and tips of femora pale yellowish-brown; tibiae blackish-brown, with bases rather broadly, and tips rather narrowly yellowish-brown; tarsi dark brown above, light brown below; femora with silvery-white shimmer, when seen in certain lights. Legs microscopically pubescent; no ciliation behind middle femora; hind femora not shining on inner side. Wings distinctly pale brown;

2nd costal segment quite clear and transparent; 3rd twice as long as the 4th; stigma distinct, but ill-defined on inner side; 4th longitudinal vein curved outwards in a bow after quitting the posterior crossvein and possessing an appendix, commencing as far from the junction of the 4th longitudinal crossvein and extending more than half-way to the wing-border; anterior crossvein exactly over centre of discal cell; basal part of wing rather clear, but extreme base pale yellowish. Halteres brownish-yellow.

Length. 3.0 mm (excl. head and ovipositor).

Described from a single ♀ in the Indian Museum from Margherita, Assam.

iii. SUBGENUS *CLARAEOSPHAERA* KAPOOR & GREWAL

Claraeosphaera Kapoor & Grewal, 1985, Int. J. Ent., U.S.A., 27(4):395-400, ♀. Type species : *Pipunculus* (*Claraeosphaera*) *suranganiensis* Kapoor & Grewal.

This subgenus fits between the subgenera *Claraeola* Aczel and *Cephalosphaera* Enderlein. With the former it shares the characters like bare propleura, presence of stigma, vein M_{1+2} forked, and M_2 present as an appendix of the 4th vein. It differs from *Claraeola* by having the 3rd antennal segment acuminate, longer than 1st and 2nd segments combined, and the 3rd costal section 2x the length of the 4th section. With *Cephalosphaera* it shares the characters like lacking ocellars, well deveoped mesonotal and scutellar bristles and vein M_{1+2} appendiculate. It differs from *Cephalosphaera* by the position of crossvein r-m and the presence of an incision between the auxillary lobe and alula. It differs from both *Claraeola* and *Cephalosphaera* by the presence of an appendix on the crossvein m. Because of its resemblance to both these subgenera, it has been named *Claraeosphaera*.

Pipunculus (Claraeosphaera) suranganiensis Kapoor & Grewal.

(Fig. 85)

Pipunculus (*Claraeosphaera*) *suranganiensis* Kapoor & Grewal, 1985, Int. J. Ent., U.S.A., 27 (4) : 395-400, (♀). Type loc. : Surangani, (H.P.).

♀. Small, black with abdomen yellow. Head black, broader than thorax; occiput swollen with small whitish hair; ocellar triangle black, ocellar bristles absent; eyes reddish black, not holoptic; frons black with whitish dust; face black with silvery pollinose, oral groove with well developed proboscis; genal plates triangular with a few whitish small hairs. Antennae (fig. 85B) brownish yellow; 1st segment brown; 2nd brownish yellow with 2 small dark bristles on dorsal surface and 1 long black bristle on ventral; 3rd segment pale yellow, acuminate, 1.5x as long as 1st and 2nd combined; arista black except yellow at base, bare. Thorax black, as long as head; dorsum covered with greyish dust; chaetotaxy rudimentary; scutellum yellowish, inflated; humeral plates yellow; propleural fan absent. Halteres yellowish with knob black apically. Legs yellow; hind trochanter trapezoidal (fig. 85C); femora yellow, fore and mid femora with 1 row of black setae dorsoapically and 1 ventroapically, hind femur with 2 rows of black setae dorsoapically and 1 ventroapically; tibiae yellow with 2 rows of black setae dorsally and 4 rows ventrally; tarsi yellow with black setae and pretarsus with 6-9 large black bristles; pulvilli yellow, well-developed; claws sickle-shaped, yellow with tip black. Wing hyaline (fig. 85A); humeral crossvein oblique; 3rd costal section 2x as long as 4th; 3rd and 4th costal sections combined 1.5x as long as 5th; stigma occupying whole of angle of R_1 with costa; r-m crossvein situated at about basal 2/5 of discal cell; appendix of 4th vein (M_{1+2}) short, not reaching margin and situated at a distance equal to length of m crossvein, appendix of crossvein m located at about its anterior 1/4; auxillary lobe not well developed, a small incision present between auxillary lobe and alula. Abdomen clavate, yellowish brown; terga yellow with brownish bands at anterior margins, hind border black, venter entirely brown; 6th abdominal tergum equal in length to 5th; hind margin entire, lacking groove or cleft; ovipositor (fig. 85D) large and pointed, reaching to base of 2nd sternum, brown.

Length. Body : 4.00 mm; wing : 5.00 mm.

♂. Unknown.

Specimen examined. Holotype ♀, Surangani, Chamba (H.P.), 4.vi.1984, coll. V. K. Kohli.

Etymology. Named after its type-locality.

iv. SUBGENUS *PIPUNCULUS* LATREILLE

The representatives of this subgenus are recognized by having the anterior portion of mesonotum evenly setose at least to the suture, or in most species to a level with the notopleural calli; the dorsocentral hairs are not differentiated and the propleural fan consists of long, conspicuous hairs. It is known by only one subspecies in India. Since we could not collect its specimens, the description is reproduced from Brunetti (1923).

Pipunculus (*Pipunculus*) *campestris himalayensis* Brunetti

Pipunculus campestris himalayensis Brunetti, 1912, Rec. Indian Mus., 7 : 487 (♂). Type loc. : Darjeeling, India.

Pipunculus (*Pipunculus*) *campestris himalayensis* : Hardy 1975, Cat. Dipt. Orient. Reg., 2 : 297.

♂. Head : frons blackish-grey, with a little grey shimmer above the antennae; vertex shining black; antennae black, somewhat short, 3rd joint with a grey shimmer; arista only twice as long as the antennae; eyes contiguous for a considerable distance, facets almost uniform in size; back of head dark grey, occiput rather well puffed out. Thorax blackish, side lighter, scutellum shining blackish; metanotum with silvery-grey tinge. Abdomen blackish, greyish towards the sides, the colour with a tendency to extend a little along the margins of the segments; hypopygium black, short, wide, with a distinct depression in centre. Legs black, dull; femora brownish-yellow at base and tip, with some traces of a greyish shimmer; basal half of tibiae and under side of part of tarsi brownish-yellow; middle femora with ciliation of hairs on hinder side. Wings clear; stigma pale brown; 3rd costal segment a little longer than the 4th; anterior crossvein at about 1/3rd of the discal cell; 4th longitudinal vein slightly curved after quitting the posterior crossvein. Halteres black.

Length. Body : 2.75 mm.

Described from 2 ♂ in the museum collection of Zoological Survey of India, Calcutta at Darjeeling, 29.v.1910 (type) and 29.ix.1908, coll. Brunetti.

Remarks. One specimen in the museum collection of Zoological Survey of India having data as Maddathoray (west base of western ghat), Travancore, 17.xi.1908 (no. 1930/H_1) is in poor condition. It was about 3 mm long, having 3rd costal section 0.8x of 4th and r-m crossvein slightly before middle of discal cell. The other specimen (no. 1920/H_1) was missing with only its collection data available as from Darjeeling, 29.xi.1908. Its actual type specimen could not be located.

5. GENUS *CHALARUS* WALKER

Chalarus Walker, 1834, Ent. Mag. (Lond.), 2 : 269. Type species, *Cephalops spurius* Fallen, by designation of Westwood (1840 : 135).

The members of this genus are characterised by the incomplete wing venation (vein M_{1+2}, anal vein and m crossvein lacking); by the presence of ocellar bristles; hemispherical head; and very narrow occiput.

Chalarus spurius (Fallen)
(Fig. 86)

Cephalops spurius Fallen, 1816, Syrphici Sveciae:16 (♀). Type-loc. : Sweden.
Chalarus spurius : Westwood, 1840, Synopsis genn. Brit. Ins., p. 135.

♂. Small, black, hairy. Head hemispherical, 1.57x as long as broad, 1.27x as broad as thorax; eyes brown, dichoptic; ocelli dark brown; post-ocellar bristles, ocellar bristles and frons dull black, opaque; lower portion about 5 facets long with silvery white pubescence, narrow in the middle, about 1.5x as broad as median ocellus; face b'ack covered with silvery white pubescence near antenna, as broad as lower end of frons and 1·5x near proboscis; occiput black not visible from lateral side. Antenna black (fig. 86B); 1st segment very small, hardly visible; 2nd segment quadrangular, black with 2 dorsal and 1 ventral large black bristles; 3rd segment black with rounded apex; arista black, about 2·5-3x as long as 3rd antennal segment. Proboscis dark brown. Thorax black, opaque, ca 1.27x as long as broad; dorsum of thorax and scutellum thickly covered with long black hairs; margins of mesonotum and scutellum with strong black bristles; metanotum and pleurae black with sparse white dust; humeri black. Halteres dark brown. Wings hyaline with slight brownish tinge (fig. 86A); venation incomplete; 3rd costal section 6x as long as 4th; 3rd and 4th combined 1.42x as long as 5th; vein M_{1+2} and crossvein m indistinct but their position is detectable; r-m crossvein at basal 1/5th of the incomplete discal cell; anal vein not very prominent. Legs totally black, fore and mid femora with a row of long strong black bristles on posterior side; hind femora with 4 to 6 long black bristles on apico-anterior side. Abdomen black with brown dust, long black bristles along the lateral side; 8th segment as long as 5th, line of articulation between surstyli and 9th segment not distinct (fig. 86C); surstyli boat-shaped, symmetrical (fig. 86D-E). Surstyli, aedeagus, ejaculatory apodeme and aedeagal guide as shown in fig. 86E-G.

Length. Body : 2.14 mm; wing : 2.57 mm.

♀. Small, black, not as hairy as in case of ♂; frons with parallel sides; upper half dull black, lower half with silvery white pubescence. Thorax with few black bristles behind humeri; 1st abdominal segment with 3-4 stout black bristles; rest of abdomen without any prominent hair; ovipositor with base black, globose, ca 0.67x as long as piercer; piercer small, brown and conical in shape (fig. 86H-I).

Length. Body : 2.14 mm; wing : partly broken.

Specimens examined. 1 ♂, 1 ♀, Kurseong (W. B.), 5.iv.1985, coll. S. K. Sharma.

6. GENUS *VERRALLIA* MIK

Verrallia Mik, 1899, Wien. Ent. Ztg., 18 : 137. Type species : *Cephalops aucta* Fallen.

Prothechus of authors, not Rondani. *Prothechus* Rondani (1856 : 139) has been suppressed by I. C. Z. N. 1961, Opinion 597 : 230.

The members of this genus are characterised by the presence of ocellar bristles, hemispherical head, narrow occiput and complete wing venation. Almost all the member species are densely hairy. In India this genus is represented by only one species of subgenus *Jassidophaga* Aczel.

SUBGENUS *JASSIDOPHAGA* ACZEL

Jassidophaga Aczel, 1939, Zool. Anz., 125 : 20. Type sp. : *Pipunculus pilosus* Zetterstedt, by original designation.

Jassidophaga was erected as a genus by Aczel (1939) for those pipunculids which have well developed ocellar bristles, scarcely developed occiput, hemisperical head and vein M_{1+2} without an appendix. Hardy (1943) also considered it as a genus. But later authors did not consider the characters of *Jassidophaga* worthy of assigning it a generic status and so treated it as a subgenus of *Verrallia* Mik. Hardy (1972b, 1975) also treated it as a subgenus. It is known by only one species, *plumbella* Brunetti from India. Since we could not collect the species of this subgenus and its type specimen (no. 1941/ H_1) in the museum collection of Zoological Survey of India is in extremely bad condition, its description has been reproduced from Brunetti (1923).

Verrallia (Jassidophaga) plumbella Brunetti

Verrallia plumbella Brunetti, 1912, Rec. Indian Mus., 7 : 495 (♀). Type-loc. : Kurseong, India.

Verrallia (*Jassidophaga*) *plumbella* : Hardy, 1975, Cat. Dipt. Orient. Reg., 2 : 296.

♀. Head : vertex black; fronto-facial groove of uniform width, with white shimmer; facets in front considerably larger than the others; back of head only just projecting beyond the post-ocular orbit, grey with a whitish reflection. Antennae (missing). Proboscis yellow. Thorax and scutellum black, moderately shining; sides and metanotum apparently concolorous; scutellum with a row of minute hairs on posterior border. Abdomen shining lead colour, with a few microscopic hairs; the base of each segment, narrowly in the centre and more broadly towards the sides, dead jet black; 6th segment the longest, bearing a thick blackish grey pointed genital organ; terminating in a long shiny brown ovipositor. Legs (middle pair missing) black, barely shining; tips of femora rather narrowly, and base of tibiae broadly, reddish yellow. Base of tarsi yellowish brown, tips black, with a few hairs; claws small, pulvilli distinct and white; legs microscopically pubescent and the fore femora with a few very small bristles below near the tip. Wings quite clear; stigma pale brownish yellow, stigmatic segment barely longer than following segment, anterior crossvein just before middle of discal cell; 4th longitudinal vein moderately sinuous after quitting the posterior crossvein.

Length. Body : 3.25 mm.

Described from a single specimen in the Indian Museum taken by Dr. Annandale at Kurseong (5000 ft.), 5.vii.1908.

UNPLACED SPECIES

Pipunculus mirabilis was described by Brunetti (1912). Since then, its generic status has been a matter of contradiction. Even Hardy (1975) could not assign it to any genus although he mentioned its probable inclusion in *Tomosvaryella.* Its holotype (No. 5726/9) in the museum collection of Zoological Survey of India is in extremely bad condition and thus could not be studied. We also could not collect any specimen of this species. The following description has been reproduced from Brunetti (1923).

Pipunculus mirabilis Brunetti

Pipunculus mirabilis Brunetti, 1912, Rec. Indian Mus., 7 : 492. Type loc. : Margherita, Assam.

♀. Head : front rather narrower at vertex, which is black. Frons greyish white, face below antennae similar, and with a silvery white sheen seen from above; mouth light brown; eyes light brown; the facets in the vicinity of the antennae much larger. Antennae (missing). Thorax : dorsum blackish aeneous, humeri yellowish brown; edge of dorsum and sides of thorax greyish; a broad stripe of grey with silver reflections extends across the metanotum and embraces the metapleura on each side; scutellum light yellowish brown; the posterior part and margin with pale long pubescence. Abdomen ash-grey; on the 2nd segment is a large brown round spot in the middle; on the 3rd, 4th and 5th are black basal bands, very narrow in the centre, and much widened at the sides of the segments; 6th segment with black band of uniform width and very narrow; bears a long ferrugineous brown process bent under the belly, with hairs towards its tip; whole abdomen covered with rather long (but not dense) pale hairs, mixed with a number of black ones, these latter having no relationship to the black parts in the ground colour. Legs : coxae brown, with a little silvery reflection in certain lights; remainder of legs bright lemon yellow, practically bare, but the tibiae have several rows of almost microscopic spines towards the apices; tips of tarsi dark brown; claws and pulvilli much enlarged as mentioned by Herr Becker in his species *hepaticolor*. Wings quite clear, extreme bare, very pale yellow. Anterior crossvein placed at two fifths from the base of the discal cell; 4th longitudinal vein taking an outward curve on quitting the posterior crossvein; 3rd costal segment twice as long as 4th and about equal in length to the 5th. Halteres pale yellow.

Length. Body : 4.00 mm (without ovipositor).

Described from a perfect ♀ from Margherita, Assam, in the Indian Museum Collection. A very striking and beautiful species and apparently closely allied to Becker's *hepaticolor*, from which it is differentiated as follows: there is no darkening of the stigma; the thoracic dorsum is blackish not greyish, the abdominal marks are somewhat different, the femora have no black streaks above; and the anterior crossvein is placed distinctly before the centre of discal cell.

7. LIST OF WORLD PIPUNCULIDS & THEIR HOSTS

Pipunculid Parasitoids	Homopteran hosts	Distribution	Author's reference
I. CHALARINAE			
Genus *Chalarus* Walk.			
1. *fimbriatus* Coe	*Eupteryx urticae* (Fab) (Cicadelloidea : Typhlocybinae : Typhlocybini); *Zygina alneti* (Dahlbom) (Erythroneurini)	England	Jervis, 1980c
2. *latifrons* Hardy	*Agallia* sp (Cicadellidae : Agallinae)	U.S A.	Hardy, 1943
	Empoasca sp	U.S.A.	Hardy, 1943
	Kybos butleri (Edwards); *K. smaragdula* (Fallen) (all of Empoascini)	England	Jervis, 1980c
3. *parmenteri* Coe	*Alebra albostriella* (Fallen) (Typhlocybinae : Alebrini); *Empoasca vitis* (Gothe) (Empoascini); *Fagocyba cruentata* (Herrich-Schaffer), *Typhlocyba quercus* (Fab.) (Typhlocybini)	England	Jervis, 1980c
4. *pughi* Coe	*Edwardsiana geometrica* (Schrank); *Eupteryx aurata* (Linn.); *E. urticae* (Fab.) (all Typhlocybini)	England	Jervis, 1980c
5. *spurius* (Fallen)	*A. albostriella*	England	Jervis, 1980c
	Empoasca sp	U.S.A.	Hardy, 1943
	Edwardsiana geometrica, *E. hippocastani*	England	Jervis, 1980c
	Edwardsiana lethierryi (Edwards)	France	Giard, 1889
	E. rosea (Linn.); *Eupteryx*	England	Jervis, 1980c

	urticae; *Eurhadina concinna* (Germar), *E. pulchella* (Fallen), *F. cruentata* (all Typhlocybini)		
	Fagocyba douglasi (Edwards)	France	Giard, 1889
	Ribautina tenerrima (Herr.-Sch.)	England	Jervis, 1980c
	R. ulmi; *T. quercus* (all Typhlocybini)	U.S.A. and Europe	Hardy, 1943
	Erythroneura sp. (Erythroneurini)		
Unidentified species			
i) *Chalarus* sp.	*Idiocerus* sp. (Idiocerinae)	U.S.A.	Hardy, 1943
ii) *Chalarus* sp.	*Forcipata loca* Delong & Caldwell (Typhlocybinae : Dikraneurini)	U.S.A.	Freytag, 1985
iii) *Chalarus* sp.	*Zygina alneti*	England	Jervis, 1980c
Genus *Verrallia* Mik			
6. *aucta* (Fallen)	Various cercopids	England	Jenkinson, 1903
		Denmark	Waloff, 1975; Lyneborg, 1975
	Philaenus spumarius; *Nephilaenus lineatus*	Belgium	Meyer & Brune, 1984
7. *beatricis* Coe	Various cercopids	Denmark	Lyneborg, 1975
8. *pillosa* (Zettersted)	Various cercopids	Denmark	Lyneborg, 1975
9. *setosa* Verrall	Various cercopids	Denmark	Lyneborg, 1975
	Macropsis flavicollis (Linn.) (Cicadellidae : Macropsinae)	England	Waloff, 1980
10. *villosa* Von Roser	*Saratoga* sp, *Aphrophora saratogensis* (Fitch) (Cercopidae)	U.S.A. : Maine	Linnane and Osgood, 1978
11. *virginea* Banks	Cercopids	Denmark	Lyneborg, 1975

II. PIPUNCULINAE

Genus *Dorylomorpha* Aczel			
12. *haemorrhoidalis* (Zett.)	*Cicadula quadrinotata* (Fab.) (Deltocephalini)	England	Waloff, 1980
13. *lini* (Perkins)	*Nephotettix cincticeps* Uhler (Deltocephalini)	Taiwan	Chu & Hirashima, 1981
14. *rufipes* Meigen	*C. quadrinotata*	England	Waloff, 1975
15. *tridentata* Hardy	*Thamnotettix* sp (Deltocephalini)	U.S.A.	Waloff, 1975
16. *xanthopus* Thompson	*Polyamia weedi* (Van Duzee); *Psammotettix confinis* (Dahlbom).	England	Waloff, 1975
	Diplocolenus bensoni (China); *Euscelis obsoletus* (Kirschbaum) (all Deltocephalini)	England	Waloff, 1980
Genus *Eudorylas* Aczel			
17. *absonditus* (Hardy)	*Cicadulina pastusae* Ruppel & De Long	U.S.A. : Columbia	Hardy, 1962
	(Deltocephalinae : Macrostelini)	U.S.A. : California	Hardy, 1964a
18. *aequus* (Cresson)	*Graminella mohri* De Long (Deltocephaline)	U.S.A.	Freytag, 1985
19. *anomalus* Hardy	*Sogatella furcifera* Horvath (Delphacidae);	England	Waloff, 1980
	Nephotettix spp., *Nilaparvata lugens* (Stal), *Recilia* (*Inajuma*) *dorsalis* (Motch.) (Deltocephalini), *Cofana spectra* (Dist.) (Cicadellinae)	England	May, 1979
20. *arundani* Hardy	*Arundanus* sp. (Deltocephalini)	U.S.A. : Georgia	Hardy, 1954b
21. *chlorionae* Frey	*chloriona* sp. (Delphacidae)	Germany	Lindberg, 1946

22. *cruciator* (Perkins)	*Hecalus immaculatus* Kirkaldy (Cicadellidae : Hecalinae);	Australia : Queensland	Perkins, 1905; Hardy, 1964
	N. cincticeps (Deltocephalini)	Japan	Shimada, 1972
		Taiwan	Chu & Hirashima, 1981
23. *erinus* (Perkins)	*Batrachomorphus* sp. (Cicadellidae : Iassinae)	Australia : Queensland	Perkins, 1905; Hardy, 1964
24. *eucalypti* (Perkins)	*Ledropsin crocina* Dist. (Ledrinae)	Australia & Taiwan	Hardy, 1964
25. *fascipes* Zett.	*Macrosteles sexnotatus* (Fall.), *M. variatus* (Fall.) (Deltocephalinae : Macrostelini); *Grypotes puncticollis* (Herr.-Sch.) (Deltocephalini)	England	Waloff, 1980
	Arthaldeus pascuellus (Fall.), *Errastunus ocellaris* (Fall.), *P. confinis* (Dahl.)	England	Waloff, 1975
	Solenphyx sulphurella (Zett.) (Deltocephalini)	Sweden	Boheman, 1855
26. *hawaiensis* (Perk.)	*Perkinsiella saccharicida* Kirk. (Delphacidae)	U.S.A.: Hawaii	Williams, 1919; Thompson, 1951
27. *helluo* (Perk.)	A deltocephaline leafhopper	Australia : Queensland	Perkins, 1905; Hardy, 1964
28. *hylaeus* (Perk.)	*Batrachomorphus* sp	Australia : Queensland	Perkins, 1905; Hardy, 1964
29. *javanensis* de Meijere	*N. cincticeps* Uhler	Taiwan; Oriental	Hardy, 1972; Liu, 1974; Chandra, 1979; Yano, 1979.

30. *jenkinsoni* Coe	*A. pascuellus* (Fall.); *Errastunus ocellaris* (Fall.) (Deltocephalini)	England	Waloff, 1975
31. *juvator* (Perk.)	*P. saccharicida*	U.S.A. : Hawaii	Williams, 1919; Thompson, 1951
32. *koebeli* (Perk.)	*Nesophrosyne* sp (Deltocephalini)	U.S.A.	Hardy, 1953
	Neoclartus sp or *Vulturnus* sp (Cicadellidae : Penthimiinae); *Thaumatoscopus* sp (Iassinae)	Australia : Sydney	Perkins, 1905; Hardy, 1964
33. *lamellifer* (Perk.)	*Campbellinella fatigondus* (Kirk.) (Deltocephalini)	Australia : Queensland	Perkins, 1905; Hardy, 1964
34. *monas* (Perk.)	jassid (name not given)	Australia : Queensland	Perkins, 1905; Hardy, 1964
35. *montium* (Becker)	*Cicadula quadrinotata* (Fab.), *Mocydia crocea* (Herr.-Sch.) (Deltocephalini)	England	Waloff, 1980
36. *mutillatus* Loew	*Nephotettix cincticeps* Uhler, *N. virescens* Dist., *N. nigropictus* (Stal.), *N. malayanus*, *N. parvus* Ishiara & Kawasee (Deltocephalini)	Oriental, African, Pacific, Palaearctic	Koizumi, 1959; Hardy, 1968, 1972; Shimada, 1972; Kathirithamby, 1974; Yano, 1979; Chandra, 1979.
37. *obliquus* Coe	*A. pascuellus* (Fall.); *E. ocellaris* (Fall.), *P. confinis* (Dahl.) (Deltocephalini)	England	Waloff, 1975
	C. quadrinotata (Fab.); *Euscelis* sp; *Mocydia crocea* (Herr.-Sch.); *Speudotettix subfasculus* (Fall.) (Deltocephalini)	England	Waloff, 1980

38. *obscurus* Coe	*A. pascuellus* (Fall); *E. ocellaris* (Fall.); *P. confinis* (Dahl.)	England	Waloff, 1975
	D. bensoni (China)	England	Waloff, 1980
39. *orientalis* (Koizumi)	*N. cincticeps* Uhler	Oriental	Koizumi, 1959; Hardy, 1972; Shimada, 1972; Liu, 1974; Yano, 1979
40. *picrodes* (Perk.)	*Tartessus* sp (Cicadellidae : Tartessinae)	Austrialia	Perkins, 1905
41. *roralis* (Kertesz)	*Nephotettix* spp	Oriental	Hardy, 1972; Liu, 1974; Chandra, 1979; Yano, 1979
42. *semifumosus* (Kowarz)	*Conomelas anceps* (Germar), *Delphacodes fairmairei* (Perris), *D. pellucida* (Fab.), *Crimorphus pteridis* (Spinola), *Megamelodes venosus* (Germar) (Delphacidae)	British Isles	Rothschild, 1964
43. *subfascipes* Collin	*E. ocellaris* (Fall.); *G. puncticollis* (Herr.-Sch.); *P. confinis* (Dalh.) (Deltocephalini)	England	Waloff, 1975
44. *subopacus* (Loew)	*Circulifer tenellus* (Baker) (Deltocephalini)	U.S.A.	Dorst, 1938
	Scaphytopius acutus (Say) (Deltocephalinae : Scaphytopiini)	U.S.A.	Hardy, 1964
45. *subterminalis* Collin	*E. ocellaris* (Fall.), *G. puncticollis*	England	Waloff, 1975

	(Herr.-Sch), *P. confinis* (Dahl.), *Verdanas abdominalis* (Fab.)		
	Arundanus sp, *D. bensoni* (China) (all Deltocephalini)	England	Waloff, 1980
	Euscelis incisus (Deltocephalini)	Berlin	Huq, 1984
46. *teryii* (Perk.)	*P. saccharicida*	U.S.A. : Hawaii	Williams, 1918
47. *beneficiens* Perk.	*Deltocephalus* sp, *Phrynophyes* sp	U.S.A.	Hardy, 1943
48. *cinerascens* Perk.	leafhoppers on *Melaleuca* plant	U.S.A.	Hardy, 1964c
Unidentified species			
i) *Eudorylas* sp	*A. pascuellus* (Fall.), *opsius* sp (Deltocephalini)	Germany	Coe, 1965
Genus *Pipunculus* Latreille			
Subgenus *Cephalops* Fallen			
49. *annulifemur* Brunetti	*Amritodes atkinsoni* (Lethierry); *Idioscopus clypealis* (Leth.) *I. niveosparsus* (Leth.) (Cicadellidae : Idiocerinae)	India	Subramaniam, 1922
50. *curtifrons* Coe	*Stenocranus minutus* (Fab.) (Delphacidae)	England	Waloff, 1975 May, 1979
Subgenus *Pipunculus* Lat.			
51. *anthracias* Perk.	*Balclutha* sp (Deltocephalinae : Balcluthini)	Australia	Perkins, 1905; Hardy, 1964
52. *ater* (Meigen)	*Paraphlepsius irroratus* (Say) (Deltocephalini); *Forcipata* sp (Dikraneurini)	U S.A.	Hardy, 1943
53. *campestris* Lat.	*Macrosteles laevis* (Ribaut) (Deltocephalinae : Macrostelini);	Germany	Coe, 1966

	A. pascuellus (Fall.); *C. quadrinotata* (Deltocephalini)		
	M. laevis	Poland	Bankowska, 1973
	Euscelis plebejus (Fall.); *Solenopyx sulphurella* (Zett.) (Deltocephalini)	England	Waloff, 1975
	Macrosteles sexnotatus (Fall.); *M. laevis* (Macrostelini); *D. bensoni*; *Euscelis obsoletus* (Kirschbaum) (Deltocephalini).	England	Waloff, 1980
	Psammotettix confinis (Dahl.), *Euscelis incisus* (Kirsh.)	Belgium	Meyer & Brune, 1984
	Euscelis incisus	Berlin	Huq, 1984
54. *cressoni* (Johnson)	*Arundanus* sp	U.S.A	Hardy, 1943
	Stenocranus arundineus Metcalf (Delphacidae)	U.S.A.	Hardy, 1964c
55. *fonescoi* Coe	*Doratura stylata* (Boheman) (Deltocephalini)	England	Waloff, 1980
56. *macrothrix* Hardy	*Nesophrosyne* sp (Deltocephalini)	U.S.A.	Hardy, 1964bc
57. *mauritianus* Hardy	*P. saccharicida* (Delphacidae); *Dicrapteris muiri* (Fulgoridae)	Mauritius	Hardy, 1956; Williams, 1957
58. *obscuratus* Hardy	*Nesosydne ipomoeicole* Kirk.; *Nesophrosyne* sp (Deltocephalini)	U.S.A : Hawaii	Hardy, 1953
59. *perkinsiellae* (Hardy)	*P. saccharicida*	U.S.A. : Hawaii	Perkins, 1905; Hardy, 1953
		Australia	Bull, 1973
60. *thomsoni* Becker	*S. sulphurella* (Deltocephalini)	England	Waloff, 1975

61. *timberlakei* Hardy	*Nesophrosyne* sp	U.S.A.	Hardy, 1953
62. *ulehe* Hardy	*Nesophrosyne* sp	U.S.A.	Hardy, 1953
63. *varius* Cresson	*Megamelus davisi* Van Duzee (Deltocephalini)	U.S.A.	Wilson & Mcphenson, 1981
64. *zygmayeriae* Kowarz	*Graphocraerus ventralis* (Fall.)	England	Waloff, 1980
Genus *Tomosvaryella* Aczel			
65. *appendipes* (Cresson)	*Scaphytopius nitridus* (De Long) (Deltocephalinae : Scaphytopiini)	U.S.A.	Pierce, 1972
66. *brevijuncta* Hardy	*Hecalus* sp (Cicadellidae : Hecalinae)	U.S.A.	Hardy, 1943
67. *epichalca* (Perk.)	*N. cincticeps*; *N. lugens*	Cambodia;Taiwan Philippines; Australia	Perkins, 1905; Liu, 1974; Chu & Hirashima, 1981
68. *frontata* (Becker)	*Opsius stactogalus* Fieber	France	Parker, 1967
69. *inazumae* (Koizumi)	*Reclia (I.) dorsalis*	Japan;Orient	Koizumi, 1960 Hardy, 1971
70. *itoi* (Koizumi)	*Psammotettix striatus* (Linn.) (Deltocephalini)	France Japan, Orient	Koizumi, 1960 Hardy, 1971
71. *kuthyi* Aczel	*P. confinis* (Dahl.)	England	Waloff, 1975
72. *lepidipes* Hardy	*Colladonus germinatus* (Van Duzee) (Deltocephalini)	U.S.A.	Hardy, 1954b; Kaloostian, 1956
73. *oryzaetora* Koizumi	*Nephotettix* spp; *N. parus*; *N. lugens*; *Reclia (I)* *dorsalis*; *C. spectra*	Orient; Japan	Koizumi, 1960 Coe, 1966; Hardy, 1971; Liu, 1974; Hsich, 1975; Chandra

			1979; Kathirithamby 1978; Yano, 1979; Chu & Hirashima, 1981
74. *palliditarsis*	*Verdanas abdominalis* (Fab.) (Deltocephalini)	England	Waloff, 1975
75. *pseudophanes* (Perk.)	*Hecalus immaculatus* Kirkaldy (Cicadellidae: Hecalinae)	Australia	Perkins, 1905; Hardy, 1964b
76. *spiculata* Hardy	*N. cincticeps*	Taiwan; Philippines	Hardy, 1971
77. *subvirescens* (Loew)	*Graphocelphala versuta* (Say) (Cicadellinae)	U.S A.	Ashmead, 1895
	Nephotettix spp; *N. parvus*, *Circulifer tenellus* Baker	Widespread in Orient but actually cosopo-litan	Thompson, 1957; Coe, 1956; Hardy 1971; Liu, 1974 Chandra, 1979; Yano 1979; Kathirithamby, 1978; Chu and Hirashima 1981.
		India ; Ludhiana	F.
78. *sylvatica* (Meigen)	*Macrosteles quadrilineatus* (Forbest) (Macrostelini)	Canada	Hardy, 1964c
	N. cincticeps, *P. striatus*	Taiwan	Hardy, 1971
		Thailand	Yano, 1979
	A. pascuellus	Poland	Bankowska, 1973
	E. ocellaris (Fab.)	England	Waloff, 1975
	Grypotss puncticollis (Herr-Sch.)	England	Waloff, 1980
	E. bensoni (China)	England	Waloff, 1980
	Graminella nigrifrons (Forbes)	U.S.A.	Freytag 1985

	(Deltccephalini)		
79. *synadelpha* (Perk.)	*Divitiacus hospes* (Kirk.)	Australia	Perkins, 1905; Hardy, 1964
80. *troangulatus* sp. n.	*N. cincticeps*	India : Ludhiana	F.
81. *vagabunda* Knab.	*Circulfer tenellus* (Baker)	U.S.A.	Dorst, 1938
UNKNOWN PIPUNCULIDS			
	i) *Ballana* sp (Deltocepholini)	U.S.A.	Hardy, 1943
	ii) *Opsius stactogalus* Fieber (Deltocephalini)	Italy	Vidano, 1962
	iii) *Athysanella altenuata* Becker (Deltocephalini)	U.S.A.	Blocker, 1967
	iv) *Athysanella emarginata* (Osborn) ; *Exitianus exitiosus* (Uhler);*Flexamia atlantica* (De Long) ; *Graminella mohri* De Long;*Laevicephalus parvulus* (Gillette);*Mocuelus collinus* (Boheman) (Deltocephalini)	U.S.A.	Blocker *et al*, 1972
	v) *Aceratagallia* sp (Cicadellidae: Agallinae) *Agallia constrieta* (Agallinae)	U.S A. U S.A.	Pierce, 1972 Freytag, 1985
	vi) *Hecalus* sp	Thailand U.S.A.	Waloff, 1975 Baldridge & Blocker, 1980
	vii) *Macosteles quadrilineatus* (Forbes)	U.S.A.	Baldridge & Blocker,

	(Deltocephalinae:Macrostelini)		1980
viii)	*Athysanella argenteola* (Uhler); *A. redacta* Blocker; *A.* sp; *Chlorotettix spatulatus* (Osborn & Ball) ; *Flexamia picta* (Osborn); *Gilletiella atropuncta* (Gillette); *Laevicephalus* sp (Deltocephalini)	U.S.A.	Baldridge & Blocker 1980
ix)	*Amblysellus curtisi* (Fitch); *Endria inimica* (Say); *Latalus sayi* (Fitch); *Planicephalus flavicostus* (Stal.) *Psammotettix lividellus* (Zett.); *Striellus bicolor* (Van Duzee) (Deltocephalini); *Dikraneura* sp (Dikraneurini)	U.S.A.	Freytag, 1985

F=First record.

Bibliography

Aczel, M. 1939a. Das system der Family Dorylaidae. Zool. Anz., 125 : 15-23.

Aczel, M. 1939b. Die untergutting *Dorylomorpha* m. von. *Tomosvaryella* m. Zool Anz., 125 (3/4) : 49-69.

Aczel, M. 1939c. *Beckerias pannonicus*, eine neue Gattung Und Art des Dorylaiden (Dip.). Dorylaiden-studien III., Zool Anz.,126 (7/8):191-192.

Aczel, M. 1940. Vorarbeiten zu einer Monograpie der Dorylaiden. Dorylaiden studien V. Zool. Anz., 132 (7/8) : 149-169.

Aczel, M, 1943 Sammelereferat der bionomisch-olcologischen Litoerature uber Dorylaiden, Ferner uber die Morphologie der junngeren Entwickunstadien (Ei. larve, puparium). Dorylaiden studien VII Dt. ent. Zt., 2:1-27.

Aczel, M. 1944 Die Gattung *Tomosvaryella* Aczel (Dipt). Dorylaiden studnie V. Ann. Nat. Hist. Mus. Natl. Hung., 37 : 75-130.

Aczel, M. 1948. Grundlagen einer Monographie der Dorylaiden., Acta. Zool. Lilloana del Inst. Mequel Lillo., 6: 5-168.

Aczel, M. 1952. Catalogo de la famila Dorilaidae (Pipunculidae) de la Region Neotropical. Rev. Soc. Ent. Argentina, 15: 237-251.

Albrecht, A. 1979a. Description of 7 new *Dorylomorpha* species from Europe (Dip.:Pipunculidae). Entomol. Scand., 10 (3) : 211-218.

Albrecht, A. 1979b. *Dorylomorpha fennica* sp. n., a new pipunculid species (Diptera) from Finland. Notulae Entomol., 59: 15-17.

Anonymous. 1979. Annual report for the year 1977. Research Branch, Dept. Agri. Sarawak, 1979. VII+257 pp.

Anonymous, 1985. Rice pests, In Annual Report of Research Branch, Deptt. of Agriculture for the year 1983, Sarawak; Ministry of Agriculture & Community development (1985), pp 37-43.

Baldridge, R. S. and Blocker, H.D. 1980. Parasites of leafhoppers (Homoptera: Cicadellidae) from Kansas grasslands. J. Kansas Ent. Soc., 53 (2): 441-47.

Bankowska, R. 1972. A review of Polish species of the family Pipunculidae (Diptera). Fragm. Faun. (wars)., 18 (14) : 257-273.

Bankowska, R. 1973a. Muchowki-Diptera-Pipunculidae. Pol. Tow. Entomol. Klucze. Oznaczana Owadow Pol., 28 (33) : 1-49.

Bankowska, R. 1973b. Muchowki-Diptera (Dip: Pipunculidae) Klucze Oznaczana Owadaw Pol., 37 (33) : 2-52.

Banks, N. 1915. Notes and descriptions of Pipunculidae. Pysche, Boston, 22 (2) : 166-170.

Becker, T. 1884. Pipunculidae,characters of Egyptian species. Mt. Mus.Berlin, 2 : 93-98.

Becker, T. 1897, Dipterologische studien-IV. Berl. Ent. Zeitschr., 42 : 25-100

Becker, T. 1900. Dipterologische Studien-V. Pipunculidae.Berl. Ent.Zeitschr., 45 : 215-252.

Becker, T. 1907. Diptera:Brachycera. Berl. Ent. Zeit., 52 : 163.

Becker, T. 1908. The Dipteran due nova ex. Hungaria. Ann. Hist. Nat. Mus. Hung. Budapast, 6 : 320.

Becker, T 1910. Dipterologische Sammelrense nach Corsica. Berl. Ent. Zeit., 55 : 635.

Becker, T. 1914. The Dipteras nouveaux recoltes par m. ch. Alluand. et. Jeannel. en. Afrique orientale. Paris. Ann. Soc. Ent. Paris., 83 : 120-130.

Becker, T. 1915 Bemerkugen. Uber. einige. *Dorylas* (*Pipunculus*) Artn. Wien. Ent. Zeit., 34 : 63-64.

Becker, T. 1921. Neue Dipteran fleiner Sammlung. Pipunculidae. Wein. Ent. Zeit., 38 : 123-132.

Becker, T. 1924. H. Sauter's Formosa-Ausbeute. Pipunculidae (Dorylaidae Diptera). Ent. Mitt., 13 (1) : 4-18.

Blocker, H. D. 1967. Classification of the western hemispherl *Balclutha* (Homoptera:Cicadellidae). Pros. U.S. Natl. Mus., 122: 1-55.

Blocker, H. D., Harvey, T. L. and Lauchbaugh, J. L. 1972 Grassland leafhoppers. I. leafhopper populations of upland seeded pastures in Kansas. Ann. Entomol. Soc. Am., 65 : 166-172.

Boheman, C. H. 1855. Utrecklingen af *Pipunculus fuscipes*. Ofvers Vetensk Akad. Forhandl., 11 : 302-305.

Brooks, K. and Jagnes, H. E. 1941. Preliminary list of Pipunculidae of Iowa. Proc. Iowa. Acad. Sci., 48 : 437-445.

Brunetti, E. 1912. New Oriental Diptera. Rec. Indian Mus , 7 (5):445-513.

Brunetti, E. 1915. Diptera of Simla district. Rec. Indian Mus., VIII. 13 : 82.

Brunetti, E. 1922. A new Pipunculidae parasitic on leafhoppers in India. Bull. Ent. Res , 12 : 469.

Brunetti, E. 1923. Pipunculidae, Syrphidae, Conopidae, Oestridae. Fauna of British India., including Ceylon and Burma. Diptera. Taylor and Francis. London, 13 : 1-123.

Brunetti, E. 1927. J. fed. Malay St. Mus., 13 : 302.

Bull, R. M. 1973. A look at the biological control of the sugarcane leafhopper Cane grower's Quart. Bull , 37 (2) : 40-42.

Cammerson, H. D. 1974. The etymology of the name *Pipunculus* Latreille & *Dorilas* Meigen. (Dip.:Pipunculidae). Great Lakes Entomol., 7 (1):31-32.

Cantoreanu, M. 1971. Observations on the parasitism of Homoptera Cercetari asupra parasitiz mului Ia cicedine (Homoptera:Auchenorrhyncha) I'n usenl. de stintele natur. Bacau studisi comunican, pp. 49-55.

Chandra, G. 1978. Natural enemies of rice leafhoppers and planthoppers in the Philippines. Internatl Rice Res. Newsletter, 3 (5) : 20-21.

Chandra, G. 1979. Taxonomy and the bionomics of the insect parasites of rice leafhoppers and planthoppers in the Philippines and their importance in natural biological control. Phillip. Ent., 4 (3) : 119-39.

Chiu, S. S. 1977. Biological control of the brown planthopper, *Nilaparvata lugens*. Memeog., Brown Pl. Hopper Symp., IRRI, pp. 37.

Chu, Y. and Hirashima, Y. 1981. Survey of Taiwanese literature on natu al enemies of rice leafhoppers and planthoppers. Esakia, 16 : 33-38.

Coe, R L. 1966a. Handbook for the identification of British Insects (Dip. : Pipunculidae). R. Ent. Soc. London., 10 (2C) : 1-83.

Coe, R. L. 1966b. Some British species of *Chalarus* and *Verrallia* (Dip : Pipunculidae). Proc. R. Ent. Soc. London (B),35 (11-12):149-160.

Coe, R. L. 1967. Notes on British Pipunculidae (Dip.). Proc. R. Ent. Soc. London (B), 36 (11-12) : 181-182.

Coe, R. L. 1969. Some Pipunculidae (Dip.) from Southern Spain with description of a New species. Ent. Meddel., 37 (11) : 1-8.

Cole, F. R. 1969. The flies of western North America. University of California Press. California I-XI : 299-302.

Collin, J. E. 1920. The British species of *sylvaticus* group of *Pipunculus*. Ent. Mon. Mag., 56 : 270-275.

Collin, J. E. 1929. Empidae and Pipunculidae. Ins. of Samoa London. Brit. Mus. (Nat Hist) Pipunculidae, 6 : 177-189.

Collin, J. E. 1931a. Platypezidae, Pipunculidae. In Diptera of Patagonia and South Chile 6 (2) : 49-61.

Collin, J. E. 1931b. Die Ausbeute des deutschen Chaco Expedition 1925/26. Diptera XXIX. Pipunculidae. Konowia, 10 (3) : 171-176

Collin, J. E. 1931c. The British species of the genus *Verrallia* (Dip.). Ent. Mon. Mag., 67 : 234-236.

Collin, J. E. 1937. The British species of the *rufipes* group of Pipunculidae (Dip.). Ent. Mon. Mag , 73 : 209–218.

Collin, J. E. 1938. A new *Pipunculus* (Diptera) from Sicily. Proc. R. Ent. Soc. London (B), 7 (1) : 81-83.

Collin, J. E. 1941. Some Pipunculidae and Empididae from Ussuri region of far Eastern border of the USSR. Proc. R Ent. Soc. (B), 10 : 218-248.

Collin, J. E. 1945. Notes on some recent work on Pipunculidae. Ent. Mon. Mag., 81 (6) : 1-6.

Collin, J. E. 1956. Scandinavian Pipunculidae. Opusc Ent., 21 : 149-169.

Collin, J. E. 1958. Pipunculidae collected by Mr Ralph L. Coe in Jugoslavia in 1955, with description of two new species. Entomologist, 91 : 96-99.

Cresson, E. T. 1911. Studies in North American Dipterology. Pipunculidae. Trans. Amer. Ent. Soc , 36 : 291-329.

Cresson, E. T. 1912. Studies of some Pipunculidae from the Eastern United States. Ent. News, Philadelphia, 23 : 452-456.

Curran, C. H. 1927. Some new North American Diptera. Canad. Ent. Orillia., 59 : 290-303.

Curran, C.H. 1928a. Records and descriptions of Diptera mostly from Jamaica in Gowdey, C. C. Calatogus Insectorum Jamaicensis. Bull. Ent. Deptt. Agric. Jamaica., 4 : 36.

Curran, C. H. 1928b. New Diptera from Africa. Bull. Amer. Nat. Hist. Mus , 50 (1) : 15-23.

Curran, C. H. 1934. The Diptera of Kartabo, Bartica District, British Guiana, with description of new species. Bull. Amer. Nat. Hist Mus., 66 (3) : 287-532.

Curran, C.H. 1936. The templetan Crocker expedition to Western Polynesian and Melanesian Islands Proc. California Acad. Sci., 22 (4):1-66.

Czechowski, W., Garbarczyk, H., Pisarski, B. and Sowoniewicz, J. 1981. Species composition and origin of the fauna of Warsaw. Part-2. Memorabilia Zoologica, 35 : 170pp

Duda, O. 1940. Neue oder ungenugend bekannete Zweiflugler der Palearktischen Region. Folio Zool. Hydrobiol. Riga., 10 : 214-236.

Dorst, H E. 1938. Flea beetle injury to sugar beets in central Utah. J. Econ. Entomol., 31 : 455-456.

Enderlein, G. 1936. Zweifluger, Diptera in Brohmer, P. G. Ehrmann & G. ulmer : Die. Tierwelt Mitteleuropas 6, Insecten, 3 : 128-129.

Esaki, T. and Hashimato, S. 1936. Reports on leafhoppers injurious to rice plant and their natural enemies. Rep. Ent Lab. Deptt Agric. Ryushu Imp. Univ., 7 : 264.

Fallen, C F. 1810. Specimen entomologicum novam Dipterorum disponendi methodum exhibens, 10 : 26 pp.

Frey, R. 1932. Neue Diptera Brachycera aus Finnland und argrenzenden Landern. II Notnl. Ent., 12 : 81-85.

Freytag, P. H. 1985. The insect parasites of leafhoppers and related groups. In the leafhoppers and Planthoppers (edited by Nault, I.R.;Rodriguez, J. G.). New York U.S.A., 423-467 pp.

Giard, A. 1889. Sur la castration parasitiaire ous *Typhlocyba pernuna* larvid hymenopterae (*Aphelopus melaleucus* Dalm) at par une larva de Diptera (*Atelenevra spuria* Meig.). comptes Rendus Hebdomadaires de L. Academie Des. Seances. Paris, 109 : 708-710

Greathead, D. J. 1983. Natural enemies of *Nilaparvata lugens* and other leaf and planthoppers in Tropical Agroecosystem and their impact on pest population. Proc 1st. Int.Workshop on leafhoppers and planthoppers of economic importance. Commonw. Inst. Ent., Lond., pp. 371-83.

Hardy, D.E. 1939.New Nearctic Pipunculidae (Diptera) J. Kansas Ent. Soc , 12 (1) : 16–35.

Hardy, D. E. 1940. Dorylaidae Notes and descriptions (Dip:Pipunculidae). J. Kansas. Ent. Soc., 13 (4) : 101-114.

Hardy, D.E. 1943. A revision of Nearctic Dorylaidae. Univ. Kansas.Sc.Bull., 29 (1) : 1-231.

Hardy, D. E. 1946. Nomenclature notes on the fam. Dorilaidae. J. Kansas Ent. Soc., 19 (4) : 135-137,

Hardy, D.E. 1947. Notes and descriptions of Dorylaidae (Dip.:Pipunculidae). J. Kansas Ent. Soc., 20 (4) : 146-153.

Hardy, D. E. 1948a. Neotropical Dorylaidae (Pipunculidae) studies. Part I. (Dip.). Pysche, 55 (1) : 1-15.

Hardy, D.E. 1948b. Notes and descriptions of Dorylaidae Part II. (Dip.:Pipunculidae). J. Kansas. Ent. Soc., 21 (3) : 88-91.

Hardy, D. E. 1948c. New and little known Neotropical Dorylaidae (Dip.:Pipunculidae) J. Kansas. Ent. Soc., 21 (4) : 124-133.

Hardy, D. E. 1949a. New & little known Diptera from the California Academy of Science Collection,Rhagionidae and Dorylaidae. The Wasmann Coll., 7 (4) : 129-137.

Hardy, D. E. 1949b. New Dorilaidae from the Belgian Congo. Bull. Inst. Royal des. Sc. Nat. de. Belg., 25 (39) : 1-10.

Hardy, D.E. 1949c. The African Dorylaidae. Mem. Inst. Royal des. Sc. Nat. de Belg., 36 (2) : 1-90.

Hardy, D.E. 1950a. Neotropical Dorilaidae studies Part II. (Dip.:Pipunculidae). Rev. de. Ent., Rio. de Janeiro, 21 (3) : 433-448.

Hardy, D. E. 1950b. Dorilaidae (Pipunculidae). Expl. du. Parc. Nat. Albert Miss. G. F. de White, (1933-35). (Fasc-62) 53 pp.

Hardy, D.E. 1952a. Contribution a letude des Dipteres de I. Urundi III. Bibionidae et Dorilaidae. Bull. Inst. Royal des. Sc. Nat. de. Belg., 28 (55):1-20.

Hardy, D. E. 1952b. Bibionidae and Dorylaidae (Dip.) of Parc. National Upemba.Belg. Cogno.-Expl. du. Parc. Nat. Albert. Miss: G. F. de White, 64 : 57-70.

Hardy, D. E. 1952c. Bibionidae and Dorylaidae in the collection of the musee du Congo Belge.-Rev. Zool. Bot. Afr., 44 (1-2) : 159-167.

Hardy, D. E. 1952d. Notes on Shanon types of Dorylaidae from Argentina. Acta Zoologica Lilloana, 10 : 299-306.

Hardy, D. E. 1953. Studies in Hawaiian Dorylaidae. (Deptera). Part I. Proc. Haw. Ent. Soc., 15 (1) : 59-73.

Hardy, D. E. 1954a. Studies in new world Dorylaidae. (Dip. : Pipunculidae). J. Kansas. Ent. Soc., 27 (4) : 121-127.

Hardy, D. E. 1954b. Neotropical Dorilaidae studies Part III. Brazilian species and a key to the known species of *Dorilas* sens. lat. Bull. Mus. Noc. Rio. de Jenerio Zool., 123 : 1-60.

Hardy, D. E. 1955. Diptera, Bibionidae and Dorilaidae. Ann. Mus. Congo. Belge Sci. Zool., 36 : 283-286.

Hardy, D. E. 1956a. Insects of Micronesia. B P. Bishop Museum. Ins. Micronesia, 13 (1) : 1-9.

Hardy, D. E. 1956b. Pipunculidae from Commonwealth Institute of Entomology. Proc. R. Ent. Soc. London (B), 25 : 180-182.

Hardy, D. E. 1959a. Dorilaidae (Dip.:Cyclorrhapha). Addendum. Parc. Nat. Albert I. Miss. G.F. de White (1933-35) Fasc., 95 (2):27-29.

Hardy, D. E. 1959b. Diptera (Brachycera) Dorilaidae-Pipunculidae. South African Animal Life. Results of the Land University Exped. in 1950-51, 6 : 390-412.

Hardy, D. E. 1960. Diptera : Dorilaidae et Bibionidae. Ann. Mus. Congo Tervuren Zool, 81 : 394-400.

Hardy, D.E. 1961. Bibionidae (Dip.:Nematocera) and Dorilaidae from Congo (Pipunculidae:Dip.:Cyclorrhapha). Parc. Natl. de la Garamba Mission H. de Saeger, 24 (3) : 111-180.

Hardy, D. E. 1962a. Notes and descriptions of Pipunculidae from the Natal. Museum South Africa. Annls of the Natal Mus., 15 (2) : 255-266.

Hardy, D. E. 1962b. Preliminary studies on the Pipunculidae of Madagascar. Varhade Naturf Ges Basel., 73 (2) : 241-269.

Hardy, D. E. 1962c. Studies in Pipunculidae (Diptera) of Colombia. Proc. Haw. Ent. Soc., 18 (2) : 259-266.

Hardy, D. E. 1964a. Diptera-Cyclorrhapha, series Aschiza. fam Lonchoptridae, Phoridae, Pipunculidae. and Syrphidae. Univ. Hawaii press, Honolulu. 11 : 458 pp.

Hardy, D. E. 1964b. A restudy of the Perkins types of Australian pipunculidae (Diptera) and the type of *Pipunculus vitiensis* Muir from Fiji. Aust, J. Zool., 12 (1) : 84-125.

Hardy, D. E. 1964c. Pipunculidae. Insects Hawaii, 11 : 302-379.

Hardy, D. E. 1965a. Neotropical Pipunculidae (Diptera) studies. part IV. Further study of Brazilian species. Arg. de Zool. Est. Sao. Paulo., 14 (1) : 1-68.

Hardy, D. E. 1965. The Pipunculidae of Argentina. De. Acta. Zoologica Lillona, 19 : 187-241.

Hardy, D. E. 1966a. A catalogue of the Diptera of the America south of the United States. Fam Pipunculidae, Syrphidae, Conopidae. Departmento De. Zoologia Secretaria De Agriculture Sao Paulo, 45 : 1-15.

Hardy, D. E. 1966b. Diptera from Nepal. Pipunculidae (Dorylaidae). Bull. Brit. Mus. (N.H.) Ent., 17 (10) : 439-49.

Hardy, D. E. 1967. Redescription of *Tomosvaryella frontata* (Dip:Pipunculidae). Ann. Ent. Soc. Amer., 60 : 116-118.

Hardy, D. E. 1968. Bibionidae and Pipunculidae of Philippines and Bismark Islands. Ent. Meddel., 36 : 417-507.

Hardy, D. E. 1971. Pipunculidae (Diptera) parasitic on rice leafhoppers in the Oriental region. Proc. Hawaii Entomol. Soc., 21 (1) : 79-91.

Hardy, D. E. 1972a. Pipunculidae-Diptera of the 1934 Swedish expedition to Burma. Zool. Scr., 1 (3/4) 121-138.

Hardy, D. E. 1972b. Studies on Oriental Pipunculidae (Diptera). Oriental Insect Supplement, nr-2 : 1-76.

Hardy, D. E. 1975. Family Pipunculidae. In : A catalogue of Diptera of the Oriental Region II. Delfinado, M. D. & D.E. Hardy eds. Hawaii Univ. Press, 296-306.

Hardy, D. E. 1980. Fam. Pipunculidae. In : Catalogue of the Diptera of Afrotropical region. Publication Br. Mus. Nat. Hist. nr-821, 37 :483-487.

Hardy, D. E., Knowlton. G. F. 1939a New and little known Pipunculidae (Diptera.) Canad. Ent , 71 : 87-91.

Hardy, D. E., Knowlton, G. F. 1939b. New & little known Western Pipunculidae (Diptera). Ann. Ent. Soc. Amer. Colombus, 32 : 113-124.

Hirashima, Y., Aizawar, K., Mirua T. and Wonsiri. T. 1979. Field studies on the biological control of leafhoppers (Hemiptera : Homoptera) injurious to rice plants in S. E. Asia. Prog. report for the year 1977. Esakia, 13 : 1-20.

Hough, G, 1899. Pipunculidae of North America. Proc. Bost. Soc. Nat. Hist., 29 : 77-86.

Hsich, C. A. 1975. Seasonal population fluctuations of green rice leafhoppers and its natural enemies. Rice. Ent. Newsletter, 3 : 29-30.

Huq, S. 1984. Breeding methods for Pipunculidae (Diptera) endoparsites of leafhoppers. Int. Rice Res. Newsletter, 9 (4) : 14-15.

Huq. S. 1985. On *Eudorylas subterminalis* Collin (Dipt. ; Pip.) as a parasite of Cicadellidae (Homo.) in West Berlin. Anzeiger fur Schadlingskunde, pflanzenschutz, Umwetschutz, 58 (8) : 147-149.

Hurting, W. F. and Severin, H.H.P. 1915 Natural enemies of the sugar beet leafhoppers in California. Mon. Bull. Calif. Comm. Hort., 3:277-279.

Jenkinson, F. 1903. *Verrallia aucta* and its host. Ent. Mon. Mag., 39 : 222-223.

Jervis M. A. 1980a. Life history studies on *Aphelopus* sp. (Hym :Dryinidae) and *Chalarus* sp. (Dip.:Pipunculidae), the primary parasites of typhlocybine leafhoppers (Homoptera : Cicadellidae). J. Natural History, 14 (6) : 769-780.

Jervis, M. A. 1980b. Studies on oviposition behaviour and larval development in species of *Chalarus* (Dip:Pip.), parasites of typhlocybine leafhoppers (Homoptera : Cicadellidae). J. Nat. Hist., 14 (6):759-768.

Jervis, M. A. 1980c. Ecological studies on the parasite complex associated with typhlocybine leafhoppers (Homoptera : Cicadellidae). Ecological Entomology, 5 : 123-136.

Jervis, M. A. 1986. Two new species of *Chalarus* Walker (Diptera : Pipunculidae) from Burma. Mitt. Schweiz Entomol. Ges., 58 (3-4) : 435-440.

Johanneson, D. A. 1884. Two new species of family Pipunculidae (Diptera). Ent. News, Philadelphia, 14:107-108.

Johnson, C.W. 1915. A new species of the genus *Nephrocerus*. Canad. Ent., 47 : 54-56.

Johnson, C. W. 1919. A revised list of the Diptera of Jamaica. Bull. Amer. Mus. Nat. Hist., 41 (8) : 421-449.

Kaloostian, C. H. and H. D. Pierce. 1972. Notes on *S. nitridus* on citrus in California. J. Econ Entomol., 65 (3) : 880.

Kapoor, V. C., Agarwal, M L. and Grewal, J S. 1977. Two new species of Pipunculidae (Diptera : Pipunculidae) from Ranikhet, Kumaon hills, India. Bull. Ent., 18 : 74-77.

Kathirithamby, J. 1974. Genital abnormalities in adult Cicadellidae (Homoptera). Ent. Mon. Mag., 110 : 193-302.

Kathirithamby, J. 1978. Studies of the *Nephotettix* spp. (Cicadellidae : Homoptera) in the Krain District, Peninsular Malayasia Malays. Agric. J., 51 (3) : 273-279.

Kathirithamby, J. 1980 Common Auchenorrhyncha (Homoptera) in the rice fields in South-East Asia Bull. Min. Agr Malaysia, 155 : 1-36.

Keilin, D. and Thompson, W. R. 1915. Sur le cycle evolutif des Pipunculidae (Diptera), parasites intracoelomique des typhlocybes (Homoptera). Comptes Rendus des Seances de la Societie de Biologie et ses Filiales, Paris, 78 : 83-87.

Kertesz, K. 1900. Bemerkungan Liber Pipunculiden (Dip.). Wien. Ent.Zeitg., 19 : 244-245.

Kertesz, K. 1903. Die gattung *Pipunculus*-Arten sud Asiens. Ann. Hist. Nat. Mus., Natl. Hung., 1 : 465-471.

Kertesz, K. 1907. Vier neue *Pipunculus* Arten. Ann. Hist. Nat. Mus. Natl. Hung. Budapest., 5 : 579-583.

Kertesz, K. 1910. Catalogus Dipterorum (Conopidae, Oesteridae, Platypezidae, Pipunculidae, Syrphidae), 7 : 1-458. Budapest.

Kertesz, K. 1912. Sauter's Formosa-Ausbeute Dorylaidae (Diptera). Ann. Hist. Nat. Mus. Natl., Hung., 10 : 285-299.

Kertesz, K. 1915. Contribution to the knowledge of Dorylaidae. Ann. Mus. Nat. Hung., 13 : 386-392.

Knab, F. 1915. Two new species of *Pipunculus* from Washington, D. C. Proc. Biol Soc. Wash., 28 : 83-85.

Knowlton, G. F. 1937. The beet leafhoppers in northern Utah. Bull. Utah. Agric. Exp. Stat , 24 : 1-16.

Koizumi, K. 1959. On four Dorylaidae parasites of green rice leafhopper

Nephotettix cincticeps Uhler (Diptera). Scient. Rep. Fac. Agric. Okayama Univ., 13 : 37-45.

Koizumi, K. 1960. A new Dorylaid parasite of Zigzag striped leafhopper *Inazuma dorsalis* and notes on other paddy field inhabiting Dorilaidae. Sci. Rep. Fac. Agric. Okayama Uuiv., 16 : 33-42.

Kowarz, G. 1887. Beitrage Zu einem Verzeichnsse der Dipteren Bohmens 6. Conopidae, Pipunculidae. Wien. Ent. Zertg., 6 : 146-154.

Kozanek, M. 1981a. Genus *Pipunculus* (Dip. : Pip.) in Czechoslovakia. Ann Zool. Bot., 142 : 1-16.

Kozanek, M. 1981b.Description of *Pipunculus lichtwardti* new sp. (Dip.:Pip.) and redescription of *P. omissinervis*. Biologia. (Bratisl), 36 (8):605-610.

Kozanek, M. 1981c. The genus *Nephrocerus* (Dip..Pip.) in Czechoslovakia. Biologia (Bratisl), 36 (5) : 395-396.

Lamb, C. G. 1922. Diptera, Asilidae, Scenopinidae, Dolichopodidae,Pipunculidae, Syrphidae. Trans. Lin. Soc. Lond., 18 (1) : 36-416. Pipunculidae 372-78.

Latreille, P. A. 1802. Histoire naturelle generale et Particuliere des crustaces et des Inscctes. 3 : 1-468.

Lauterer, P. 1981. Contribution to the knowledge of family Pipunculidae of Czechoslovakia. Acta Mus. Morav. Sci. Nat., 66 : 123-150.

Lindberg, H. 1946. Die Biologie von *Pipunculus chlorionae* Frey and die Einwirkung von dessen parasitismus auf Chloriona-Arten. Acta Zool. Fenn., 45 ; 1-50.

Liu, K. S. 1974. Notes on some natural enemies of *N. cincticeps* and *N. lugens* in Taiwan. J. Taiwan. Agric. Res., 23 (2) : 91-115.

Linnane, J. P. and E. A. Osgood. 1978. *Verrallia virginica* reared from Saratoga spittlebug in Maine Proc. Ent. Soc. Wash., 79 : 622-623.

Loew, H. 1841. Horae anatomicae Enotmetonien. 1 (1/3):1-126. Posen.

Loëw, H. 1865. Diptera Americae septentrionalis indigena Centuria sexta. Berl. Ent. Zeitschr., 9 . 127-176.

Loew, H. 1872. Diptera Americae septentrionalis indigena Centuria sexta. Berli. Ent. Zeischr., 16 : 49-124.

Lundbeck, W. 1922. Diptera Danica. Part IV: Pipunculidae, Phoridae. Copenhagen., pp 447.

Lyenborg, L. 1975. Notes on Danish Pipunculidae (Dip. : Pip.). Ent. Medd., 43 (3) : 136.

Macquart, J. 1834. Recueil des trauaux de la societa d'amateurs des Sciences de l' Agriculture et das Arts de Litte. Insectas du Nord de France (1830) : 356.

Malloch, J.R. 1912. Three new spp of Pipunculidae (Dip.)from Panama, Washington, D. C. Smithsonian Inst. Misc.Collect., 60 (1):1-4, pb nr-2141.

Malloch, J. R. 1913. New American Dipterous insects of the fam. Pipuuculidae. Proc. U. S. N. M., 43 : 291.

May, Y. Y. 1979. The biology of *Cephalops curtifrons* (Dip:Pipunculidae), an endoparsitoid of *Stenocranus minutes* (Homoptera : Delphacidae). Zool. J. Linn. Soc., 36 (1) : pp. 40.

McAlpine, J. F. Peterson, B. V., Shewell, G. E., Teskey, H. J., Vockeroth, J. R. and Wood, D.M. 1981. Mannual of Nearctic Diptera, Vol. 1., 641 pp.

McLean, I.F.G. 1979. Notes on Diptera taken in 1976.Entomol. Rec. J. Var., 9 (2-3) : 71-72.

Meigen, J. W. 1800, Nouvelle classification des mouches a deux arten (Diptera) dapres un plan. tout Nouveau. pp. 40.

Meigen, J. W. 1803. Versuch einer neuen Gattungs Eintheilung des europiischen Zweflugeligen Insekten. Mag. Insectktenk., 2 : 259-86.

Meijere, J. C. H. de. 1907. Studien uber sudostasiatische Dipteren-1. Tijds. Ent., 50 : 259-64.

Meijere, J. C. H. de. 1914. Studien uber sudostasiatische Dipteren-8. Tijds. Ent., 56 : 167-178.

Meyer, M. de. and Brune, L. de 1984. On the phenology of Pipunculidae (Diptera) in Belgium. Bull. et Annals de la Societs Royale Belge de Entomologie, 20 (4/6) : 123-131.

Mik, J. 1899. *Verrallia* gen. nov. Pipunculidarum (Dip.). Wien Ent. Zeitg., 18 : 133-137.

Mityaev, I. D. 1983. Pathological variability in Cicadas. Izv. Akad. Nauk. Kaz. SSR SER, Biol., 6 : 18-23.

Morcos, G. 1953. The biology of some Hemiptera-Homoptera (Auchenorrhyncha). Bull. Soc. Fouad. I. Ent., 37 : 405-439.

Muir, F. 1918. Pipunculidae and Stylopidae in Homoptera. Ent. Mon. Mag., 54 : 137.

Muir, F. 1921. The sugarcane leafhopper and its parasites in Hawaii. Hawaii Plant Res., 25 (2) : 108-23.

Otake, A., P. H. Somasundram and M. B. Abeykoon. 1976. Studies on Population of *Sogatella furcifera* Horwath and *Nilaparvata lugens* Stal. (Hemiptera:Delphacidae) and their parasites in Sri Lanka. App. Ent. Zool., 11 (3) : 284-94.

Parker, H. L. 1967. Notes on biology of *T. frontata*, a parasite of leafhoppers. Ann. Ent. Soc. Amer., 60 (2) : 292-95.

Perkins, R. C. L. 1903. The leafhopper of the sugarcane. Bull. Board Agric. Forestry, Hawaii, 1 : 23-24.

Perkins, R.C.L 1905. Leafhoppers and their natural enemies. Pt. 4. Pipunculidae Bull. Div. Ent. Hawaiian Sug. Plrs. Ass. Exp. Stn , 1 (4):123-157.

Perkins, R. C. L. 1906. Leafhoppers and their natural enemies. Pt-10. Dryinidae, Pipunculidae Supplement. Bull. Div. Ent. Hawaiian Sug. Plrs. Assoc. Expt Stat., 1 (10) : 481-499.

Perkins, R. C. L. 1910. Supplement to Diptera. Bull. Div. Ent. Hawaiian Sug. Plrs. Assoc. Expt. Stat., 6 (10) : 697-700.

Penar, N. and Shepard, M. 1986. Seasonal incidence of parasitism of brown planthoppers, *Nilaparvata lugens* (Homoptera : Delphacidae), green planthopper, *Nephotettix* spp and whitebacked planthoppers, *Sogatella furcifera* (Homoptera:Cicadellidae) in Loguna province Philippines. Env. Ent., 15 (2) : 263-267.

Pierce, H.D. 1971 (Pubd. 1972). *Scahytoplus nitridus* (Hemiptera,Homoptera: Cicadellidae) parasitizing by *T. appendipes* (Diptera:Pipunculidae). Environ. Ent , 1 (6) : 796-797.

Rald, E. 1977. New and rare Diptera Brachycera from Denmark. Entomol. Medd., 44 (1) : 23-27, 1976.

Rald, E. 1979. Diptera from the island of Laeso II. (Brachycera : Aschiza). Entomol. Medd., 46 (2) : 40-55.

Ramane, Reihard, & K. Schulz. 1973. Disturbances in the formation of the ectodermal female genital armature in relation to parasitic castration in cicada of the genus *Jassargus* (Homopt:Cicadellidae). Z. Wiss. Zool.,186 (½) : 108-117.

Rapp, W. F. 1943. Some new North American Pipunculidae (Diptera). Ent. News, Philadelphia, 54 : 222-24.

Rapp, W. F. 1944. Pipunculidae of New Jersey. Bull. Brooklyn Ent. Soc., 39 : 65-70.

Rapp, W. F. 1945. Types of genera and subgenera of Pipunculidae (Diptera). Canad. Ent., 77 : 209-210.

Rapp, W.F., and Cooper, J. L. 1943. Preliminary catalogue of African Pipunculidae. Ann Mag. Nat. Hist., 12 (11) : 128-129.

Rondani, C. 1856. Genera Italica ordines dipterorum ordinatim disposita et distincta et in familias et stirpes aggregata. Dipterologiae Italica Prodromus, 1 : 1-228, Parmae.

Rothschild, G. H. L. 1964. The biology of *P. semifumosus* (Kowarz) (Dipt: Pip.) with observations on the effects of parasitism on the host. Parasitology, 54 : 763-769.

Sack, P. 1935. Dorylaidae (Pipunculidae). In Lindner Die Fliegen des Palaearktischen Region. 4 (4) : 1-57.

Shannon, R C. 1927. Some new Diptera from Argentina. Rev. Soc. Ent Arg., 1 (4) : 31-42.

Shatalkin, A.I. 1981. *Claraeola crassula* sp.n. (Pip.)and *Stronglyophthalmyia raricornis* sp. n. (Stronglyophthamyiidae), new peculiar Diptera from USSR. Zoologischeski Zl., 60 (5) : 791-793.

Shimada, K. 1972. On Dorilaid parasites of the green rice leafhopper. Proc. Assoc. Plant Protection of Kyushu, 18 : 41-43.

Speight, M. C. D. 1986. *Asafhidon curtum*, *Dorylomorpha maculata*, *Selatosomus melencholicus* & *Syntormon miki*, insects new to Ireland. Ir. Nat. J , 22 (1) : 20-23.

Stahl, C. F. 1920. Studies on the life history and habits of the beet leafhoppers. J. Agric. Res., 20 : 245-252.

Strobl. 1909. Die Diptera von Steiemark Nachtrag. Craz. Mitt. Natn Ver. Steimark, 45 : 45-293.

Stubbs, A.E. 1980. The largest Pipunculid in the land:*Nephrocerus scutellata* (Macquart, 1834) (Dip.:Pipunculidae) new to Britain, with observations on its behaviour in Greece. Proc. Trans. Br. Entomol. Natl. Hist. Soc., 13 (1-2) : 46-48.

Subramanian, T. V. 1922. Some natural enemies of mango leafhopper (*Ideocerus* sp) in India. Bull. Ent. Res., 12 : 465-467.

Thompson, W. R. 1951. Host parasite Catalogue. Commonwealth Institute of Biological Control Publ. Ontario, Canada, pp. 17-18.

Thompson, F.C. 1977. *Verrallia virginica* Banks,a valid species (Dipt.:Pipunculidae). Proc. Ent. Soc. Washingtion, 79 (4):624-625.

Tonnoir, A. L. 1925. Newzealand Pipuncu'idae (Diptera). Rec. Cantenbury. Mus., 2 : 313-316.

Ulmi, M. 1976. Morphological variability of a cicadellid injurious to forage grasses in high Piedomentese pastures by *Diplocolenus* (*Verdanus*) *abdominalıs* (F.). Frag. Ent., 12 (1) : 103-112.

Verrall, G. H. 1900. Catalogue of flies of European District with reference to synonymy (Platypezidae, Syrphidae, Pıpunculidae), 3 : 1-121.

Verrall, G.H. 1901. British flies of Platypezidae, Pipunculidae and Syrphidae, 3 : 1-691.

Vidano, C. 1966. Introduzione in Italia de *Polynema striaticorne* Girault parassita oofago di *Ceresa bubulus* Fabricius. Bull. Soc Entomol. Italiana, **46** : 55-58.

Wahlgren, E. 1910. Svensk insekt Fauna (Swedish insect fauna) Diptera II. Cyclorrhapha, Aschiza (Pipunculidae,Phoridae,Platypezidae). Tijds. Ent., 31 : 209-235.

Walker, F. 1834. Some observations on the British species of Pipunculidae. Ent. Mag., 2 : 262-270.

Waloff, N. 1975. The parasitoids of the nymphal and adult stages of leafhoppers (Auchenorrhyncha:Homoptera) of acidic grassland. Trans. R. Entomol. Soc. London, 126 (4) : 637-686.

Waloff, N. 1980. Studies on grassland leafhoppers (Auchenorrhyncha:Homoptera) and their natural enemies. Advances in Ecological Research, 11 : 81-216.

Waloff, N. and P. Thompson. 1980. Census data of populations of some leafhoppers (Auchenorrhyncha:Homoptera) of acidic grasslands. J. Animal Ecol., 49 (2) : 395-416.

Wan, M. T. K. 1972. Observations on rice leaf and planthopper in Sarawak (Malaysian Borneo). Malays. Agric. J., 48 (4):308-335.

Whittaker, J. B. 1969. The biology of Pipunculidae (Diptera) parasitizing some British Cercopidae (Homoptera). Proc. Roy. Ent. Soc. Lond., Sr. A. 44 (1-3) : 13-24.

Williams, F. X. 1918 (Pubd. 1919) Some observations of *Pipunculus*, a fly which parasitizes the cane leafhopper at Pahala, Hawaii. Hawaiian Planter's Record, 19 (3) : 189-92.

Williams, F. X. and Sweezy. 1905. Leafhoppers and their natural enemies. Haw. Sugar Planters Assoc Expt. Sta. Bull., 1 (4) : 123-157.

Williams, J. R. 1957. The sugarcane Delphacidae and their natural enemies in Mauritius. Trans. Roy. Ent. Soc. Lond., 109 : 65-110.

William, S. W. 1983. In Riley, C. W. Report on a small collection of insects made during the death valley Expedition. North Amrican Fauna, 7:255.

Wilson, S. W. and J. E. Mcphenson. 1981. Life history of *Megamelus davisi* von R. with descriptions of immature stages. Ann. Ent. Soc. Am.,74 (4): 345-350.

Yang, S. L. and Y. S. Pan. 1979. Ecology of *Matsumuratettix hiroglyphicus* (Matsumura), an insect vector of sugarcane white leaf disease. In: Proc. of the R. O. C. United states cooperative Sci. Seminar on Mycoplasma disease of plants (Ed. Su, H. T., McCoy, P. E.). Taipei, Taiwan. National Sci. Council, pp. 111-117.

Yano, K. 1979. Faunal and biological studies on the insects of paddy fields in Asia. II. Esakia, 13 : 45-54.

Yano, K., Ishtani, M., Aisa, I.and Satoh, M. 1984. Faunal & biological studies on the insect of paddy fields in Asia. XIII. Pipunculidae from Japan (Diptera). Transactions of the Shikoku Ent. Soc., 16 (4) : 55-74.

Yano, K., Morokote. R , Satoh, M., & Asai, I. 1985. An evidence for behavioural change in *N. cincticeps* (Hemiptera:Deltocephalinae) parasitized by pipunculid flies. Appl. Entomol. Zool., 20 (1) : 94-96.

Zetterstedt, J. W. 1838. Insect Lapponica, 8 : pp 578.

Zetterstedt, J. W. 1849. Diptera Scandinavia, 8 : 1-320

Explanation To Figures

Fig. 1. Leafhopper nymph with pipunculid larva in its abdomen.

Fig. 2. Pipunculid larva protruding out of host's abdomen.

Fig. 3. A. Male fly in general; B. Head of Male; C. Abdomen of male; D. Female fly in general; E. Head of female; F. Abdomen of female; At. Antenna; CE. Compound eyes; MA. Membranous area; OC. Ocelli; OP. Occiput.

Fig. 4. Different parts of fly in general. A. Wing; B. Antenna; C. Terminal portion of female abdomen with ovipositor; D. Leg; E. Claspers (d v.); F. Aedeagal basal plates with aedeagus and ejaculatory apodeme; Ab. Aedeagal basal plates; Ae. Aedeagus; Ar Arista; Au. Auxillary plates; Bp Basiphallus; CC. Costal cell; Ce Cerci; Cl. Claw; Co. Coxa; DC Discal cell; Dp. Distiphallus; Ea. Ejaculatory apodeme; Em. Empodium; Fe. Femur; Pl Pulvilli; Pr. Piercer; Su. Surstylus; T. Tibia; Ti. Tarsi; Tr. Trochanter; Un. Unguitractor.

Fig. 5. *Tomosvaryella baderiensis* sp n —A. Wing; B. Antenna; C. Male terminalia (d.v.); D. Claspers (d.v.); E. Claspers (v.v.); F. Claspers (l.v.); G Aedeagal basal plates with aedeagus; H Ovipositor.

Fig. 6. *Tomosvaryella equistylis* sp.n.—A. Wing; B. Antenna; C. Claspers (d.v.); D. Claspers (l.v.); E Aedeagal basal plates with aedeagus.

Fig. 7. *Tomosvaryella guwahatiensis* sp n.—A. Wing; B. Antenna; C. Claspers (d.v); D. Claspers (v v); E. Claspers (l.v.); F. Aedeagal basal plastes with aedeagus and ejaculatory apodeme.

Fig. 8. *Tomosvaryella multisetae* sp.n.—A Wing; B Antenna; C. Hind trochanter; D. 1st abdominal segment; E. Male terminalia (d v.); F. Aedeagal basal plates with aedeagus and ejaculatory apodeme; G 9th tergum with claspers (d.v.); H. Ovipositor.

Fig. 9. *Tomosvaryella troangulatus* sp n.—A. Wing; B. Antenna; C. Hind trochanter; D. Male terminalia (d v.); E. Claspers (d.v.); F. 9th tergum with claspers (l.v.); G. Aedeagal basal plates with aedeagus and ejaculatory apodeme; H. Hind trochanter of female; I. Ovipositor.

Fig. 10. *Tomosvaryella coquilletti* Hardy.—A. Wing; B. Antenna; C. Hind trochanter; D. Male terminalia (d.v.); E. Male terminalia (l.v.); F. 9th segment with Claspers (d.v.); G Ovipositor.

Fig. 11. *Tomosvaryella curvipatis* sp.n.—A. Wing; B. Hind tibia; C. Male terminalia (d.v.); D. Claspers (d.v.); E. Aedeagal basal plates with aedeagus and ejaculatory apodeme.

Fig. 12. *Tomosvaryella dehraduniensis* sp.n.—A. Wing; B. Antenna; C. Claspers (d.v.); D. Claspers (v.v.); E. Claspers (l.v.); F. Aedeagal basal plates with aedeagus; G. Ovipositor.

Fig. 13. *Tomosvaryella denticulatus* sp.n.—A. Wing; B. Antenna; C. Hind trochanter; D. Male terminalia (d.v.); E. 9th tergum with claspers (d.v.); F. Same in v.v.; G. Aedeagal basal plates with aedeagus and ejaculatory apodeme; H. Ovipositor,

Fig. 14. *Tomosvaryella epichalca* Perkins.—A Wing; B Antenna; C. Male terminalia (d.v.); D. Claspers (d.v.); E. 9th segment with claspers (v.v.); F. Same in l.v.; G. Aedeagal basal plates with aedeagus and ejaculatory apodeme; H. Ovipositor.

Fig. 15. *Tomosvaryella eusylvatica* sp.n.—A. Wing; B. Hind trochanter; C. Male terminalia (d.v.); D. 9th segment with claspers (d.v.); E. Same in l.v.

Fig. 16, *Tomosvaryella genitalis* sp.n.—A. Wing; B. Antenna; C. 9th tergum with claspers (d.v.); D. Same in v.v.; E. Aedeagal basal plates with aedeagus and ejaculatory apodeme; F. Ovipositor.

Fig. 17. *Tomosvaryella indica* sp.n.—A. Wing; B. Antenna; C. Male terminalia (d.v.); D. Claspers (d.v.);E. 9th tergum with claspers (v.v.); F. Same in l.v.; G. Aedeagal basal plates with aedeagus and ejaculatory apodeme; H. Hind trochanter of female; I. Ovipositor.

Fig. 18. *Tomosvaryella kashipuriensis* sp.n.—A. Wing; B. Antenna; C. Male termimalia (d.v.); D. 9th tergum with claspers (d v.); E. Same in v.v.; F. Same in l.v.; G. Aedeagal basal plates with aedeagus; H. Ovipositor.

Fig. 19. *Tomosvaryella limpidipennis* (Brunetti).—A. 9th segment with claspers (d.v.).

Fig. 20 *Tomosvaryella longipygiamis* sp.n.—A. Wing; B. Antenna; C. Male terminalia (v.v.); D. Claspers (d.v.); E. 9th segment with claspers (l.v.); F. Aedeagal basal plates with aedeagus and ejaculatory apodeme.

Eig. 21. *Tomosvaryella minutus* sp.n.—A. Wing; B. Antenna; C. Claspers (d.v.); D. 9th segment with claspers (v.v.); E. Aedeagal basal plates; F. Ovipositor.

Fig. 22. *Tomosvaryella nitens* (Brunetti)—A. Wing; B. Hind trochanter; C. Male terminalia (d.v.); D. 9th segment with claspers (d.v.).

Fig. 23. *Tomosvaryella oryzaetora* Koizumi.—A. Wing; B. Antenna; C. Ovipositor.

Fig. 24 *Tomosvaryella ramnagariensis* sp.n —A. Wing; B. Male antenna; C. Hind trochanter; D. Claspers (d.v.); E. Claspers (v.v.); F. Aedeagal basal plates with aedeagus and ejaculatory apodeme; G. Female antenna; H. Ovipositor.

Fig. 25. *Tomosvaryella robusta* Hardy.—A. Wing; B. Ovipositor.

Fig. 26. *Tomosvaryella subhectena* sp n.—A. Wing; B. Antenna; C. Claspers (d v.); D. Aedeagal basal plates with ejaculatory apodeme.

Fig. 27. *Tomosvaryella subrobusta* sp.n.—A. Wing; B. Antenna; C. Male terminalia (d.v.); D. 9th segment with claspers (d v.); E. Same in v.v.; F. Same in l.v.; G. Aedeagal basal plates with aedeagus.

Fig. 28. *Tomosvaryella subvirescens* Loew—A. Wing; B Antenna; C. Hind trochanter; D. Male terminalia (d.v.); E 9th tergum with claspers (d.v.); F. Left and right claspers; G. Aedeagal basal plates with aedeagus and ejacutatory apodeme; H. Hind trochanter of female; I. Ovipositor.

Fig. 29. *Tomosvaryella surstylae* sp.n.—A. Wing; B. Antenna; C. Male terminalia (d.v.); D. 9th segment with claspers (d.v); E. Claspers (v v.); F. Claspers (l.v.); G. Left & right claspers; H. Aedeagal basal plates with aedeagus; I. Ovipositor.

Fig. 30. *Tomosvaryella sylvatica* (Meigen).—A. Wing; B Antenna; C. Hind trochanter;D. Male terminalia (d.v.);E. Claspers (d.v);F. 9th tergum with claspers (l.v.); G. 9th tergum with claspers (v.v); H. Aedeagal basal plates with aedeagus; I. Ovipositor.

Fig. 31. *Tomosvaryella tattapaniensis* sp.n.—A. Wing; B. Antenna; C. Hind trochanter; D. 9th tergum with claspers (d.v.); E. Same in v.v.; F. Same in l.v.; G. Aedeagal basal plates with aedeagus; H. Ovipositor.

Fig. 32. *Tomosvaryella longistylus* sp.n.—A. Wing;B. Antenna;C. Ovipositor.

Fig. 33. *Dorylomorpha* (*Claraeomorpha*) *appendiculata* sp.n.—A. Wing; B.

Antenna; C. 9th tergum with surstyli (d.v.); D. Aedeagus, phallotheca & ejaculatory apodeme; E. Ejaculatory apodeme and aedeagus (l.v.); F. Surstyli (v.v.); G. Left surstylus (l.v.); H. Aedeagal guide.

Fig. 34. *Dorylomorpha* (*Dorylomorpha*) *abdochaetus* sp.n.—A. Wing; B. Antenna of male; C. Antenna of female; D. Hind trochanter of male; E. Male terminalia (d.v.); F. Male terminalia (v.v.); G. 9th segment with surstyli; H. Left surstylus (v.v.); I. Right surstylus (v v.); J. Same in l.v.; K. Left surstylus (l.v.); L. Aedeagus and ejaculatory apodeme; M. Ovipositor.

Fig. 35. *Dorylomorpha* (*Dorylomorpha*) *abdoflavus* sp.n.—A. Wing; B. Antenna; C. Hind trochanter; D. Male terminalia (d.v.); E. Surstyli (d.v.); F. Left surstylus (l.v.); G. Right surstylus (l.v.); H. Aedeagus, phallotheca and ejaculatory apodeme.

Fig. 36. *Dorylomorpha (Dorylomorpha) lini* Hardy —A. Wing; B. Antenna; C. Male terminalia (d.v.); D. 9th tergum with surstyli (d.v.); E. 9th tergum with surstyli and aedeagal guide (v.v.); F. Surstyli (v v.); G. Surstyli (d v.); H. Right surstylus (l.v.); I. Left surstylus (l v.); J. Aedeagus, phallotheca and ejaculatory apodeme; K. Ovipositor (l.v); L. Ovipositor showing its two parts.

Fig. 37. *Dorylomorpha* (*Dorylomorpha*) *pterae* Kapoor & Grewal.—A. Wing; B. Antenna; C. Trochanter; D. Male terminalia (d v.).

Fig. 38. *Eudorylas acroacanthus* Hardy —A. Wing;B. Antenna;C. Ovipositor.

Fig. 39. *Eudorylas albucus* Hardy.—A. Wing; B. Antenna; C Male terminalia (d.v); D. Same in v.v. showing claspers; E. Ovipositor.

Fig. 40. *Eudorylas antennalis* sp.n.—A. Wing; B. Antenna; C. Male terminalia (d.v); D. 9th tergum with surstyli (d v.); E. Surstyli; F. Aedeagus with ejaculatory apodeme; G. Aedeagal guide; H. Ovipositor.

Fig. 41. *Eudorylas bharatiensis* sp n.—A. Wing; B. Antenna; C. Male terminalia (d v); D. 9th tergum with surstyli (d.v.);E. Surstyli (l.v); F. Aedeagus with ejaculatory apodeme; G. Aedeagal guide.

Fig. 42. *Eudorylas bicostalis* sp.n.—A Wing; B. Trochanter; C. Male terminalia (d.v.); D. 9th tergum with surstyli (d.v.); E. Surstyli (l.v.); F. Aedeagus with ejaculatory apodeme; G. Aedeagal guide.

Fig. 43. *Eudorylas corbetti* sp n —A. Wing; B. Antenna; C. Male terminalia (d.v.); D. 9th tergum with surstyli (d.v.); E. Surstyli (l.v.); F. Aedeagus with ejaculatory apodeme; G. Aedeagal guide; H. Ovipositor.

Fig. 44. *Eudorylas dextrostylus* sp.n.—A. Wing; B. Antenna; C. Male terminalia (d.v.); D. Male terminalia (p.v.); E. 9th tergum with surstyli (d.v.); F. Surstyli (l.v.); G. Aedeagus with ejaculatory apodeme; H. Aedeagal guide.

Fig. 45. *Eudorylas euciliatus* sp.n.—A. Wing; B. Antenna of male; C. Male terminalia (d.v.); D. 9th tergum with surstyli (d.v.); E. Surstyli (l.v.); F. Aedeagus with ejaculatory apodeme; G. Aedeagal guide; H. Antenna of female; I. Ovipositor.

Fig. 46. *Eudorylas eulentiger* sp.n.—A. Wing; B. Antenna; C. Male terminalia (d v.); D. 9th tergum with surstyli (d.v.); E. Surstyli (l.v.); F. Basiphallus with ejaculatory apodeme; G. Aedeagal guide.

Fig. 47. *Eudorylas extensus* (Brunetti).—Wing.

Fig. 48. *Eudorylas filicornis* (Brunetti).—A. Male terminalia (d.v.); B. Male terminalia (v.v.) showing 9th tergum with surstyli (taken as such from Hardy, 1972).

Fig. 49. *Eudorylas garhwalensis* sp.n.—A. Wing; B. Antenna; C. 9th tergum with surstyli (d.v.); D. Surstyli (l.v); E. Aedeagus with ejaculatory apodeme; F. Aedeagal guide; G. Ovipositor.

Fig. 50. *Eudorylas indiaensis* sp n —A. Wing; B Antenna; C. Male terminalia (d.v.); D. 9th tergum with surstyli (d.v.); E. Surstyli (l.v.); F. Aedeagus; G. Aedeagal guide; H. Ovipositor.

Fig. 51. *Eudorylas jacksoni* sp n.—A. Wing;B. Antenna of male; C. 9th tergum with surstyli (d.v.); D. Surstyli (l v); E. Aedeagus with ejaculatory apodeme; F. Aedeagal guide; G. Antenna of female; H. Ovipositor.

Fig. 52. *Eudorylas javanensis* (de Meijere).—A. Antenna; B. Male terminalia (d.v.); C. Male terminalia (v.v.) showing claspers; D. Ovipositor.

Fig. 53. *Eudorylas khaziarensis* sp.n —A. Wing; B. Antenna; C. Surstyli (d v.); D. Surstyli (l.v.); E. Aedeagus with ejaculatory apodeme.

Fig. 54. *Eudorylas ludhianensis* sp.n.—A. Wing; B. Antenna; C. Male terminalia (d.v.); D. 9th tergum with surstyli (d.v.); E. Surstyli (l.v); F. Aedegaus with ejaculatory apodeme; G. Aedeagal guide.

Fig. 55. *Eudorylas macropygus* (de Meijere).—A. Wing; B. Antenna; C.

Male terminalia (d.v.); D. 9th tergum with surstyli (d.v.); E. Surstyli (l.v.); F. Aedeagus with ejaculatory apodeme; G. Aedeagal guide; H. Ovipositor.

Fig. 56. *Eudorylas major* (Brunetti).—Wing.

Fig. 57. *Eudorylas manaliensis* sp.n.—A. Wing; B. Antenna; C. Male terminalia (d.v.); D. 9th tergum with surstyli (d.v.); E. Surstyli (l.v.); F. Aedeagus with ejaculatory apodeme; G. Aedeagal guide.

Fig. 58. *Eudorylas minghlanii* sp.n.—A Wing; B. Antenna; C. Male terminalia (d.v.); D. 9th tergum with surstyli (d.v); E Surstyli (l.v.); F. Aedeagus with ejaculatory apodeme; G. Aedeagal guide.

Fig. 59. *Eudorylas mutillatus* (Loew) —A Wing; B. Antenna; C. Male terminalia (d.v.); D. 9th tergum with surstyli (d v); E. Surstyli (l.v.); F. Aedeagus with ejaculatory apodeme; G. Aedeagal guide; H. Ovipositor.

Fig. 60. *Eudorylas orientalis* Koizumi—A. Wing; B. Antenna; C. Male terminalia (d v); D. 9th tergum with surstyli (d.v.); E. Surstyli (l.v.); F. Aedeagus with ejaculatory apodeme; G. Aedeagal guide (l.v.); H. Aedeagal guide (d.v.); I. Ovipositor.

Fig 61. *Eudorylas pennatus* sp n.—A. Wing; B. Antenna; C. Male terminalia (d.v.); D. 9th tergum with surstyli (d.v); E. Surstyli (l v.); F. Aedeagus; G. Aedeagal guide; H. Ovipositor.

Fig. 62. *Eudorylas pinjorensis* sp.n.—A. Wing; B. Antenna; C. Male terminalia (d.v.); D. 9th tergum with surstyli (d.v.); E. Surstyli (l.v.); F. Aedeagus with ejaculatory apodeme; G. Aedeagal guide.

Fig. 63. *Eudorylas poantaensis* sp.n.—A. Wing; B. Antenna; C. 9th tergum with surstyli (d.v.); D. Surstyli (l.v.); E. Aedeagus with ejaculatory apodeme; F. Aedeagal guide.

Fig. 64. *Eudorylas roralis* (Kertesz).—A. Wing; B. Antenna; C. Male terminalia (d.v.); D. 9th tergum with surstyli (d.v.); E. Surstyli (l.v.); F. Aedeagus with ejaculatory apodeme; G. Aedeagal guide; H. Ovipositor.

Fig. 65. *Eudorylas scutellatus* sp.n.—A. Wing; B. Antenna; C. Male terminalia (d.v.); D. 9th tergum with surstyli (d.v.); E. Surstyli (l.v.); F. Aedeagus with ejaculatory apodeme; G. Aedeagal guide; H. Ovipositor.

183

Fig. 66. *Eudorylas thekkadiensis* sp.n.—A Wing; B. Antenna; C. Male terminalia (d.v.); D. 9th tergum with surstyli (d.v.); E. Surstyli (l.v.); F. Aedeagus with ejaculatory apodeme; G Aedeagal guide; H. Ovipositor.

Fig. 67. *Eudorylas tibiatus* sp n.—A. Wing; B. Antenna; C. Male terminalia (d.v.); D. 9th tergum with surstyli (d.v.); E. Surstyli (l.v.); F. Aedeagus with ejaculatory apodeme; G. Aedeagal guide.

Fig. 68. *Eudorylas tuberculatus* sp n.—A. Wing; B. Antenna; C. Ovipositor (d.v.); D. Ovipositor (l v.)

Fig 69 *Eudorylas uniformis* (Brunetti)—A. Wing; B. Antenna of male; C. Male terminalia (d.v.); D. 9th tergum with surstyli (d.v.); E. Surstyli (l.v.); F. Aedeagus with ejacultory apodeme; G. Cross section of vesica cup; H. Cross section of ejaculatory apodeme; I. Aedeagal guide; J. Antenna of female; K Ovipositor.

Fig. 70. *Pipunculus (Cephalops) chandiensis* sp.n.—A. Wing; B. Antenna; C. Hind femur; D. Male terminalia (d.v.); E. 9th tergum with surstyli (d v.); F. Surstyli (l.v.); G Aedeagus with ejaculatory apodeme; H. Aedeagal guide; I. Ovipositor.

Fig. 71. *Pipunculus (Cephalops) deminitens* Hardy.—A. Wing; B. Antenna of Male; C. 9th tergum with surstyli (d.v.); D. Surstyli (l.v.); E. Aedeagus with ejaculatory apodeme; F. Aedeagal guide; G. Antenna of female; H Ovipositor.

Fig. 72. *Pipunculus (Cephalops) eufraternus* sp.n.—A. Wing; B. Antenna; C. Male terminalia (d.v.); D. Male terminalia (l.v.); E. 9th tergum with surstyli (d.v.); F. Surstyli (l v.) G. Aedeagus with ejaculatory apodeme; H. Aedeagal guide; I Ovipositor.

Fig. 73. *Pipunculus (Cephalops) flavocinctus* Brunetti.-A. Wing; B. Antenna; C. Ovipositor (l.v.); D Ovipositor (d.v.).

Fig. 74. *Pipunculus (Cephalops) kashmirensis* sp n.—A. Wing; B. Antenna; C. 9th tergum with surstyli (d.v.); D. Surstyli (l.v.); E. Aedeagus with ejaculatory apodeme; F. Aedeagal guide.

Fig. 75. *Pipunculus (Cephalops) kumaonensis* sp.n.—A. Wing; B. Antenna; C. Male terminalia (d.v.); D. Male terminalia (l.v.); E. 9th tergum with surstyli (d v.); F. Surstyli (l.v.); G. Aedeagus with ejaculatory apodeme; H. Aedeagal guide; I. Ovipositor.

Fig. 76. *Pipunculus* (*Cephalops*) *kurseongiensis* sp.n.—A. Wing; B. Antenna; C. 9th tergum with surstyli (d.v.); D. Surstyli (l.v.); E. Aedeagus with ejaculatory apodeme; F. Aedeagal guide.

Fig. 77. *Pipunculus* (*Cephalops*) *mashobraensis* sp.n.—A. Wing; B. Antenna; C. Male terminalia (l.v.); D. 9th tergum with surstyli (d.v.); E. 9th tergum with right surstylus (l.v.); F. 9th tergum with left surstylus (l.v.); G. Aedeagus with ejaculatory apodeme; H. Aedeagal guide.

Fig. 78. *Pipunculus* (*Cephalops*) *palawanensis* Hardy.—A. Antenna of Male; B. Male terminalia (d.v.); C. Male terminalia (v.v.) showing surstyli; D. Ovipositor; E Antenna of female; F. Wing of female

Fig. 79. *Pipunculus (Cephalops) spenceri* Hardy.—A. Wing; B. Antenna; C. Male terminalia (d.v.); D. Male terminalia (p.v.); E. 9th tergum with surstyli (d.v.); F. Surstyli (l.v.); G. Aedeagus with ejaculatory apodeme; H. Aedeagal guide; I. Wing of female; J. Antenna of female; K. Ovipositor.

Fig. 80. *Pipunculus* (*Cephalops*) *subaeneus* Brunetti —A. Antenna; B. Male terminalia (d.v.); C. Male terminalia (v.v.) showing surstyli.

Fig. 81. *Pipunculus* (*Cephalops*) *subdolosus* sp.n.—A. Wing; B. Antenna; C. Male terminalia (d.v.); D. 9th tergum with surstyli (d.v.); E. Aedeagus with ejaculatory apodeme; F. Aedeagal guide; G. Ovipositor.

Fig. 82. *Pipunculus* (*Cephalops*) sp.nov. near *microdes* Perkins.—A. Wing; B. Antenna; C. Ovipositor.

Fig. 83. *Pipunculus* (*Cephalops*) sp.nov. near *philippinensis* Brunetti.—A. Wing; B Antenna; C. Ovipositor.

Fig. 84. *Pipunculus* (*Cephalosphaera*) *motichoorensis* sp.n.—A. Wing; B. Antenna; C. Ovipositor.

Fig. 85. *Pipunculus* (*Claraeosphaera*) *suranganiensis* Kapoor & Grewal.—A. Wing; B. Antenna; C. Hind trochanter; D. Ovipositor.

Fig. 86. *Chalarus spurius* (Fallen).—A. Wing; B. Antenna; C. Male terminalia (d.v.); D. 9th tergum with surstyli (d v.); E. Surstyli (l.v.); F. Aedeagus with ejaculatory apodeme; G. Aedeagal guide; H Female terminalia (d.v.); I. Ovipositor (l.v.).

INDEX

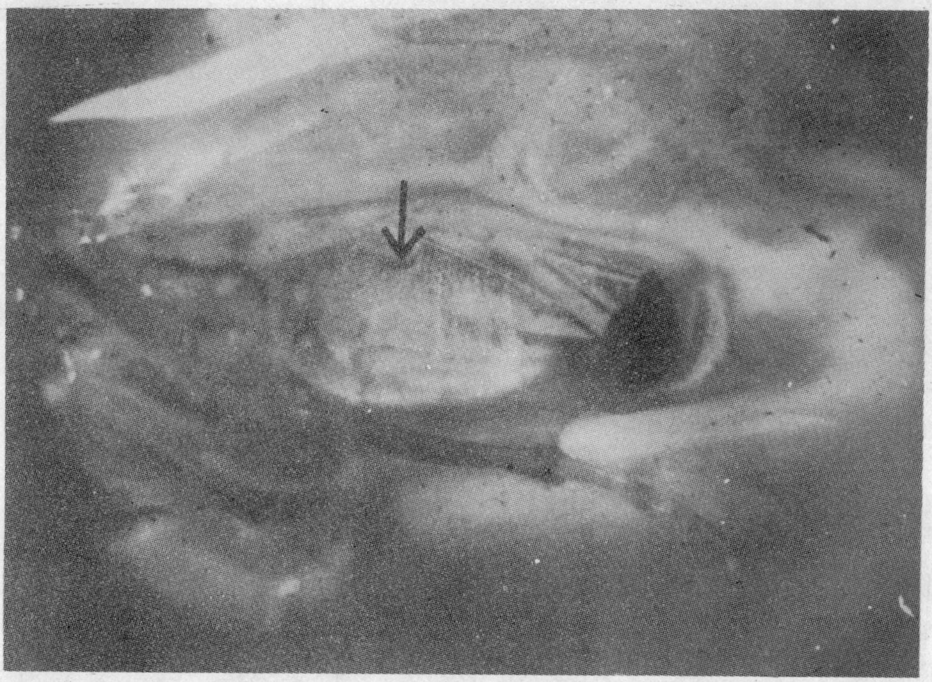

Fig. 1

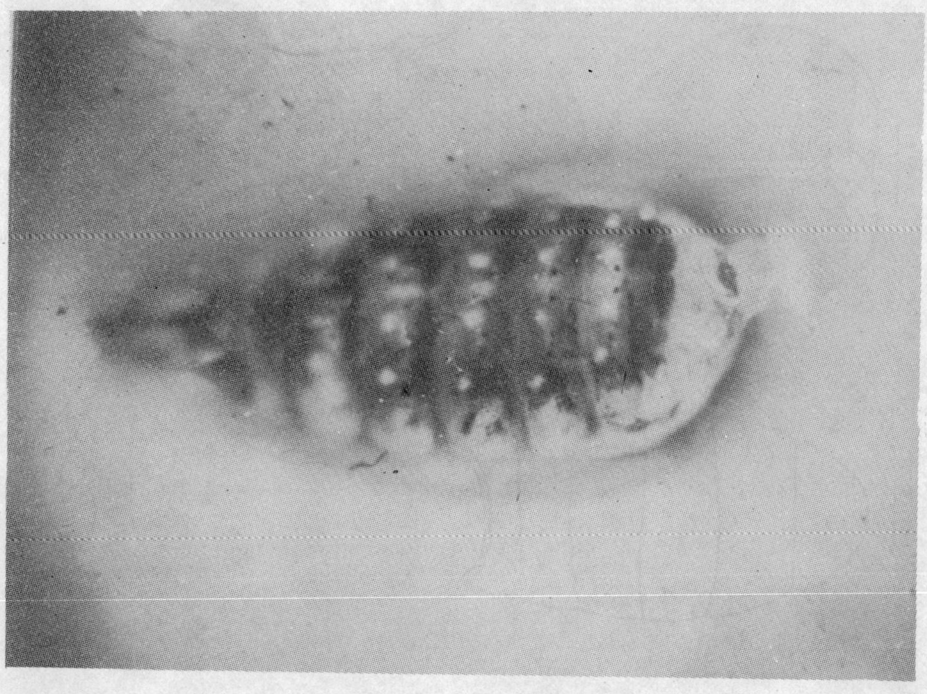

Fig. 2

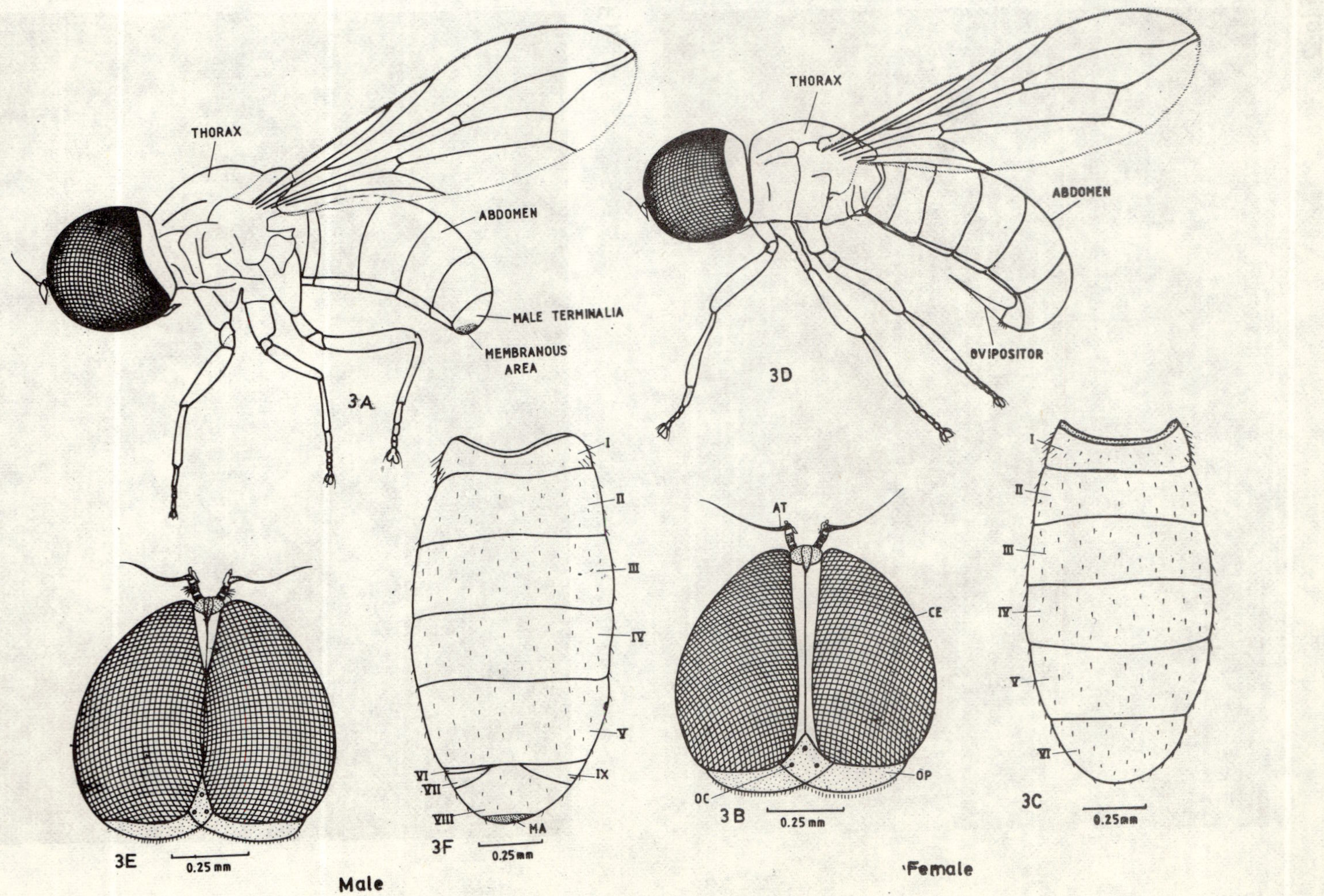
THORAX
ABDOMEN
MALE TERMINALIA
MEMBRANOUS AREA
3A
THORAX
ABDOMEN
OVIPOSITOR
3D
I
II
III
IV
V
VI
VII
VIII
IX
MA
3F
0.25 mm
3E
0.25 mm
Male
AT
CE
OP
OC
3B
0.25 mm
I
II
III
IV
V
VI
3C
0.25 mm
Female

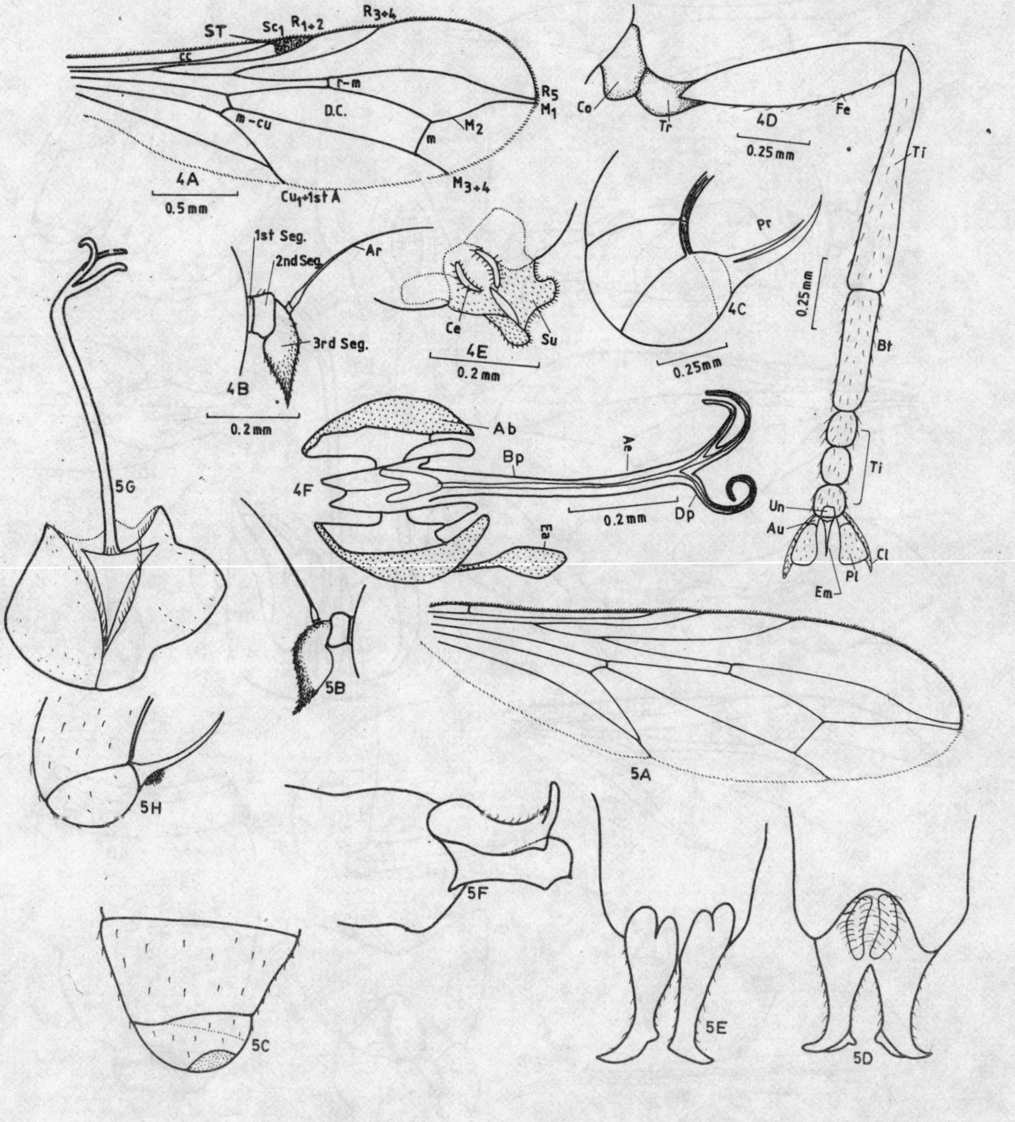
ST
Sc1
R1+2
R3+4
cc
r-m
R5
M1
D.C.
M2
m-cu
m
4A
0.5 mm
Cu1+1st A
M3+4
Co
Tr
4D
Fe
0.25 mm
Ti
Pr
4C
0.25mm
1st Seg.
2nd Seg.
Ar
3rd Seg.
4B
0.2 mm
Ce
Su
4E
0.2 mm
0.25mm
Bt
Ab
Ae
Bp
4F
0.2 mm
Dp
Ea
Ti
Un
Au
Cl
Pl
Em
5G
5B
5A
5H
5F
5E
5D
5C

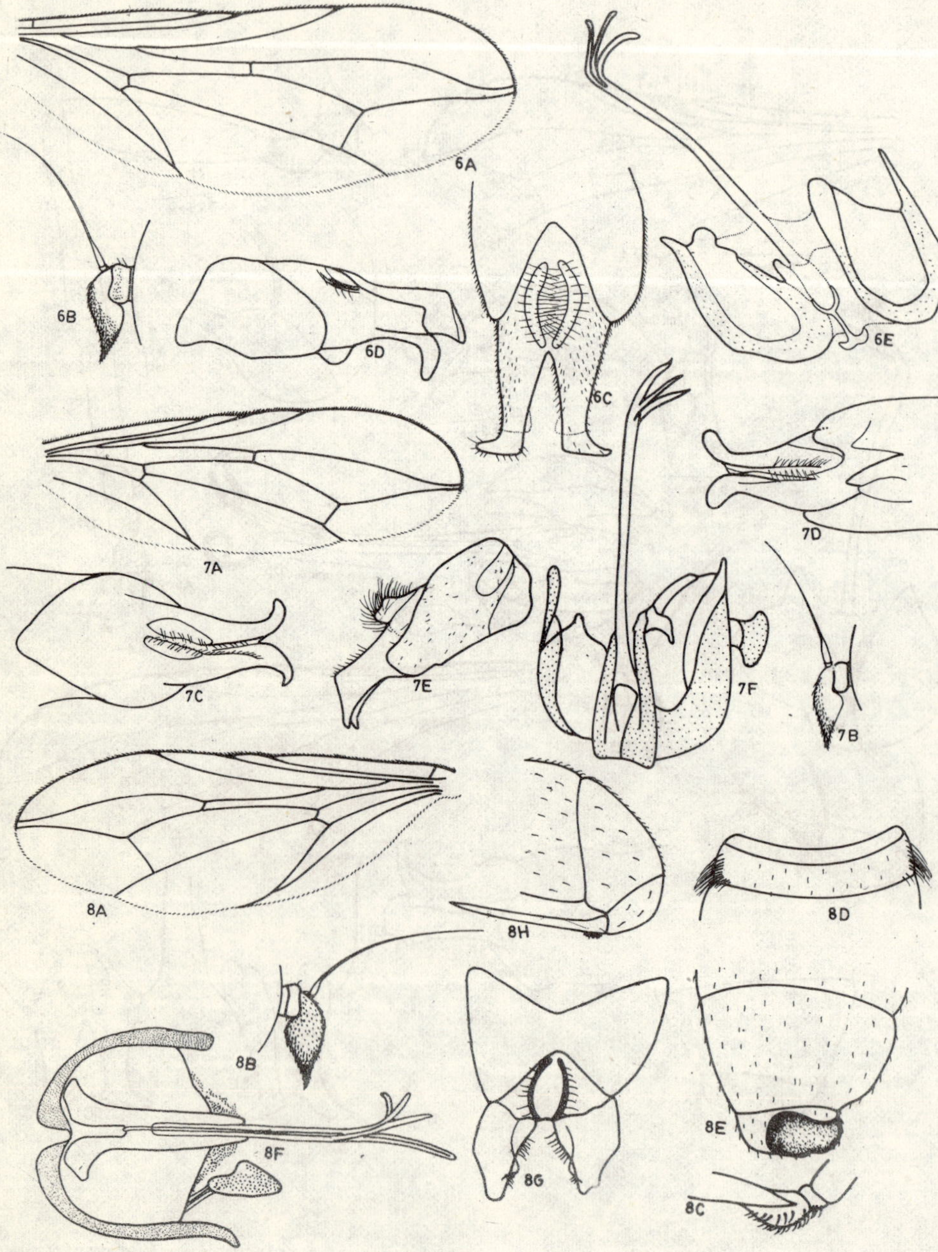
6A
6B
6C
6D
6E
7A
7B
7C
7D
7E
7F
8A
8B
8C
8D
8E
8F
8G
8H

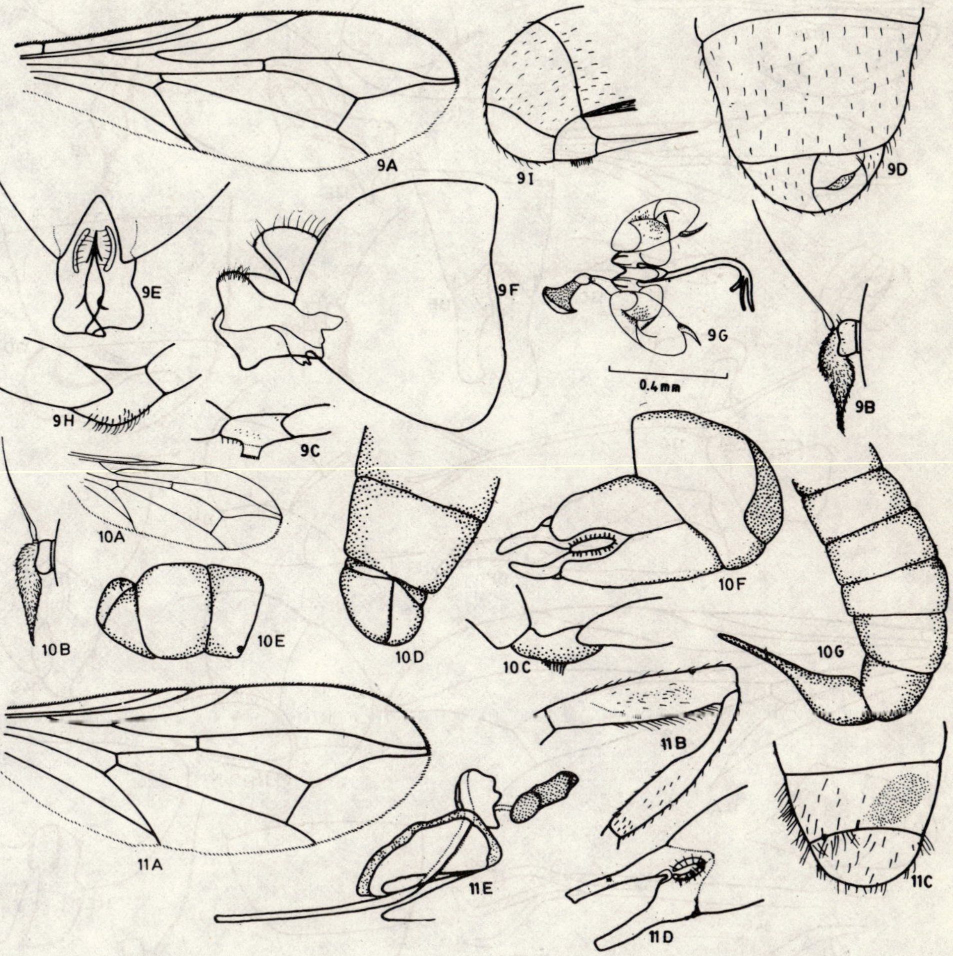
9A
9I
9D
9E
9F
9G
0.4 mm
9H
9C
9B
10A
10B
10E
10D
10C
10F
10G
11B
11A
11E
11C
11D

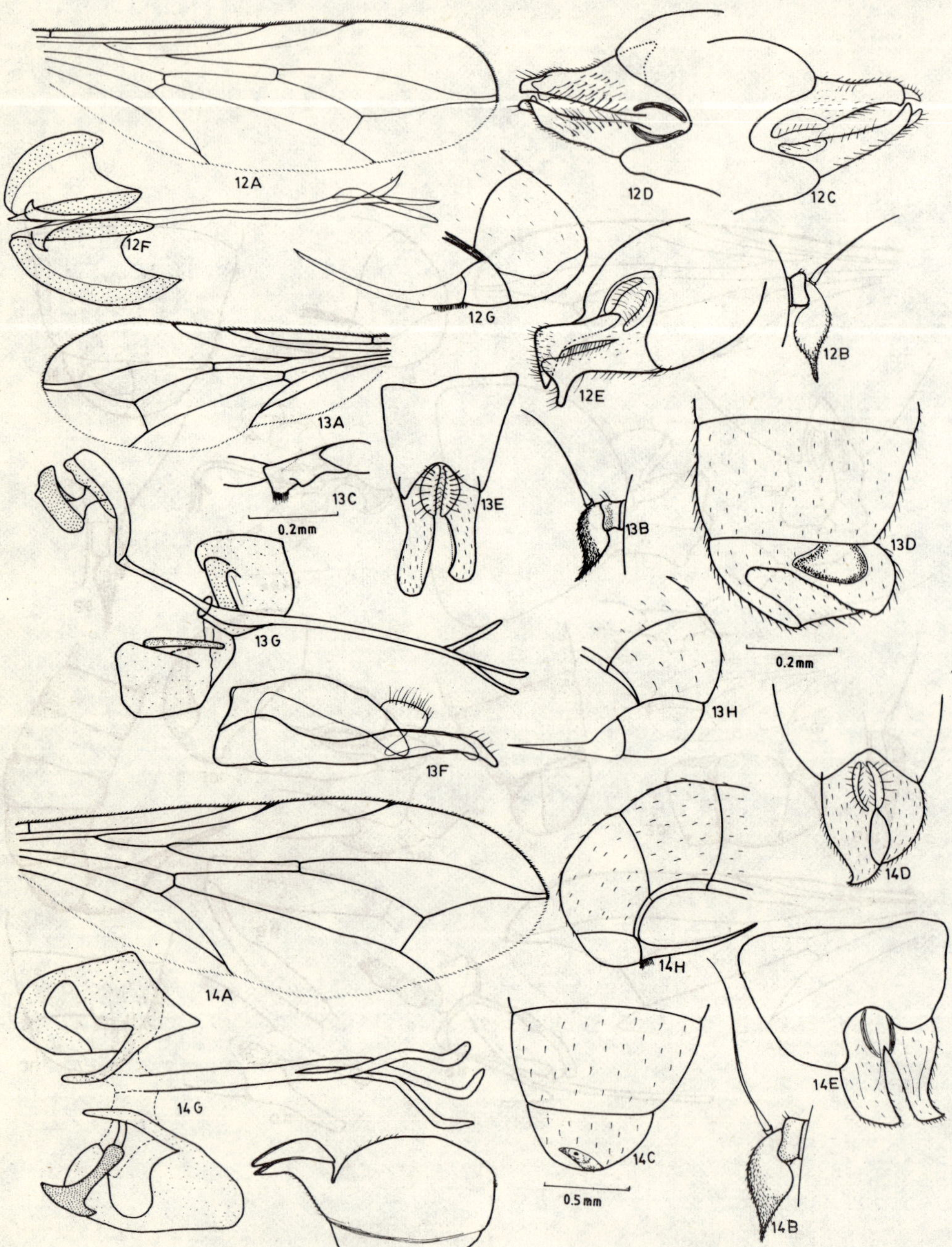
12A
12D
12C
12F
12G
12E
12B
13A
13C
0.2 mm
13E
13B
13D
0.2 mm
13G
13H
13F
14D
14A
14H
14E
14G
14C
0.5 mm
14B
14F

15A
15B
15C
15D
15E
16A
16B
16C
16D
16E
16F
17A
17B
17C
17D
17E
17F
17G
17H
17I

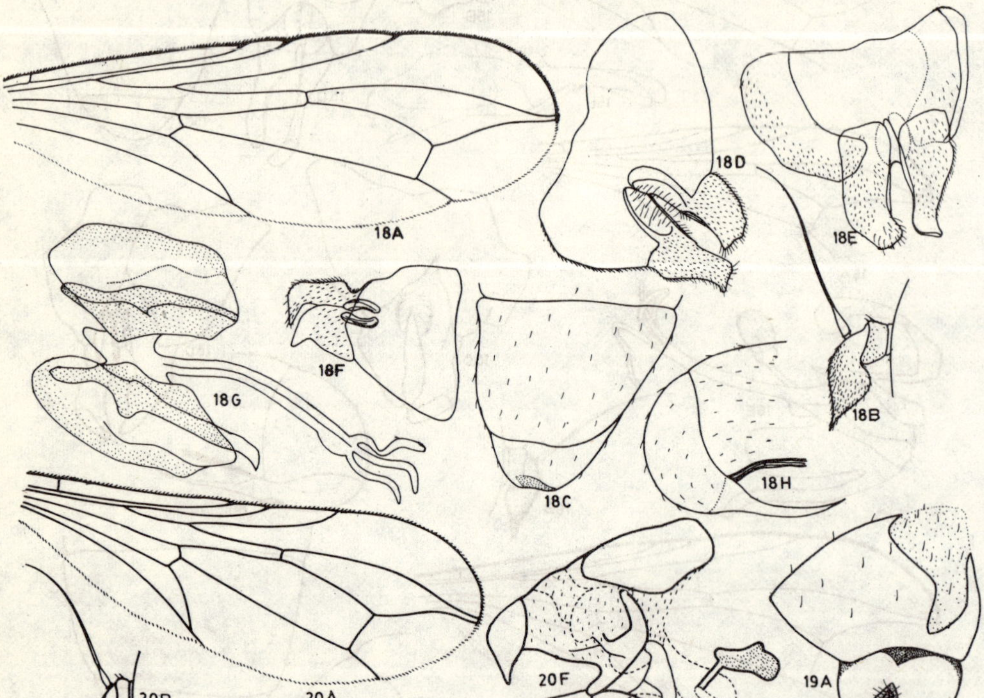
18A
18B
18C
18D
18E
18F
18G
18H
19A
20A
20B
20C
20D
20E
20F
21A
21B
21C
21D
21E
21F

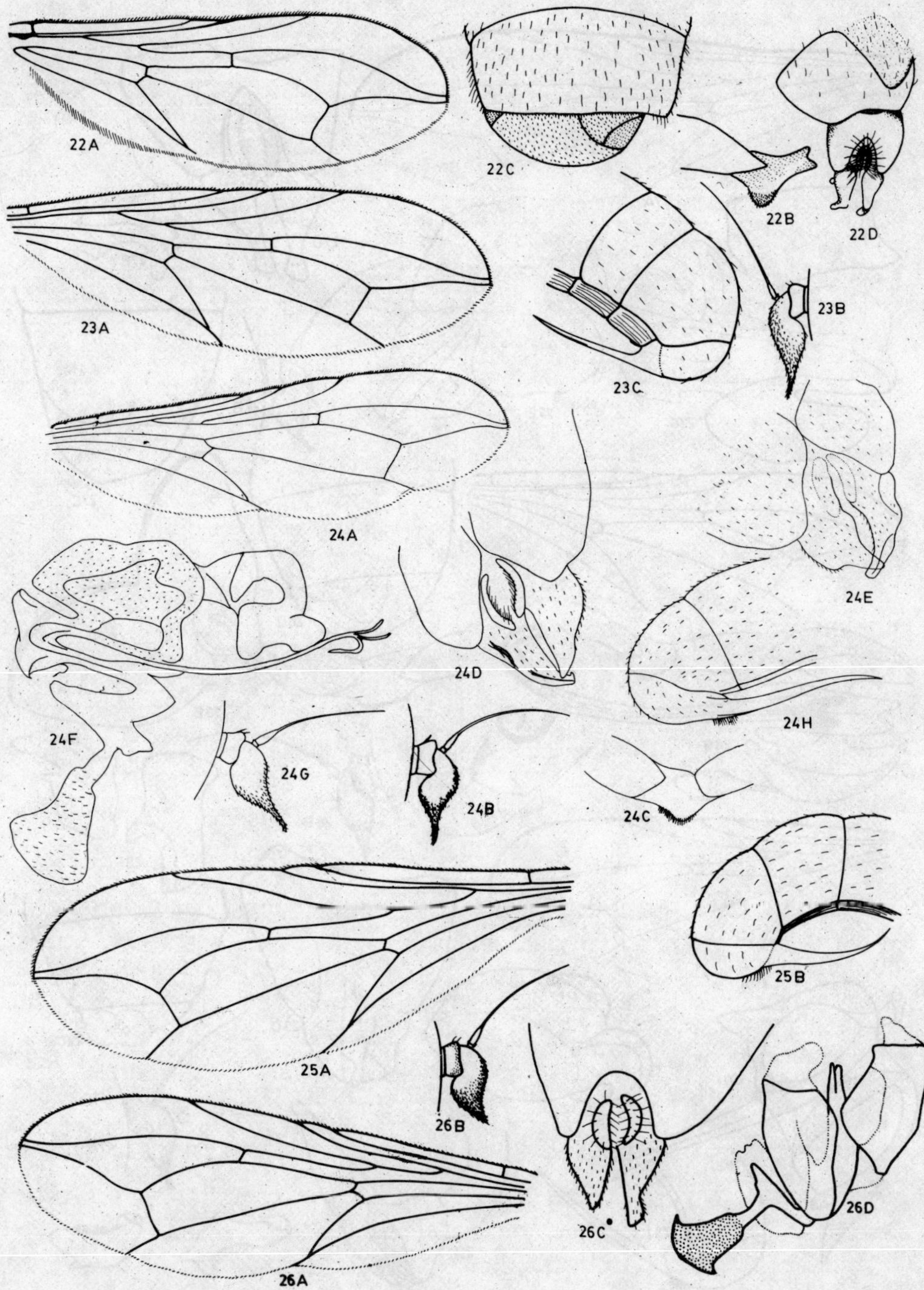
22A
22C
22B
22D
23A
23C
23B
24A
24E
24D
24H
24F
24G
24B
24C
25A
25B
26B
26A
26C
26D

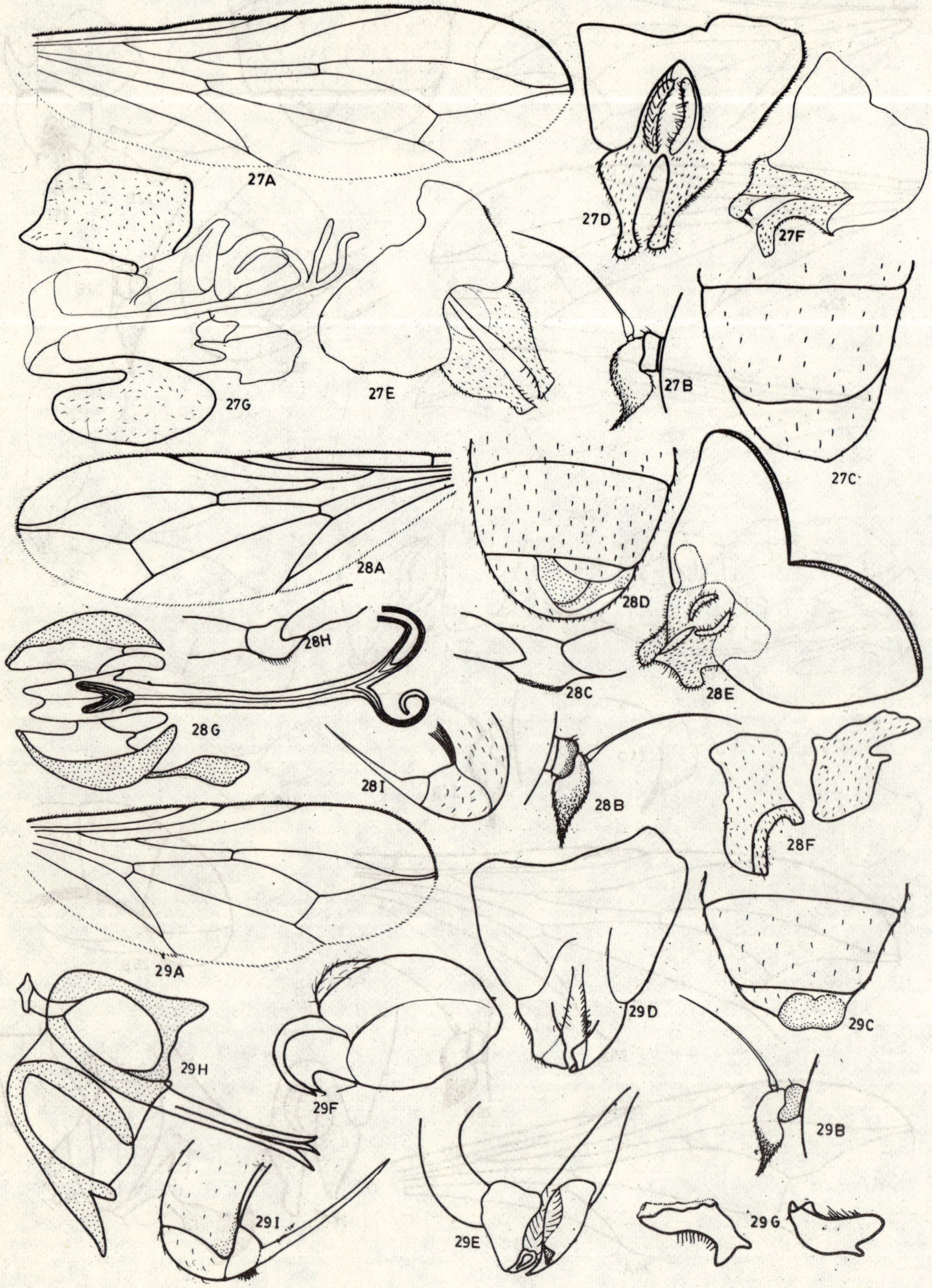
27A
27B
27C
27D
27E
27F
27G
28A
28B
28C
28D
28E
28F
28G
28H
28I
29A
29B
29C
29D
29E
29F
29G
29H
29I

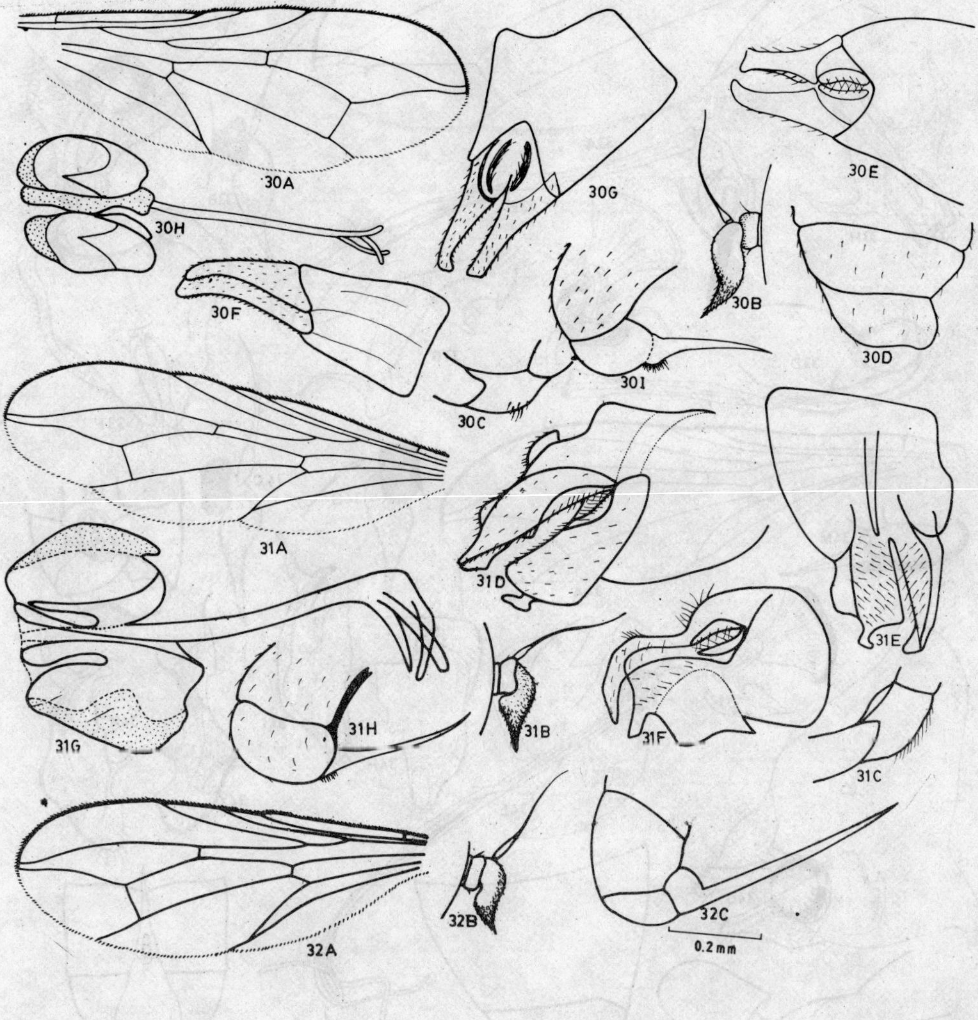
30A
30H
30G
30E
30F
30B
30I
30D
30C
31A
31D
31E
31G
31H
31B
31F
31C
32A
32B
32C
0.2 mm

33A
33B
33C
33D
33E
33F
33G
33H
34A
34B
34C
34D
34E
34F
34G
34H
34I
34J
34K
34L
34M
34N

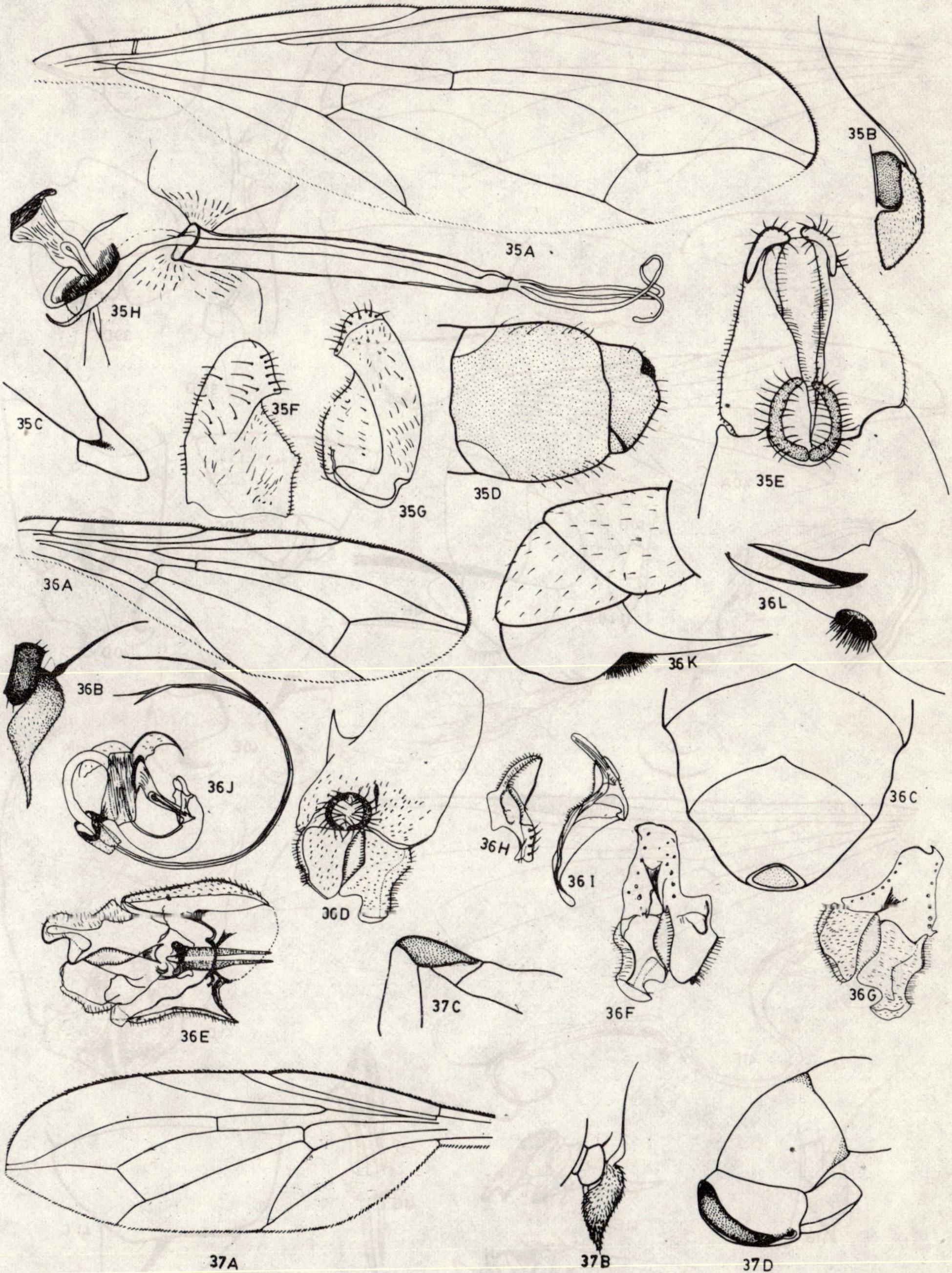

35A
35B
35C
35D
35E
35F
35G
35H
36A
36B
36C
36D
36E
36F
36G
36H
36I
36J
36K
36L
37A
37B
37C
37D

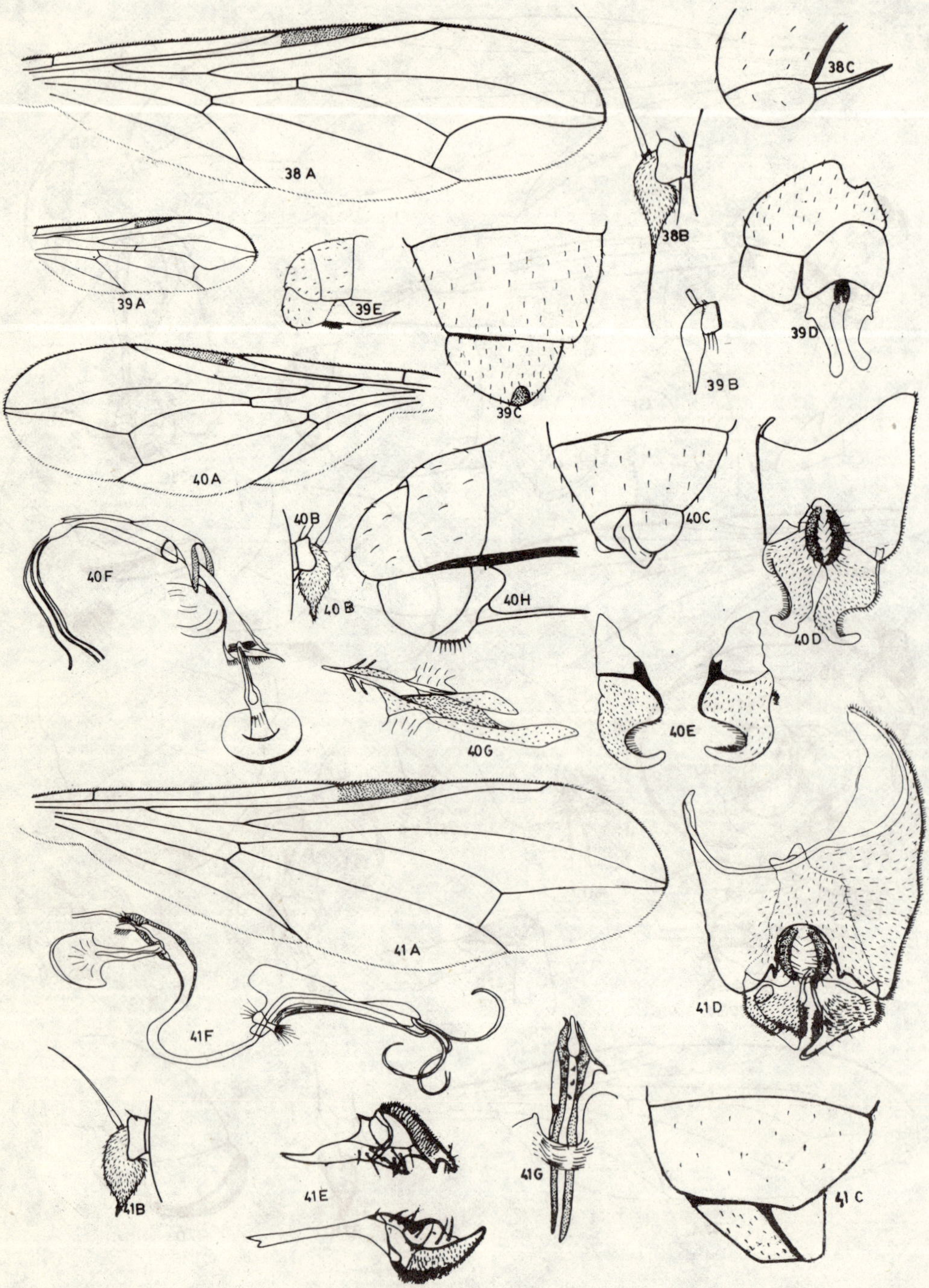
38 A
38B
38C
39 A
39E
39C
39 B
39D
40A
40B
40 B
40C
40D
40F
40H
40G
40E
41 A
41D
41F
41B
41E
41G
41 C

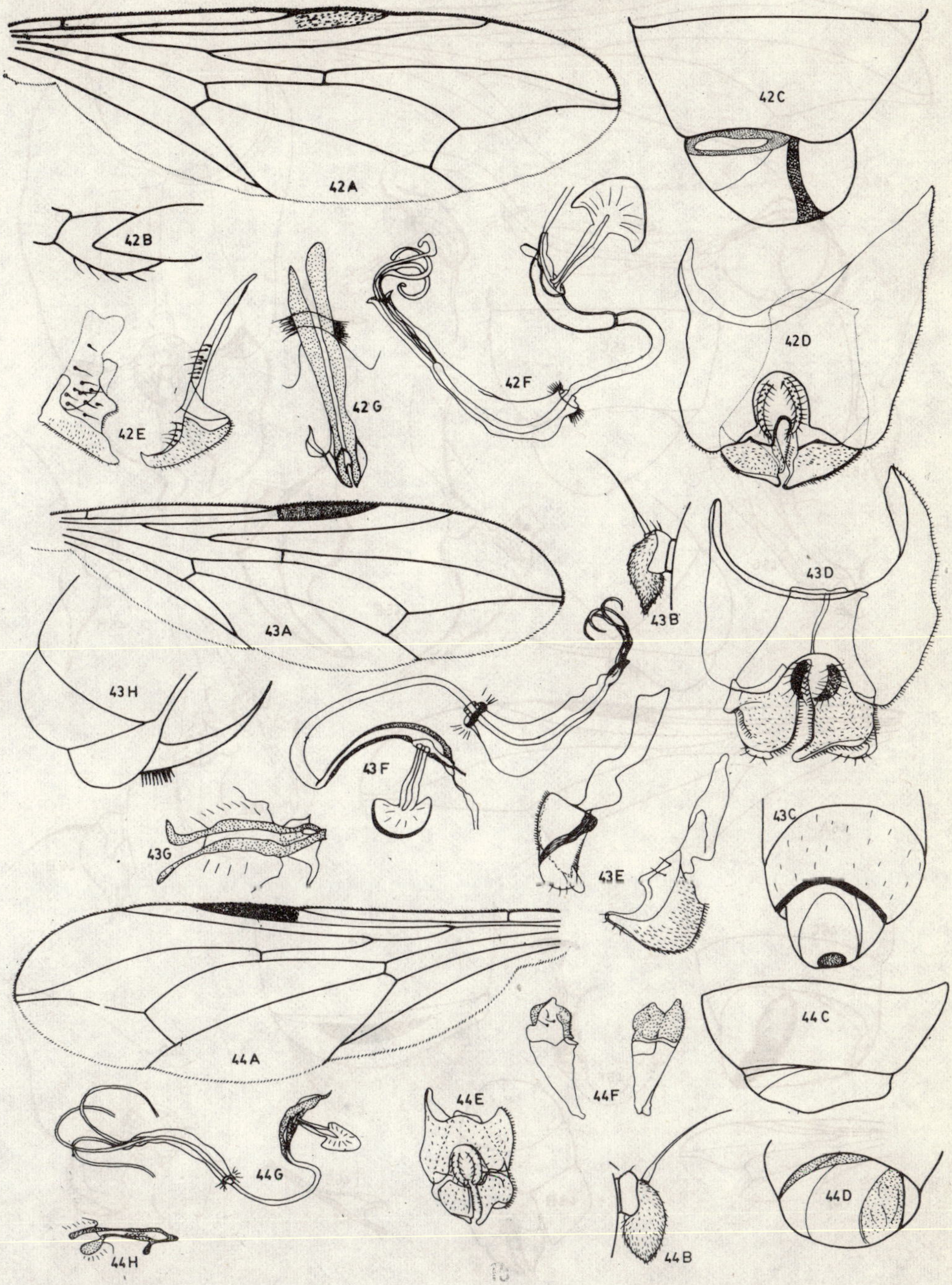
42A
42B
42C
42D
42E
42F
42G
43A
43B
43C
43D
43E
43F
43G
43H
44A
44B
44C
44D
44E
44F
44G
44H

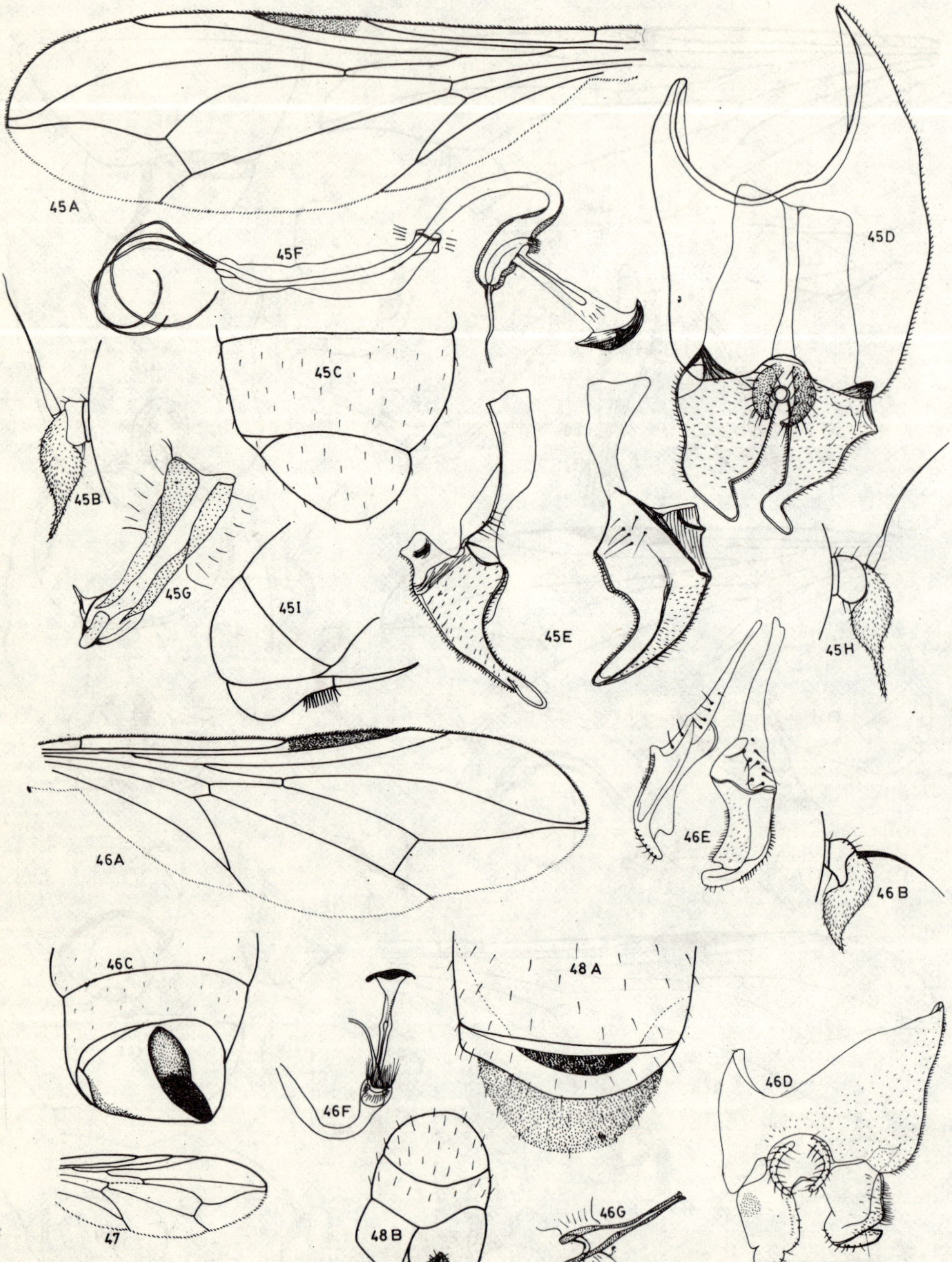
45A
45F
45D
45B
45C
45G
45I
45E
45H
46A
46E
46B
46C
48 A
46F
46D
47
48 B
46G

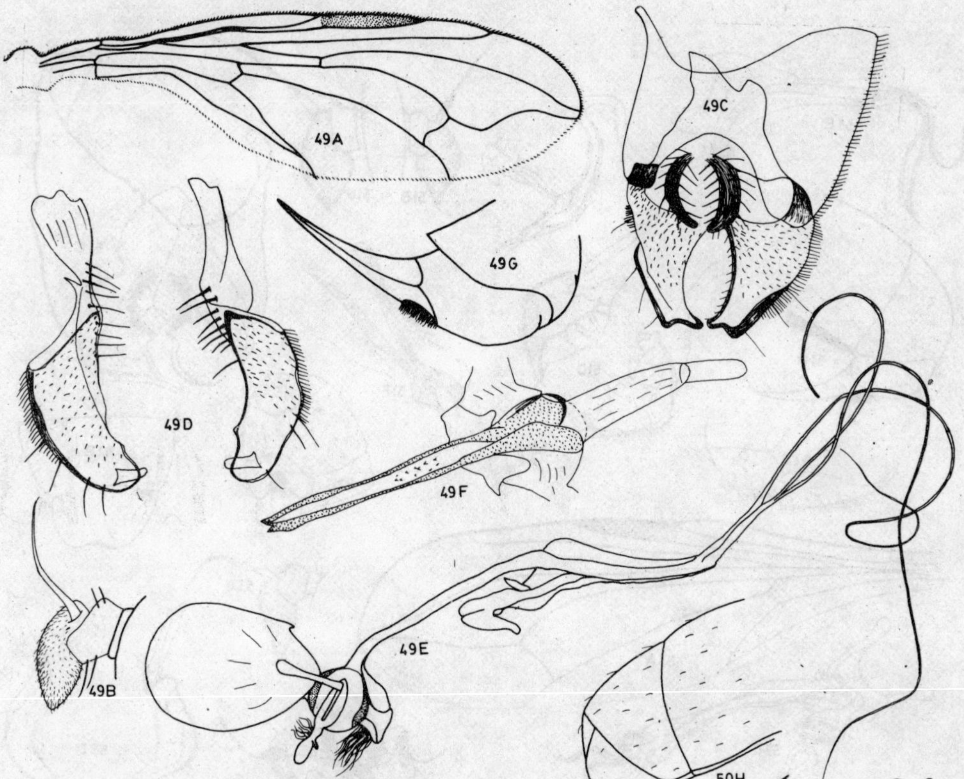
49A
49C
49G
49D
49F
49E
49B
50H
50G
50C
50A
50F
50E
50B
50D
51A

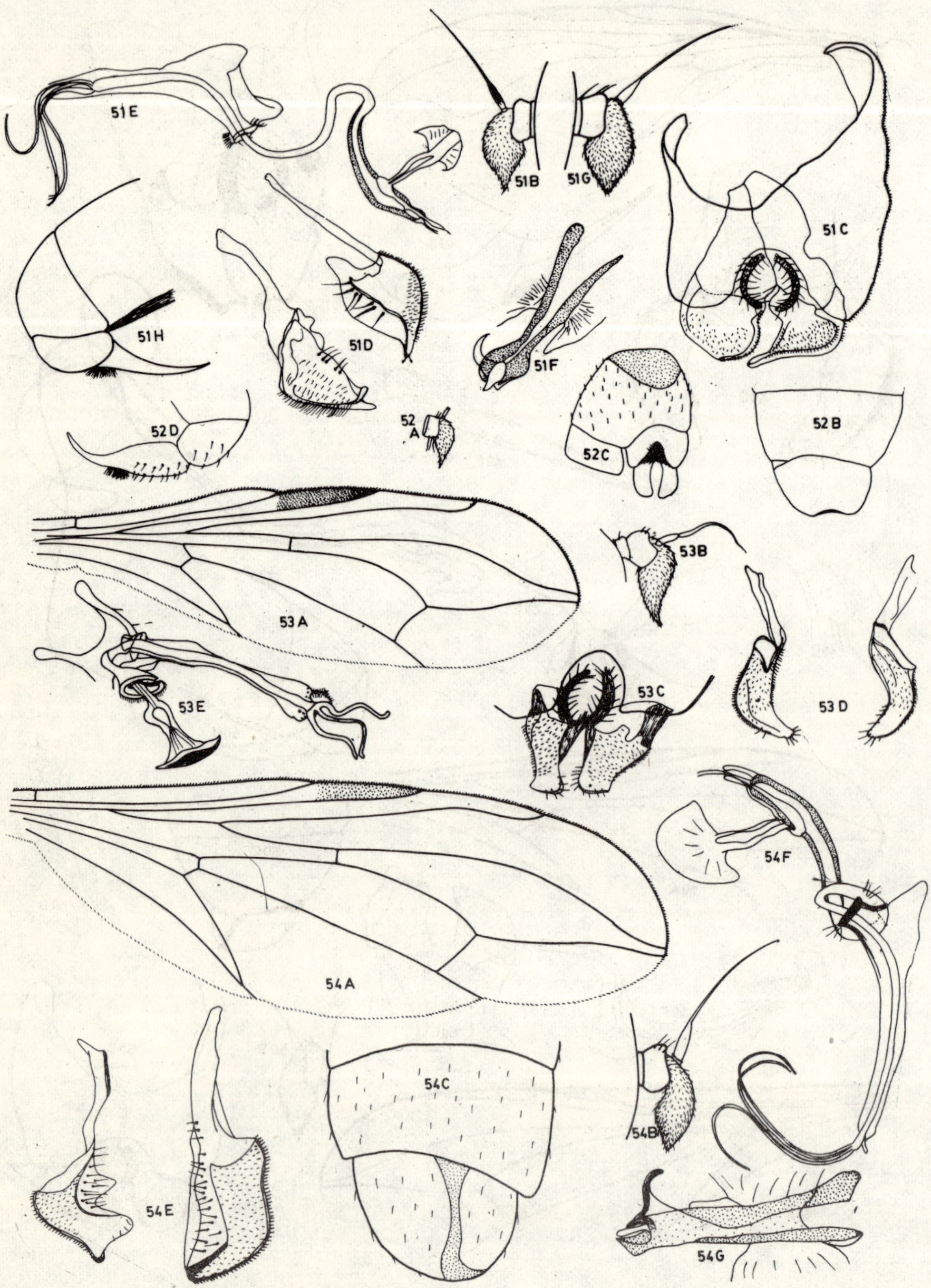
51E
51B
51G
51C
51H
51D
51F
52D
52
A
52C
52B
53B
53A
53C
53D
53E
54F
54A
54C
54B
54E
54G

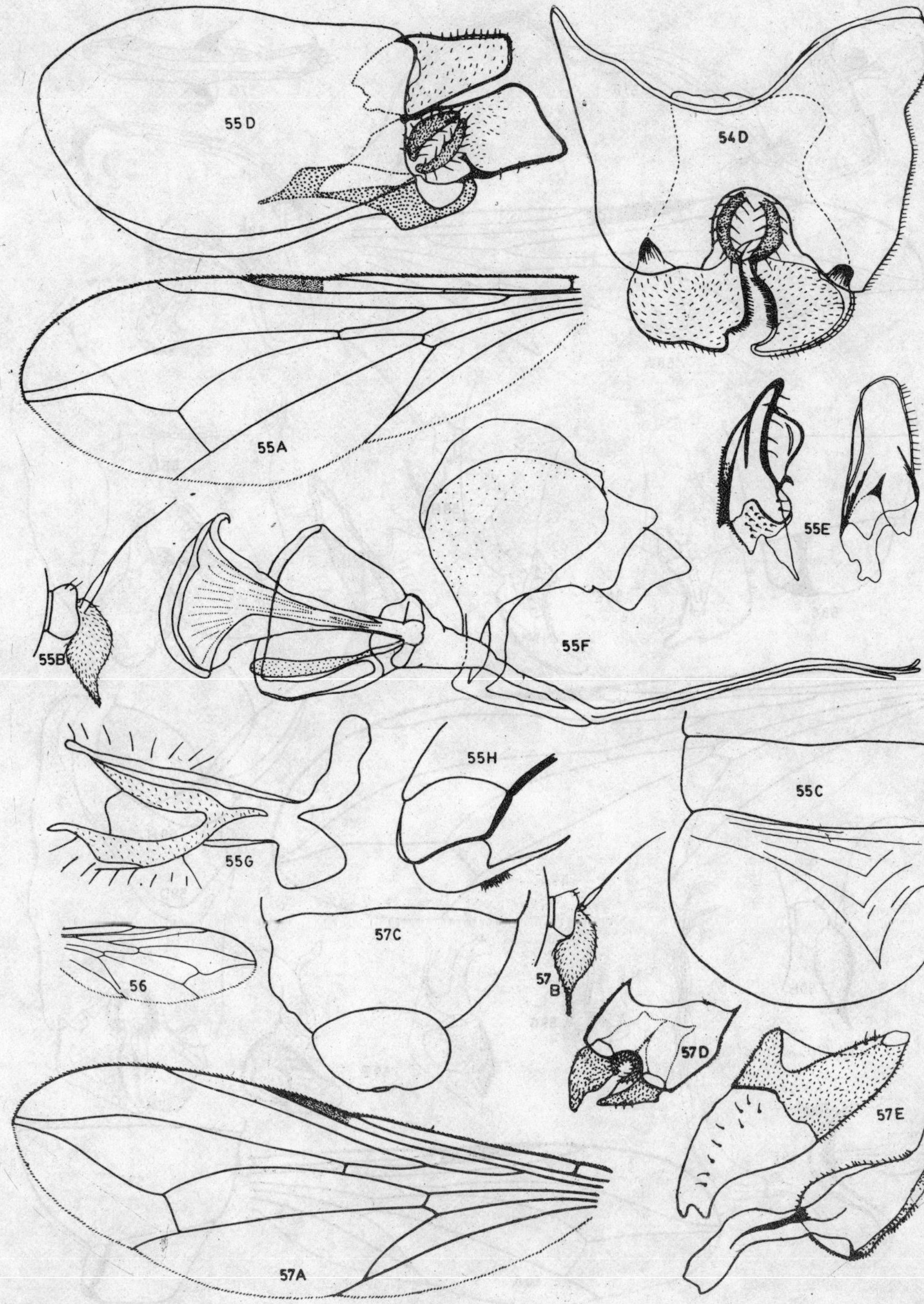
55D
54D
55A
55E
55B
55F
55H
55C
55G
57C
56
57 B
57D
57E
57A

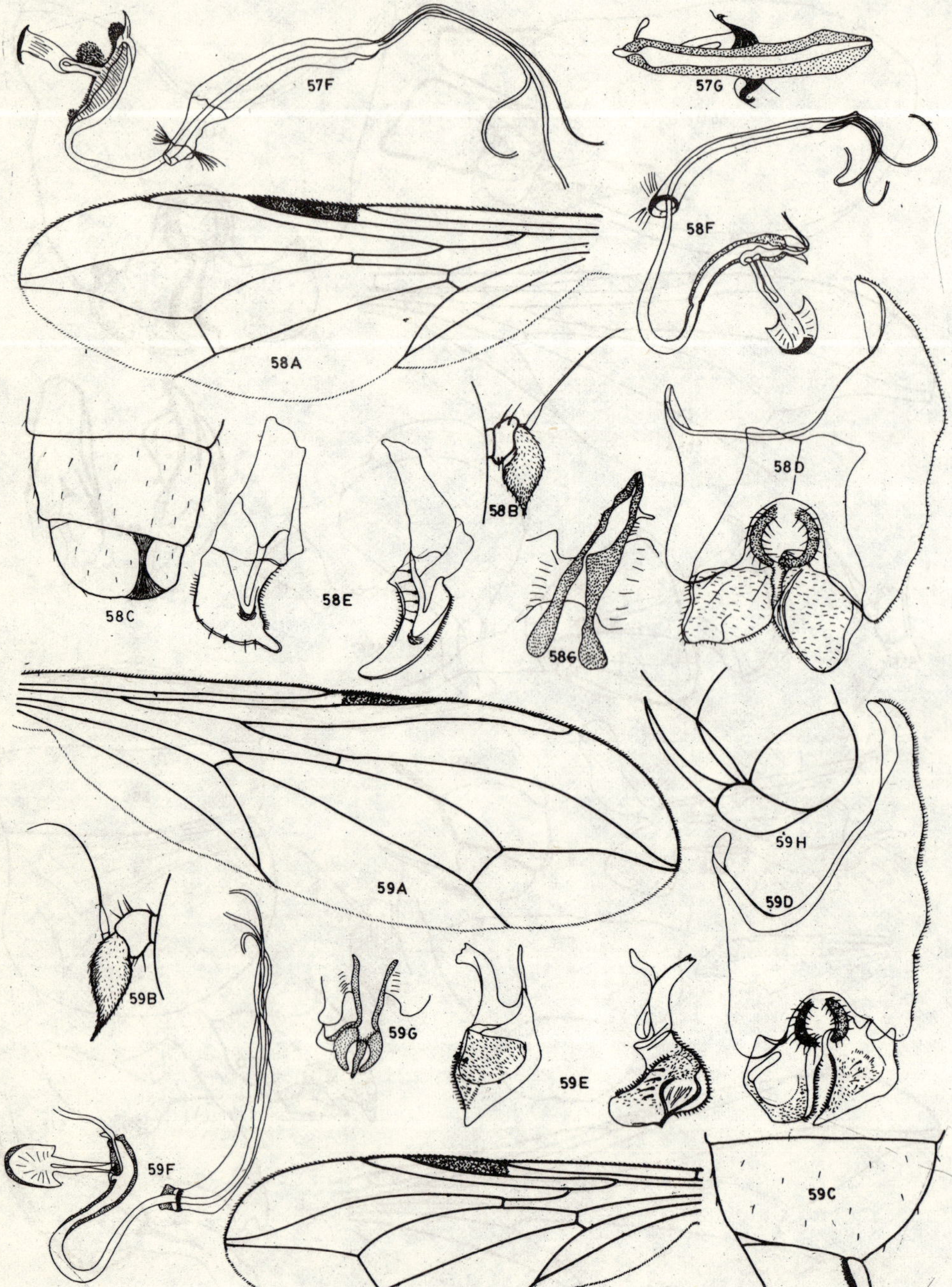
57F
57G
58F
58A
58D
58B
58C
58E
58G
59H
59A
59D
59B
59G
59E
59F
60A
59C

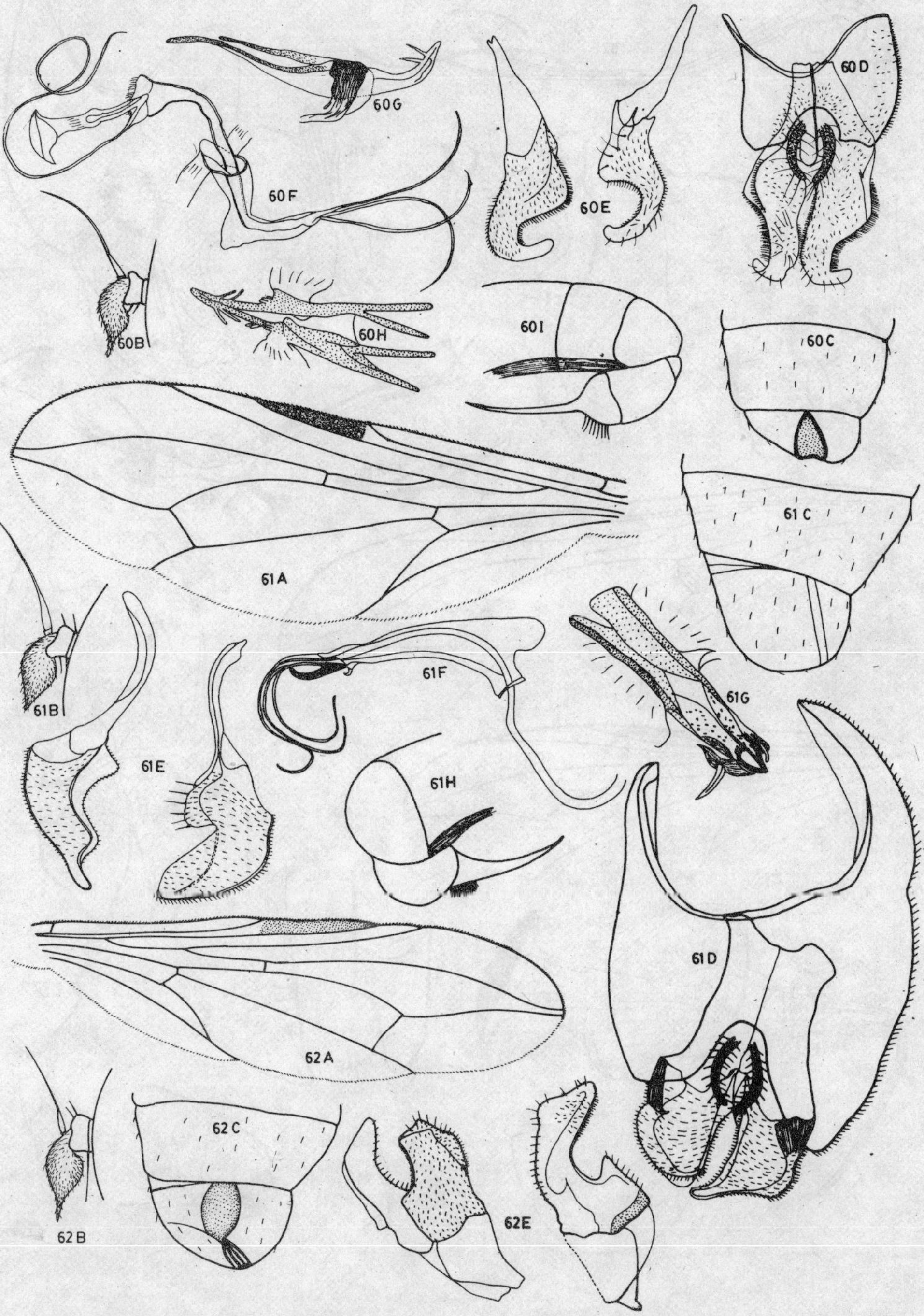
60G
60F
60E
60D
60B
60H
60I
60C
61A
61C
61B
61F
61G
61E
61H
61D
62A
62B
62C
62E

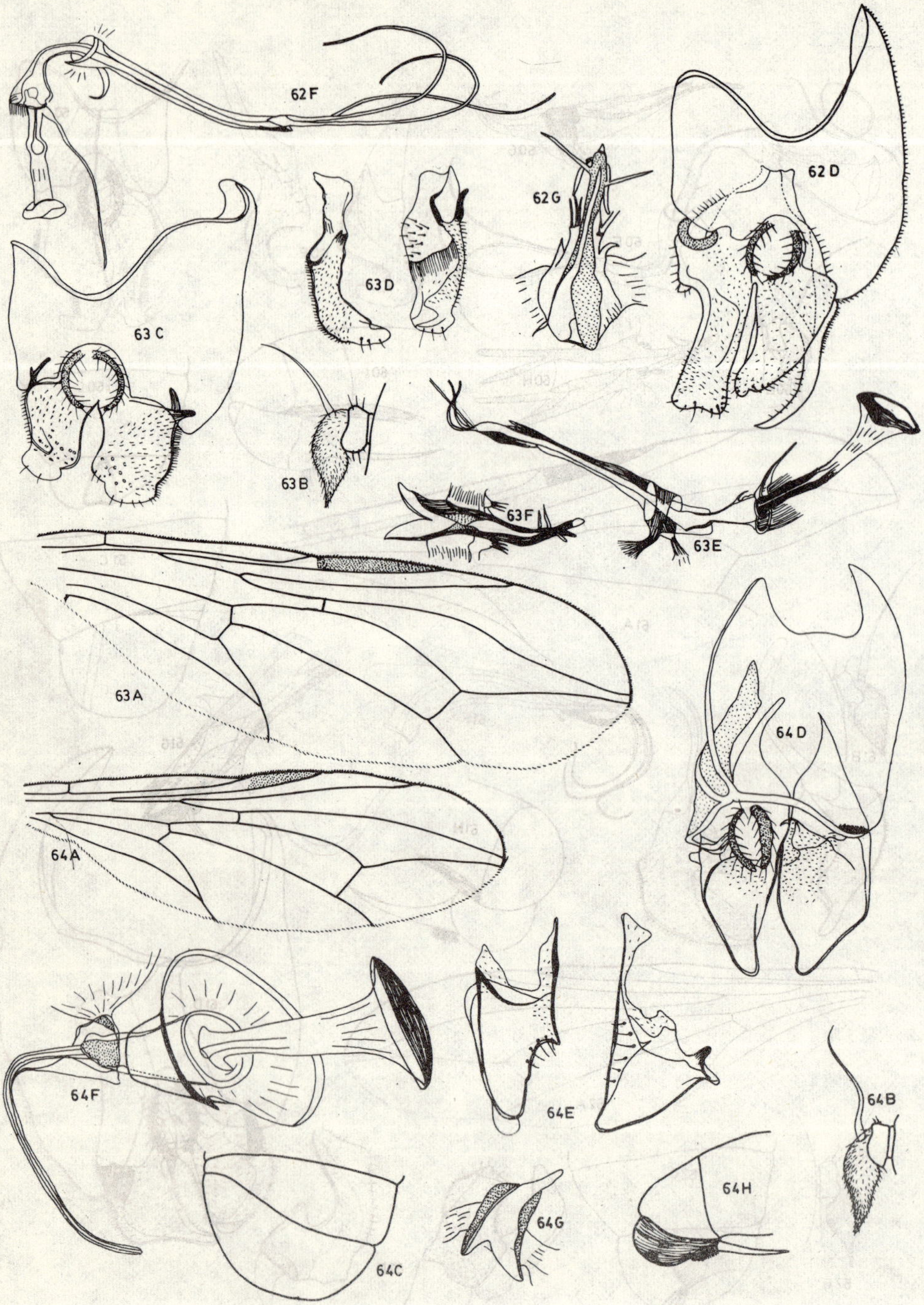

62F
62D
62G
63C
63D
63B
63F
63E
63A
64D
64A
64F
64E
64B
64C
64G
64H

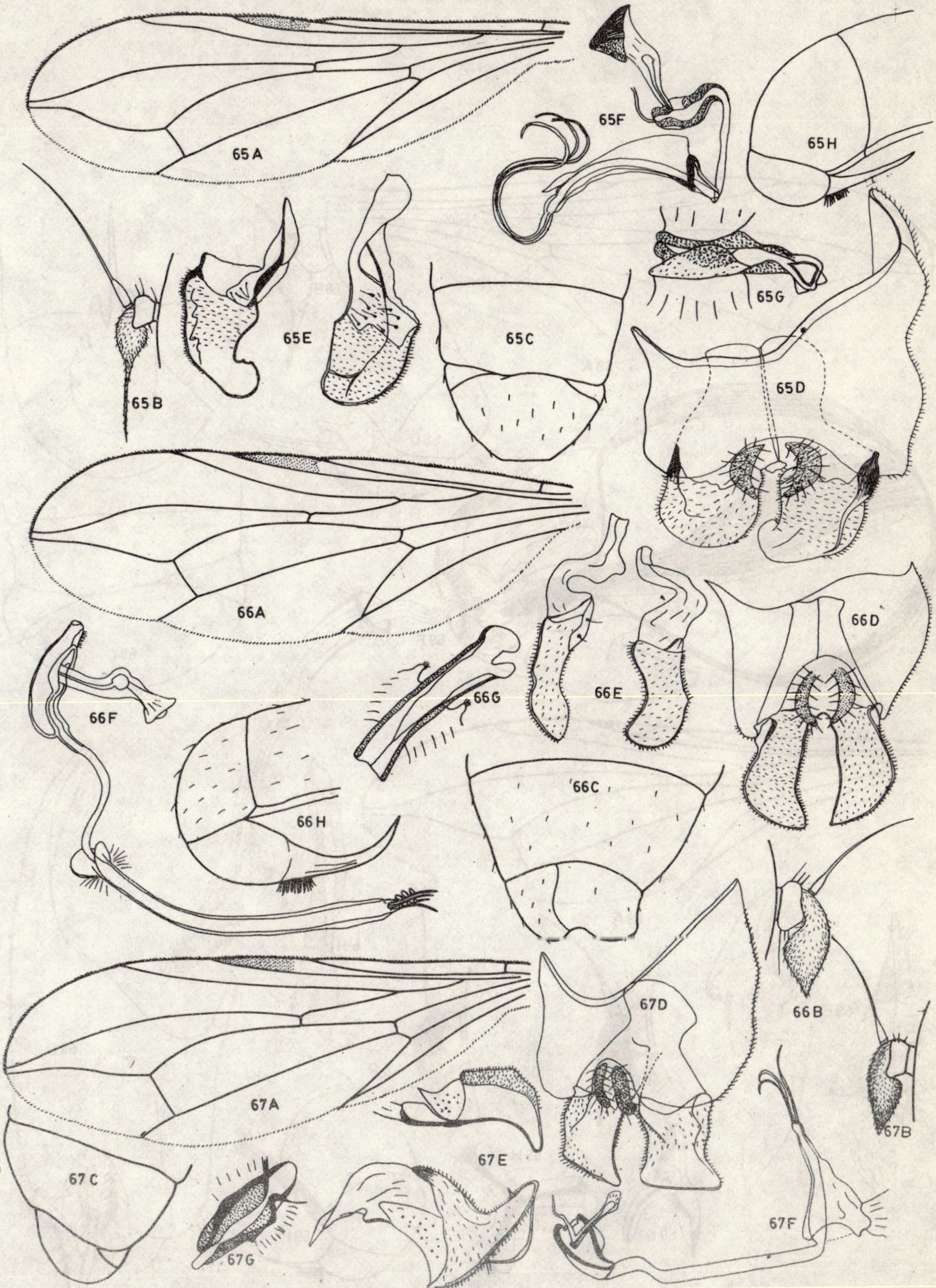
65A
65F
65H
65B
65E
65C
65G
65D
66A
66E
66D
66F
66G
66H
66C
66B
67D
67A
67B
67E
67C
67G
67F

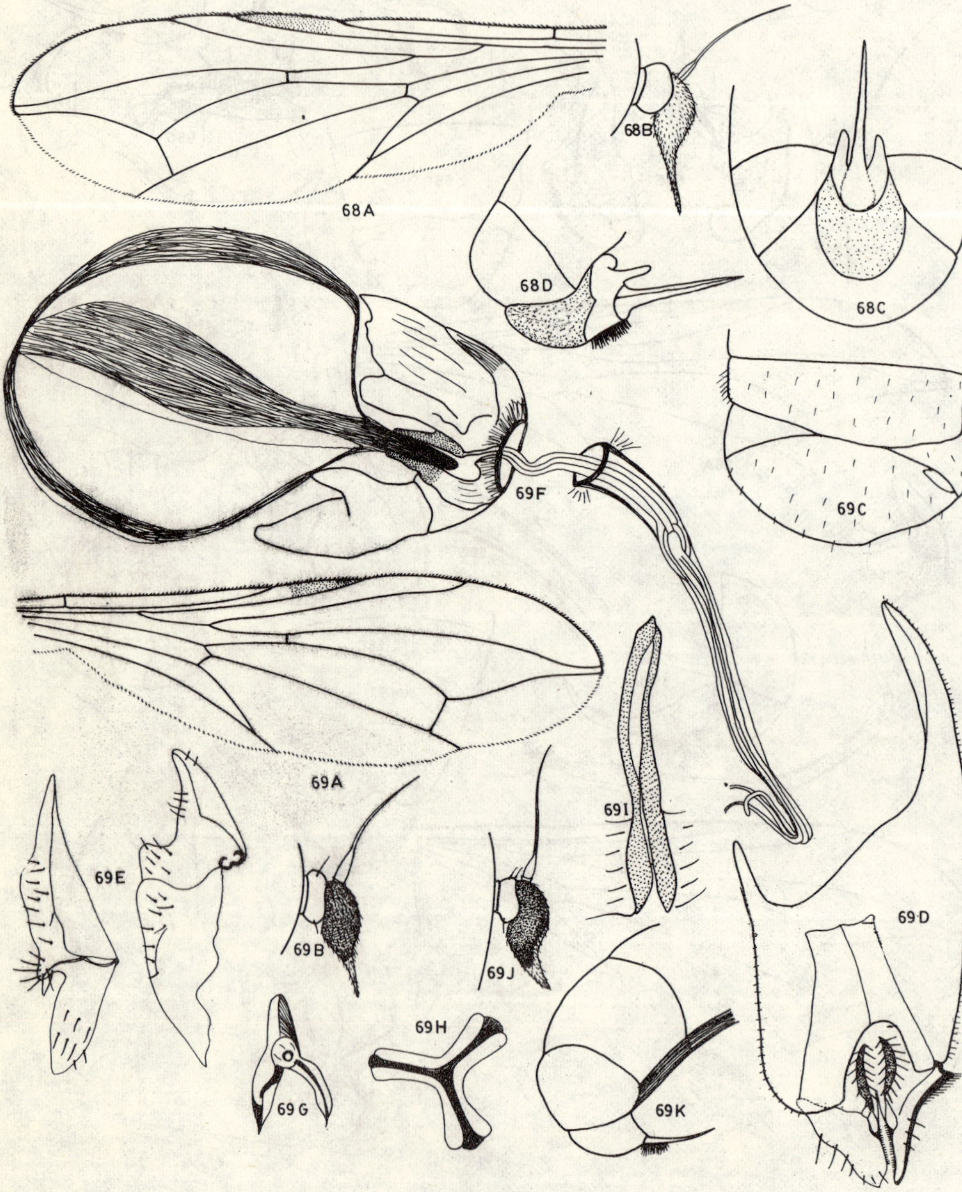
68A
68B
68C
68D
69A
69B
69C
69D
69E
69F
69G
69H
69I
69J
69K

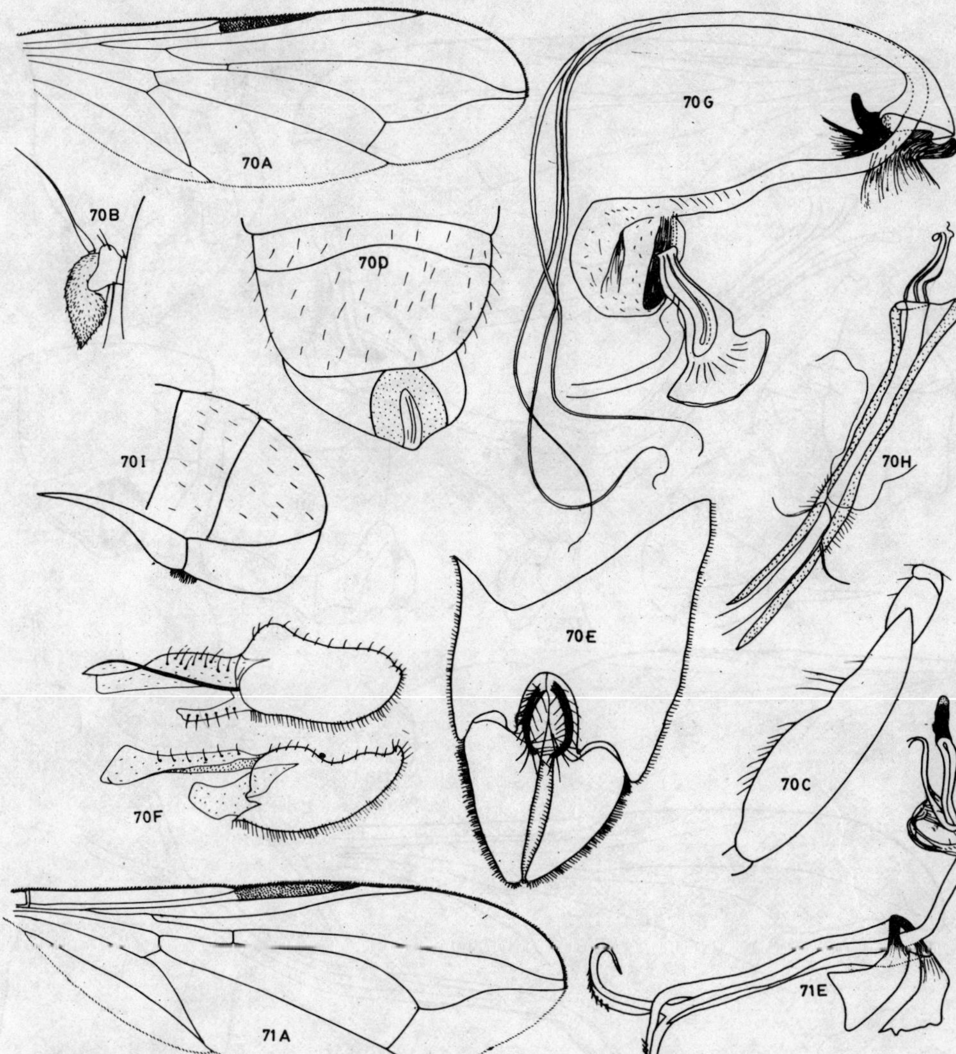
70A
70B
70D
70G
70H
70I
70E
70F
70C
71E
71A
71D
71H
71C
71G
71B
71F

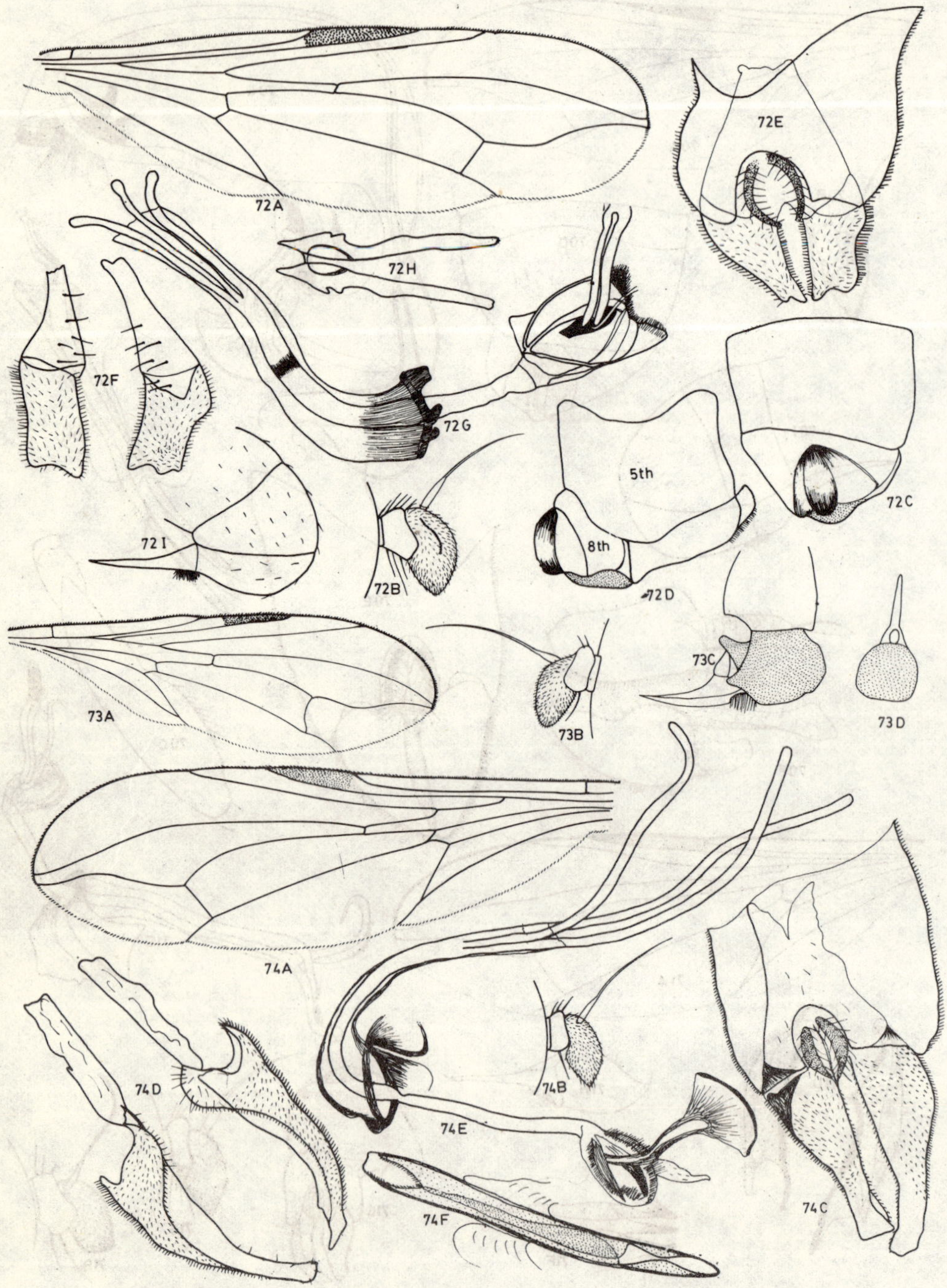
72A
72E
72H
72F
72G
5th
8th
72C
72I
72B
72D
73A
73B
73C
73D
74A
74B
74D
74E
74C
74F

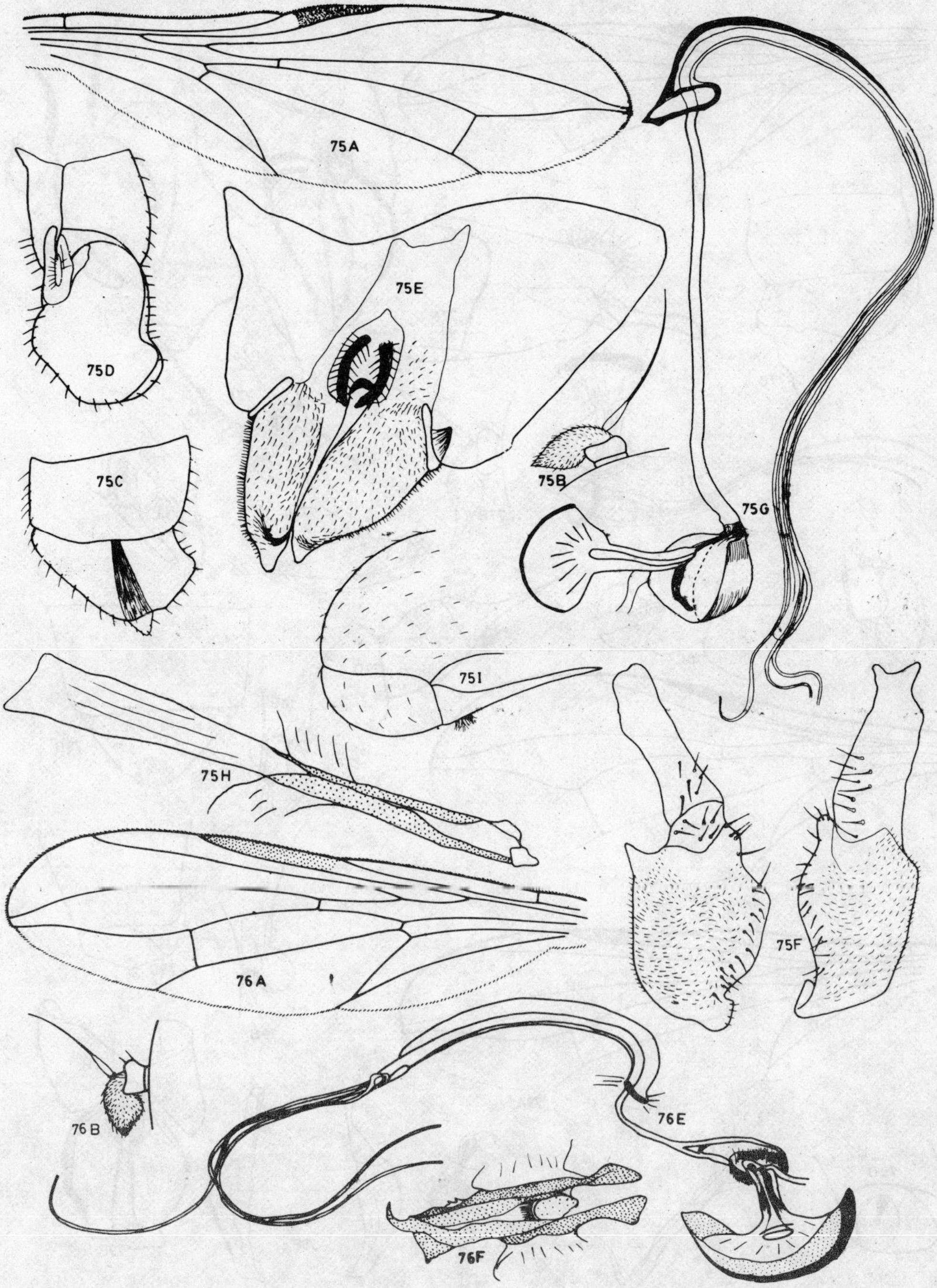
75A
75D
75E
75C
75B
75G
75I
75H
75F
76A
76B
76E
76F

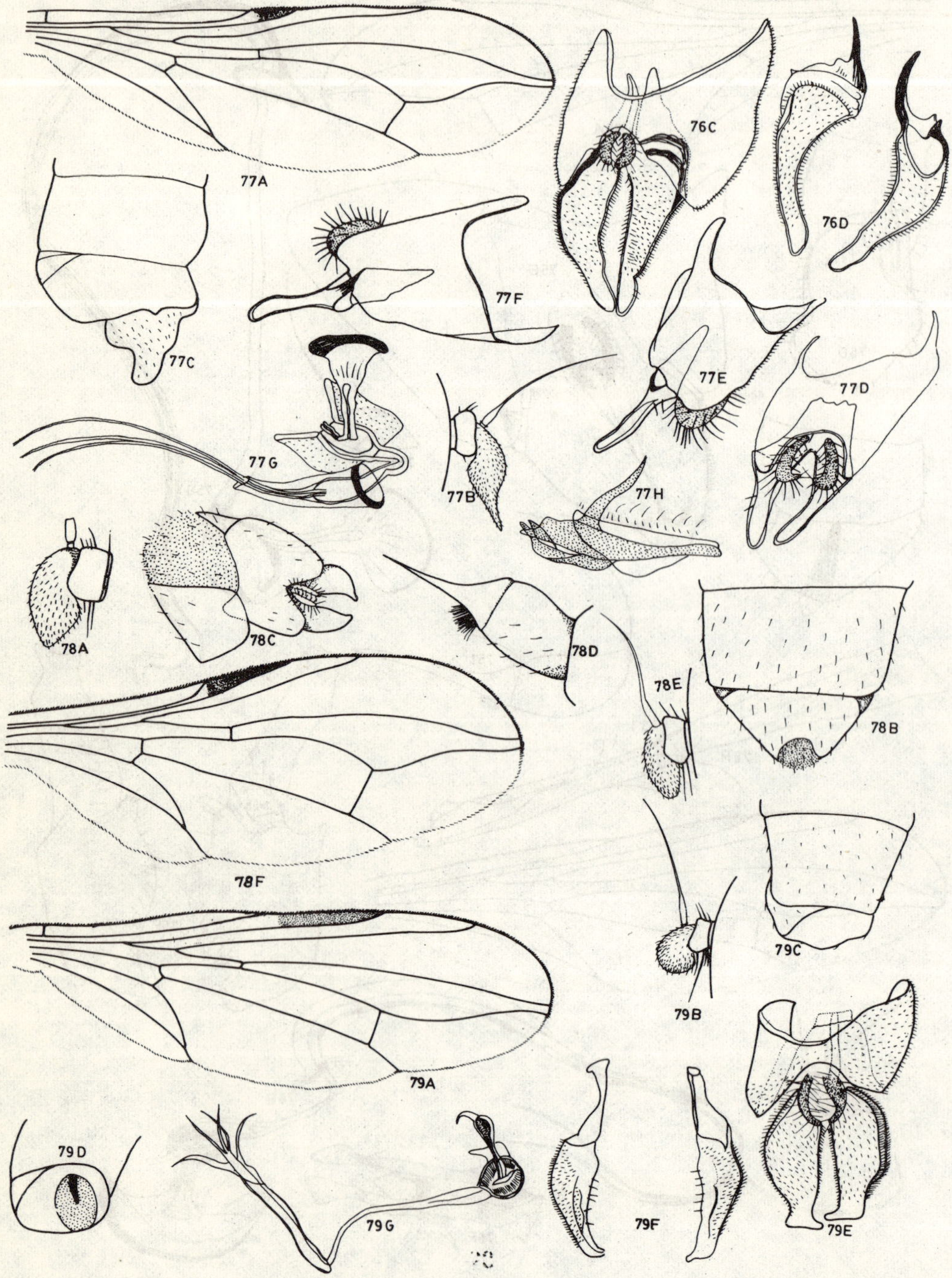
77A
76C
76D
77F
77C
77E
77D
77G
77B
77H
78A
78C
78D
78E
78B
78F
79C
79B
79A
79D
79G
79F
79E

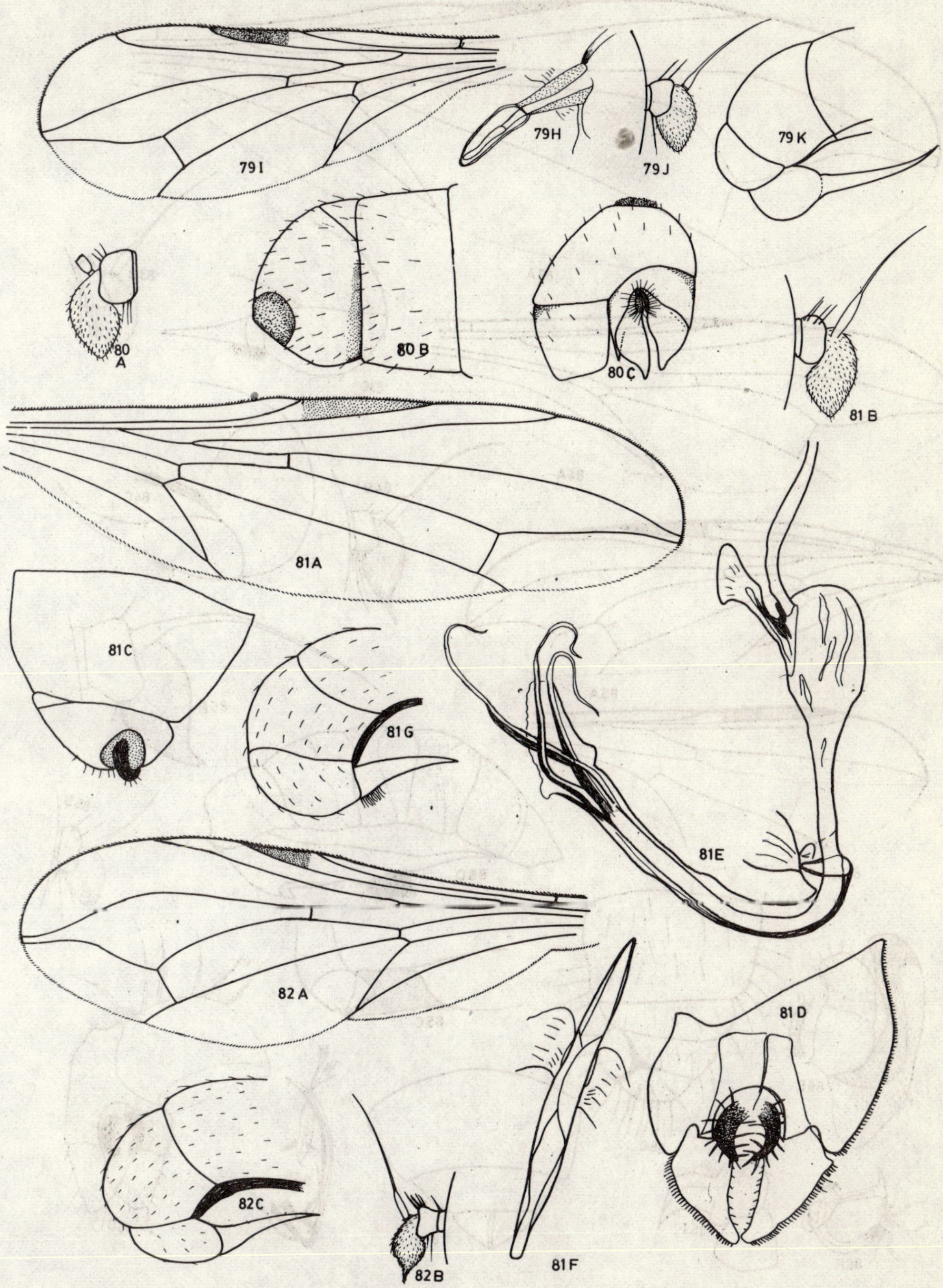
79 I
79 H
79 J
79 K
80 A
80 B
80 C
81 B
81 A
81 C
81 G
81 E
82 A
81 D
82 C
82 B
81 F

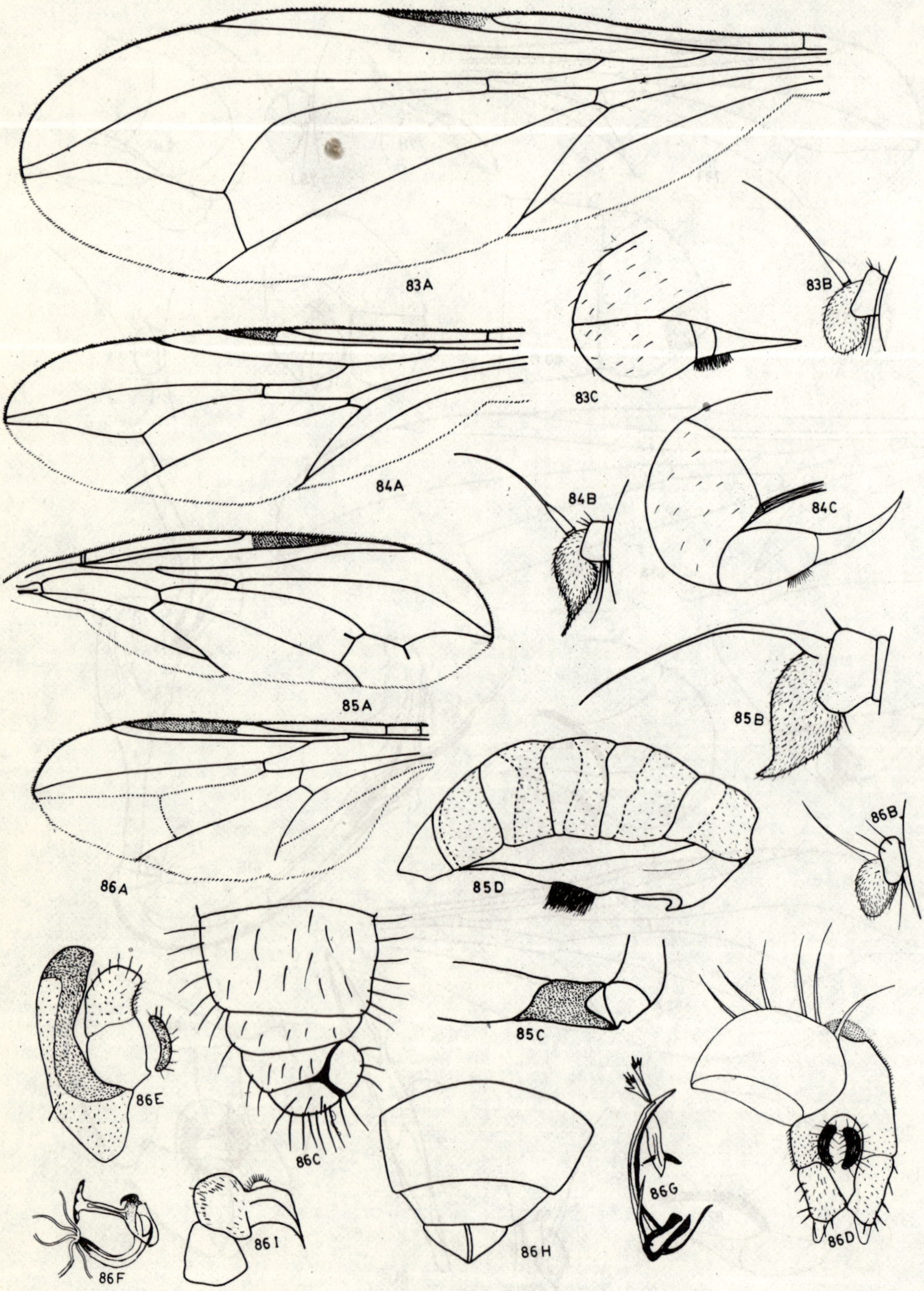
83A
83B
83C
84A
84B
84C
85A
85B
85C
85D
86A
86B
86C
86D
86E
86F
86G
86H
86I

ERRATA

Page	Para	Line	Read	As
1	3	5 from above	Hoshimato	Hashimato
2	1	3,6 from above	javaensis	javanensis
2	1	last	hoppes	hoppers
3	2	4 from above	javaensis	javanensis
3	last	last	Clareosphaera	Claraeosphaera
4	4	2 from below	Allonevra	Alloneura
5	4	4 from above	Willam	Williams
6	2	4 from above	England	Finland
6	4	5 from above	Collinas	Collinias
7	2	8 from below	news pecies	new species
8	1	last	Nearetic region	Nearctic region
8	last	last	Dorylomorpna	Dorylomorpha
9	1	1	Acording	According
9	1	6 from above	usuall	usually
9	1, 2	9 & 16from above	Coe (1966)	Coe (1966a)
11	heading	—	Devlopment	Development
12	2	3 from below	in to	into
12	3	4 from above	in	is
12	3	5	elther, letter	either, latter
12	4	2nd	Kathiritham by	Kathirithamby
12	4	8	macropter-	macropterous
12	4	9	anpeps	anceps
12	4	7 from below	pellucica	pellucida
12	4	5	membrance	membrane
13	1	6	parasiteoid	parasitoid
14	2, 3	4 from below & last	javaensis	javanensis
15	1	3 from below	Pina	Pena
15	2	6 from above	Chloriana	Chloriona
15	2	9 from above	Marcos	Morcos
15	2	9 from below	pellucids	pellucida
16	1	1	that	than
16	1	4 from below	verius	varius
18	last	1	aqeuous	aqueous

Indian Pipunculids

Page	Para	Line	Read	As
18	last	3 from below	mathod	method
19	3	2 from below	fig. 2	fig. 1
19	4	3 from below	Cerefully	Carefully
27	8th couplet	1	a symmetrical	asymmetrical
35	1	12 from above	tringe	tinge
35	2	3 from above	broder	broader
36	4	5 from below	Hoshiarpur	Hoshiarpur (Pb.);
42	—	6	Lenght	Length
45	Remarks	2	Chaetotxy	Chaetotaxy
47	1	2 from below	aceagus	aedeagus
47	last	3 from below	Jahankhelen	Jahankhelan
48	1	11 from below	pubesence	pubescence
52	3	2 from below	synadephoides	synadelphoides
54	1	12 from above	Halters	Hateres
54	1	15 from above	slighttly	slightly
55	2	2	structure	structure (fig. 24H)
56	2	2 from below	Ranikhat	Ranikhet
58	Etymology	—	Name	Named
58	title	—	Tomosvasyella	Tomosvaryella
61	2	2 from below	Hoshiarpur, Chandigarh (Punjab)	Hoshiarpur (Punjab); Chandigarh (U.T.)
62	1	2 from below	aedegal	aedeagal
65	last	7 from below	Crossuein	crossvein
67	5th couplet	alternate	situated of	situated on
67	After keys	last line of Claraeomorpha	Vain	Vein
69	1	2 from below	stractures	structures
70	1	1	pubescene	pubescence
70	1	3 from above	pubesecence	pubescence
70	1	5 from above	costel	costal
70	1	2 from below	clasers	claspers
70	—	15	Lenght	Length
70	Remarks	1	species	species is
70	Remarks	1	D. etranslucenrs	D. translucens
70	Remarks	last	Handy	Hardy